Perfecting Social Skills

A GUIDE TO INTERPERSONAL
BEHAVIOR DEVELOPMENT

APPLIED CLINICAL PSYCHOLOGY

Series Editors: Alan S. Bellack and Michel Hersen

University of Pittsburgh, Pittsburgh, Pennsylvania

PARTIAL HOSPITALIZATION: A Current Perspective
Edited by Raymond F. Luber

HANDBOOK OF MARITAL THERAPY: A Positive Approach to Helping
Troubled Relationships
Robert P. Liberman, Eugenie G. Wheeler, Louis A.J.M. DeVisser, Julie
Kuehnel, and Timothy Kuehnel

PERFECTING SOCIAL SKILLS: A Guide to Interpersonal Behavior
Development
Richard M. Eisler and Lee W. Frederiksen

HANDBOOK OF BEHAVIOR MODIFICATION WITH THE MENTALLY
RETARDED: Future Perspectives in Behavior Therapy
Edited by Johnny L. Matson and John R. McCartney

THE UTILIZATION OF CLASSROOM PEERS AS BEHAVIOR CHANGE
AGENTS
Edited by Philip S. Strain

A Continuation Order Plan is available for this series. A continuation order will bring delivery of each new volume immediately upon publication. Volumes are billed only upon actual shipment. For further information please contact the publisher.

Perfecting Social Skills

A GUIDE TO INTERPERSONAL BEHAVIOR DEVELOPMENT

Richard M. Eisler
AND
Lee W. Frederiksen

Virginia Polytechnic Institute and State University
Blacksburg, Virginia

PLENUM PRESS • NEW YORK AND LONDON

Library of Congress Cataloging in Publication Data

Main entry under title:

Perfecting social skills.

(Applied clinical psychology)
Includes index.
1. Interpersonal relations. 2. Social adjustment. 3. Interpersonal relations—Study and teaching.
4. Social adjustment—Study and teaching. I. Eisler, Richard M. II. Frederiksen, Lee W. III. Title:
Social skills: a guide to interpersonal behavior development. IV. Series.
HM132.P39   302   80-21209
ISBN 0-306-40592-X

© 1980 Plenum Press, New York
A Division of Plenum Publishing Corporation
227 West 17th Street, New York, N.Y. 10011

Printed in the United States of America

To Dane, Danielle, Nathan, and Andrew

Preface

That man is a social being is almost axiomatic. Our interpersonal relationships can be sources of the most rewarding or the most painful of human experiences. To a large measure our accomplishments in life depend on the facility with which we interact with others—our social skill. The acquisition of social skills is, of course, a natural part of the overall socialization process. However, in many instances it becomes necessary or desirable to develop further an individual's social facilities. Such skill development is the topic of this book.

Two major goals were kept in mind in the writing of this book. The first was to provide a conceptual framework within which to view social skills. Such a framework allows one to understand why it is important to develop social skills, and the effects that such skill development should have. If the reader has a thorough understanding of the concept of social skills and their development, it becomes possible to make appropriate innovations and adaptions to his or her own circumstances. Without such a framework, social-skills training becomes little more than a collection of disjointed techniques. Also, without a conceptual understanding, procedural innovations are difficult to incorporate into training.

Second, important as a conceptual framework is, theory alone is not sufficient. The "skills trainer" must also have a solid grasp of the techniques and practical aspects of training. To this end we have tried to emphasize the practical application of the basic principles. How does one actually go about identifying, measuring, and modifying social behavior? Actual case material has been included to illustrate points and help the reader attain a feel for how the principles can be applied. Although this should help the reader develop an appreciation of useful training methods (social-skills training is itself an interpersonal skill!), it must be remembered that specific training methods can usually be improved on. Thus, we have tried to avoid a rigid "cookbook" approach. Likewise, this is not intended to be a "do-it-yourself," self-improvement guide to social skills.

In the broadest sense, this book is intended for those who within some professional training capacity seek to increase the effectiveness of his or her clients' interpersonal effectiveness. The underlying principles and basic training procedures are applicable to a wide variety of individuals and specific kinds of populations. For example, social-skills training may be used to teach chronic psychiatric patients how to engage in elementary conversation. The same principles and similar procedures could be used to instruct a corporate executive how to give more effective feedback to subordinates. Although some elements of these skills may be worlds apart, similar concepts are involved in the identification, assessment, and training procedures for both situations. Thus, the same principles may find applications in areas as diverse as mental health, industry, education, business, health care, government work, etc. In short, almost any area of human endeavor that involves effective social behavior can profit from the principles set forth here.

We have attempted to present the material in a factual, yet not highly technical, way. It is expected that professionals or nonprofessionals familiar with basic psychological processes will be able to use this book as a primary means of learning to employ social-skills training procedures in practice. The book is also appropriate for use as a text accompanying courses in psychology, education, social work, nursing, organizational behavior, and personnel management, which emphasize practical training in social-skills development.

We wish to acknowledge the creative contribution of all our colleagues and students who have constructively challenged and helped us refine our notions about social-skills training. Special appreciation also goes to Linda Burnsed, Lucy Wallace, and Daphne Palmer, whose assistance in typing and editing the manuscript through its many stages has been invaluable. Finally, we reserve our greatest thanks for the many individuals who have participated in social-skills training with us. We have learned much from observing their successes and disappointments as they have improved and developed their abilities. Hopefully we have grown with them.

RICHARD M. EISLER
LEE W. FREDERIKSEN

Contents

I

Introduction to Social Skills

The purpose of this introductory section is to provide the reader with practical perspectives on the nature of social skills, what they accomplish for us, and how skills may be improved by almost anyone who receives appropriate training.

Chapter 1 presents a model of interpersonal skill based on social-learning principles. Then working definitions of social skill are provided which translate the model into conceptualizations of social skills which can be used when we discuss the specifics of assessment and training in the next sections. Finally some of the objectives of training are outlined, as well as an introduction to the basic training techniques.

In Chapter 2, the theoretical and research bases for social-skills training are reviewed. The purpose here is not to summarize all of the work on social skills, but to give the reader an appreciation of how various training techniques were developed, and which ones are likely to be effective in particular circumstances. Armed with a conceptual grasp of the issues presented in this section, the reader should be able to make greater use of information presented in the subsequent chapters on assessment, training, and specific applications.

1

On the Nature of Social Skills

Overview

- Historically, the relationship between an individual's social competence and his or her successful functioning in society has been overlooked by our major educational and remedial institutions.
- Traditionally, "mental health" approaches to social functioning have had difficulties in defining interpersonal behavior problems in ways which were conducive to effective assessment and remediation.
- The social-learning model as a practical and useful framework for understanding and changing social behavior is described.
- Some working conceptualizations of social skill are proposed, with an eye toward establishing a framework for assessing their functional utility in different situations.
- General training considerations stemming from the social-learning model are described, with an overview of the following areas: assessment of interpersonal problems; establishing the objectives of training; the process of training; maintenance and transfer of improvements following training; and evaluation of results.

Throughout history, the ability of a person to develop mutually satisfying relationships with his fellows has been regarded as one of mankind's most significant attributes. In contemporary society, the ability to function successfully with others requires mastery of relatively complex social skills. This is true whether the objective is to find mutual satisfaction from a diversity of relationships with one's spouse, children, friends, and members of the community, or to promote oneself successfully in a chosen vocation or career. Although no single definition of social skill is either adequate or sufficiently comprehensive to describe all social interactions, there appear to be some characteristics of a basic interpersonal process which may be regarded as necessary for demonstration of social skill. Included among these would be the development of a repertoire of effective social behaviors, an awareness of the social norms governing social behavior in various situations, the ability to select the most effective responses from available alternatives, the ability to perceive accurately the feedback from others, and the ability to change one's social behavior based on this feedback. In practical terms, this means that individuals need to learn how to develop skills in negotiation and compromise, how to display assertion appropriately, how to listen effectively, how to use or respond to humor, and when to accede tactfully to the wishes of another, to mention a few.

In earlier times, when interactive roles prescribed for the individual were relatively unambiguous, and the number of social systems that an individual was required to interact with were few, social experiences with family, peer groups, and adult models provided sufficient developmental influences. Owing to the expansion of roles in society today, with a trend toward more egalitarian marital, school, and work relationships and with changing standards of acceptable interpersonal conduct, there is an increased awareness of the need to develop greater facility in social exchanges.

Unfortunately, our universities and our secondary and vocational schools have focused almost exclusively on teaching a practically infinite number of technical skills, from mathematics to scuba diving, which do not necessarily prepare individuals to function effectively with others. This technical emphasis has resulted in parents who do not know how to relate positively to each other or their children, and physicians, lawyers, and other professionals who do not know how to direct the activities of their employees effectively.

Individuals who have demonstrated extreme deficits in social functioning have often found themselves either in mental institutions or in correctional facilities, depending on how unacceptable, maladaptive, or antisocial their behaviors have been perceived to be. Individuals sent to mental-health facilities have usually been stigmatized as being "mentally ill," and in need of "treatment." Unfortunately, treatment methods have often been based on methods of alleviating the *symptoms* of the emotionally or behaviorally disturbed individual, for example, anxiety, depression, or hyperaggressiveness, rather than on teaching the individual more successful ways to cope with his or her interpersonal environment.

Another problem with the mental-illness approach is that a person has had to show rather obvious signs of emotional instability or antisocial behavior before becoming a candidate for remedial attention. This means that many people within the "normal" range of adjustment, who sometimes experience interpersonal stress with their families, spouses, peers, or members of their community, have no legitimate place to go for assistance in solving their human problems. To the present writers, the enhancement of the social functioning of all individuals who need or desire such improvements would appear to be a desirable goal. One does not need to be "ill" in order to benefit from enhanced interpersonal functioning.

Traditional Mental-Health Approaches to Social Skills

Earlier attempts to conceptually differentiate good from poor interpersonal functioning relied on theories of relatively unchanging personality attributes. In this model, personality traits such as empathy, emotional stability, maturity, and needs for affiliation or affection were seen as motivating forces which promoted positive interpersonal functioning. On the other hand, personality characteristics such as "introversion," "neuroticism," and "dependency" were associated with unsuccessful or deviant social functioning.

In retrospect, it appears that personality traits were really shorthand descriptions of how individuals typically behaved or how they described their behavior in various social situations. Unfortunately, many theorists and practitioners working within the personality-trait framework tended to attribute casual significance to personality variables. Therefore, an individual was viewed as behaving passively in social situations *because* he possessed the trait of introversion. Another problem with the concept of personality traits was that they were used to predict that individuals would exhibit similar behaviors in many different social situations. A person high on the trait of "aggression" would, for example, be expected to behave aggressively in all interpersonal situations. We now have evidence that specific attributes of *interpersonal situations* heavily influence a person's behavior so that trait descriptions frequently do not predict how effectively an individual will respond in any particular situational context (Mischel, 1973).

A second notion of personal competence utilized the concept of social attainment. That is, competence was based on the individual's ability to achieve and maintain interpersonal relationships necessary to succeed in a number of socially important areas of life, such as marriage, education, and occupation. Using criteria in these areas as a yardstick of social competence, Zigler and Phillips (Phillips & Zigler, 1961, 1964; Zigler

& Phillips, 1960, 1962); found that hospitalized psychiatric patients evidenced greater impoverishment in social achievement than nonhospitalized individuals from the same socioeconomic strata of society. Further, psychiatric patients who had demonstrated relatively adequate social functioning prior to their hospitalization tended to have shorter periods of institutionalization, and also made better adjustments on returning to community life than did patients with more inadequate social skills. Although diagnostic studies relating social achievement to "Mental health" were very impressive, the findings did not lend themselves to the measuring of specific skills which determined how or why some individuals were successful in the aforementioned categories of social functioning, and others not.

Recently, an increasing number of therapeutic or reeducative approaches have been developed which have aimed to influence social functioning. These remedial techniques, administered individually and in group workshops, have been described by a bewildering array of labels, including "milieu therapy," "gestalt therapy," "rationale-emotive therapy," "transactional analysis," and a variety of "encounter therapies." Although many individuals in treatment at various mental-health resources, including those at psychiatric hospitals, mental-health centers, and drug or alcohol treatment clinics, have experienced one or more of these treatment approaches, others who have wanted to improve their personal effectiveness have also sought these self-improvement experiences.

Unfortunately, many of the aforementioned therapeutic experiences tend to be portrayed as the culmination of some unique theory of human behavior. Most require that therapists and clients alike learn a special jargon for describing social interactions. An additional problem is that none of the labels adequately describes a unique set of therapeutic operations which are demonstratively different from the others. For adherents to these therapies, treatment objectives tend to be vague, like "personal growth," so that participants may not know what specific outcomes to expect from the experience. Finally, attempts at evaluation of results on specified criteria are rare. Since the failure to specify measurable objectives cannot help but lead to insufficient attention to evaluation, most of these popularized "social therapies" are perpetuated by ardent believers despite the possibility that some may be ineffective or possibly detrimental.

For the counselor who must assess and develop a remedial approach for a specific problem, such as how to manage a dysfunctional family or what to do with a shy college student, the best course is often elusive. For the average person who wants to "get along better" with others, or the company president who wants to train his executives in managing personnel more efficiently, the choice of whom to consult or what workshop to attend is often confusing.

A major purpose of this book is to describe a systematic approach to the teaching of interpersonal skills to a variety of individuals, ranging from those who are quite handicapped interpersonally to those who merely want to function more effectively with others. The approach is based on established principles of social learning which have received at least some empirical verification through psychological research. It assumes that maladaptive or deficient social skills are among the necessary conditions which lead to the psychological impairment experienced by many individuals. Although it is recognized that there are genetic, physiological, and other biological influences which may predispose individuals to interpersonal dysfunction, remediation may begin by systematically teaching new and more effective social behaviors.

The Social-Learning Model

A useful starting point is a model of interpersonal behavior based on principles of social learning. Since a comprehensive treatment of social-learning principles goes beyond the scope of this book, we will only highlight some of the major points relevant to our purposes. For a more detailed perspective the reader is referred to Bandura (1969, 1974). Mahoney (1974), Meichenbaum (1974, 1977), and Mischel (1973).

The social-learning view of interpersonal behavior rests on the assumption that a person's responses to social situations are acquired through previous experience and are being continually modifed or maintained by social consequences delivered by others. In addition, the individual is not viewed as a passive recipient influenced solely by the behavior of others. The interaction is viewed as one of reciprocal influence whereby each actor can modify the social behavior of the other. Finally, there is no automatic relationship between social situations and the individual's responses. Responses are mediated by cognitive processes which include the motivations, intentions, expectations, discriminations, and choices of each actor in the process of interaction.

In this model, the individual is neither impelled by inner thoughts or emotions nor is he entirely controlled by conditions operating in his social environment. When a person is confronted with a social situation, he or she develops anticipations of what to expect from the other person in the interaction. Then, the individual must anticipate the probable consequences that any particular response may elicit. The response chosen will be influenced by what the individual has found most likely to produce desirable consequences with others in the past. Also, the individual can imitate or model his or her response after one that he or she has witnessed someone else use in similar situations.

No matter how it has been learned, the response selected will elicit social consequences from others. Depending on how positively the individual views the social consequences of his or her response, he or she will tend to employ similar responses in that situation in the future.

Thus, social behavior is conceptualized on the basis of *reciprocity* and *mutual influence*. Not only is the individual influenced by responses from others; the individual also helps create his or her social environment by influencing others to modify their behavior. The ability with which the individual can create a favorable social climate in which others respond according to his or her expectations and desires is a measure of the individual's social skill.

Toward a Definition of Social Skill

As pointed out earlier, recent advances in social-learning conceptions of effective psychological functioning have been divorced from earlier notions of mental health or mental illness. Presumably, principles governing the acquisition of abnormal or maladaptive social behavior should apply to the acquisition of socially appropriate functional behaviors. Theoretically, a model of interpersonal functioning based on social skill or social competence should have applicability to a wide range of individuals from varying social backgrounds and levels of achievement in their social, occupational, and educational lives. A skill-development approach to social behavior should be as useful for those who are severely deficient in interpersonal skills as it is for those whose interpersonal behaviors are relatively adaptive in many situations.

At first glance, the concept of social skill is one that most of us can readily identify with in assessing the behavior of others. On an intuitive basis most of us presume to know whether those we come into contact with are relatively skilled or unskilled in dealing with people. However, once we attempt to define social skill in a functional manner, the apparent simplicity of the concept becomes more elusive. Some of the questions which typically arise are: (1) How many social skills are there? (2) Can a person be socially skilled in some situations and not in others? (3) How does one judge whether a person's social behavior is effective or not? (4) Who should judge whether skillfulness has been demonstrated, the actors in the interaction or an outside observer? (5) Why do various explicit social behaviors appear to work well for some individuals and not for others? (6) How can we account for the discrepancy when an individual says that he is socially adept, and others report that he is tactless?

These questions point to the fact that social skill is a multidimensional construct. Definitions of social skill which appear appropriate and functional for one set of circumstances, for example, getting a date, do not appear fruitful for another, such as getting a job. This penomenon has frustrated researchers attempting to develop skill-training methods as much as it has hindered practitioners attempting to apply them.

Behavioral Components of Skill

Perhaps an analogy between our use of the term "social skill" and the concept of "athletic skill" will be useful in highlighting the problems, and help us arrive at a tentative solution. First, there are some measurable behavioral elements comprising social skill across many social situations, just as there are definite attributes of general athletic ability. For social skill, empirical research has shown that there are specific component behaviors which differentiate between assertive and unassertive individuals (Argyle, 1969; Eisler, Hersen, Miller, & Blanchard, 1975). Among these are nonverbal behaviors such as eye contact, gestures, tone of voice, and appropriate emotional expression. Verbal abilities are also necessary, such as to ask direct questions, to state one's position clearly, and the ability to reinforce the other actor with praise or show of appreciation. In the case of athletic ability, some of the basic measurable ingredients might be perceptual-motor coordination, speed, stamina, and strength.

Cognitive Components of Skill

In our analogy between social skill and athletic ability there are some cognitive elements which are difficult to observe directly. These cognitive elements refer to the person's expectations, thoughts, and decisions about what should be said or done next during the interaction.

Since thoughts are invisible to a witnessing observer, they are frequently correctly or sometimes incorrectly inferred from what the observed person has said or done. In the case of social skills, cognitive abilities might include skills in the accurate perception of the other person's wishes or intentions, or insight into which response will be most likely to influence his or her partner's opinion. For athletic skill, the cognitive dimensions might include an ability to develop alternative strategies of attack based on the opponent's perceived weaknesses or knowing when to conserve energy. In both kinds of skill the aforementioned cognitive abilities about "how to play the game" are, to a large extent, responsible for success or failure.

At this point we have identified some general components of social and athletic skills that are relatively easy to measure behaviorally, and some which may be inferred from observing performance. However, observed behavior and inferred cognitive abilities do not by themselves outline all the parameters of social skill.

Generality of Skills

An additional parameter is the generality or utility of these skills in a variety of different situations. In the case of athletic skill, the situational aspect becomes apparent when we consider that a person may be skillful in dealing with peers of the same sex, but relatively unskillful in dealing with persons of the opposite sex.

Clearly, although there is some generality of athletic ability in that a good football player may possess skills required by a good baseball player, each sport may require different levels of various kinds of ability. For example, though both football and baseball require strength and agility, nimble movements may be more important than strength for fielding in baseball, whereas strength may be more important for blocking in football. Likewise, poise and apparent self-confidence may be important social skills both for dating and for obtaining a job. However, the ability to be humorous and entertaining is probably a more important skill for getting a date than for obtaining a job.

Skill Effectiveness

Another parameter which applies to both athletic and social skills involves the functional effectiveness or impact of the component skills. In a sport such as baseball, getting a hit or throwing a strike is an observable measure of the athlete's combined skills. In boxing, the outcome is shown by a fighter's ability either to knock his opponent down for ten seconds or to win more rounds than his opponent, as judged by a referee. The knockdown is an effect that everyone can easily observe. Winning rounds is based on the subjective impressions of referees, who may have different criteria for boxing skill, which sometimes leads to a "split decision." Nevertheless, boxing skill is often judged by the effects it has on the opponent.

In the area of social behavior it is possible to judge the skillfulness of the actor's behavior by its effects on the respondent. The person interacting with a girl gets a date with her as he intended. We could count the number of dates this person gets per number of attempts as a measure of his dating skill, just as we rate the skill of a field-goal kicker by the number of scores per attempt. Note, the emphasis is on the *effects* of the behavior, not which behaviors were employed to be successful. Getting a hit, scoring a knockdown, or getting a date are all successful outcomes demonstrating that a certain combination of behaviors does in fact produce the intended results. Skills employed by different individuals to obtain a date or a job, or to win a boxing match, may vary considerably. The point is that different combinations of skills used by different athletes or socially skilled persons to attain their ends may be successful as gauged by the criteria of intended effects. It would be an oversimplification, therefore, to suggest that any one set of social skills should be employed by everyone to obtain specified objectives in any particular set of interpersonal situations.

Rules of the Game

Finally, athletic contests and interpersonal interactions are governed by certain rules or norms. In case of athletic events, scores have to be made within certain time limits according to certain rules of the game. Athletes are penalized for rule infractions. In football, interference with the receiver may result in the loss of yardage toward the goal. In boxing, hitting "below the belt" can result in the loss of points. Similarly, there are social norms governing what is considered to be appropriate behavior in different interpersonal situations. For instance, it may be permissible and functionally effective to ask a waitress to take your dinner back. The consequences of requesting the same from your mother-in-law might be quite dysfunctional and lead to the loss of your dinner. To upbraid your son for leaving his room untidy might be entirely appropriate, whereas requesting your boss to clean up her office might be perceived at best as inappropriate or at least unwise. Both these examples point to the fact that there are norms governing what is considered appropriate during particular kinds of interactions with different kinds of people, such as son, boss, waitress, and mother-in-law. Additionally, various groups of individuals who hold different social values may perceive the same event differently. For example, if a youngster confronts his teacher for making an error, the boy's peers may view the confrontation positively and applaud his behavior, whereas the teacher may view it negatively, and provide punishing consequences.

To summarize this section, it is clear that our conceptualization of social skill must include several dimensions. One dimension has to do with a number of observable behaviors which may be noticed by anyone in a social situation. In some instances we may expect to assess these abilities with relatively objective measures of performance. In other instances, cognitive skills will be inferred from our observations of social behavior, or by asking the person what he was thinking before he did thus and so.

Another dimension of social skill has to do with the interaction between the performance of certain social behaviors and the environmental context in which it occurs. Put simply, this means that the utility of explicit social skills depends, in part, upon the situations in which they are employed. Thus, social skills employed to get a promotion on the job may not be effective when used to change the behavior of one's spouse in a marital relationship. Therefore, changes in the social environment from one situation to the next evoke different responses from others which require different skills.

There are several ways of looking at social adroitness apart from observing the constellation of behaviors displayed by the actor. Another view of his skill is provided by observing the effects of his behavior on the other actor. Just as we can judge a basketball player's skill by the number of points he scores in a game, so we can assess social ability in relation to the degree to which the other actor produces the desired reciprocal behavior.

Last, it is possible to judge social skill on the dimension of social acceptability. A bully may produce the responses he desires in an interaction by threats and intimidation. A liar may produce similar results by deception. However, one must remember that individuals and social groups have norms and values as to ethical and unethical means in obtaining personal objectives. To the extent that the actor violates these rules, a social cost may accrue in the form of anger and retaliatory behavior. Thus, social acceptability must also be taken into account when making judgments about the effectiveness of social skills.

Training Considerations: An Overview

At this point we have discussed, in general terms, some of the reasons why social skill or interpersonal effectiveness is preferable to focusing on concepts of normality and abnormality in describing interpersonal behavior. In addition, we have noted that traditional theories of personality are of little value, in that they (a) assume that social behavior is relatively constant in different situations, and (b) do not give us many clues as to how social behavior can be changed. Although various methods of changing interpersonal behavior in the context of treatment or therapy have been devised, many of these are based on fad or untestable theories rather than on empirically derived principles of social learning. In this section we shall discuss briefly some issues relevant to the application of the social-learning model. The objective will be to describe a basis for social-competence training, rather than to provide specific details (which will be presented later in the book). The following parameters must be considered carefully in the development of social-skills training: (1) assessment of the interpersonal problem(s); (2) establishing the objectives of training; (3) the process of training; (4) maintenance and transfer of improvements following training; and (5) evaluation of results.

Assessment of Interpersonal Problems

Assessment of interpersonal problems depends on detailed observations and accurate reports of clearly specified behavior in social situations. Although self-report inventories and personal interviews have always been useful in discovering how a person relates to his social environment in a general way they do not provide us with a detailed basis for social-skills training. In other words, evaluations of a client's performance communicated through written inventories and verbal interviews provide us with only a partially complete view of how he or she actually interacts in social situations. The majority of us have trouble remembering exactly what we have said and done in a particular social situation. We also have difficulty in reporting precisely how the other person behaved. In addition, few of us can assess fully the impact of the social situation on ourselves and the other person at the time of the exchange because of all the complexities and subtle nuances of social interaction.

In order to comprehend more fully the client's difficulties, there must be some demonstration of his typical performance in social interactions so that we can select targets for change. Some sample of social behavior must be elicited and observed in such a fashion that we can determine functional and nonfunctional aspects of the behavior which requires improvement. The assessment situations must have the characteristics of allowing observation of social exchanges by the trainer and must also be highly related to how the client functions in his natural environment without the presence of the trainer. This permits a more precise identification of what the client says, how he says it, how he responds to the maneuvers of the other person, and the likely consequences of his behavior. In addition, more subtle indications of what the client is thinking and feeling about the interactions are brought forward in time for his report immediately following the interaction. Here, too, targets for remedial attention can be identified. In some instances, the client has misconceptions about the effectiveness of his own behavior or fails to perceive the other person's intentions accurately. Sometimes the client does not exhibit potentially effective behavior because he misjudges the appropriateness of his behavior for a particular social situation. The beliefs and attitudes that the client has about certain kinds of social behavior must be scrutinized, as well as the performance itself.

Samples of interpersonal behavior to be improved are typically obtained in one of two ways. One method is to set up hypothetical problems which are then role-played by client and trainer. A second more direct way is to observe the client interacting with a natural life partner, such as his spouse with whom he is having difficulty. Observations of simulated or naturally occurring interactions are vital to a valid assessment of interpersonal behavior.

Objectives of Training

Following a careful assessment of the problem(s), the objectives of training must be agreed on by the client and the trainer. In some instances, the objective will be to change the client's performance in dealing with certain people, such as spouse, peers, or boss. In others, the objectives will be to change his behavior in a whole class of situations, for example, how to get a date, or how to become a more effective supervisor. In still other cases, the classes of behavior to be changed may be more general in that the client may wish to become more assertive with a variety of people. Based on our social-learning model, the general objectives can then be broken down into more specific steps or learning tasks.

For example, suppose a client identifies his major problem as having difficulty with his temper. We observe that, in dealing with a variety of people, this person attempts to coerce his partner to fulfill his requests by threats, demands, and other socially unacceptable behaviors. This aggressive social discourse eventuates in the other person's typically avoiding him or engaging in nonproductive counterattacks. We also observe that this person typically is unassertive when other people treat him unfairly. Goals of training which could be specified for the individual might be: (1) how to request tactfully that someone do something for you; (2) how to show appreciation to others when they have done something you liked; (3) how to determine more accurately that another person is being noncompliant because your presentation does not demonstrate appropriate concern for his feelings; (4) how to express irritation in a socially appropriate manner which will elicit sympathy and respect for your rights. Note that once the social deficits and excesses have been assessed in behaviorally relevant terms, training goals can be established which focus on changing specific social behaviors to such as have a higher probability of success than those previously displayed.

The Training Process

The objective of training is to facilitate the acquisition of interpersonal skills which will be more functional than the social behaviors demonstrated during assessment. Training can be viewed as an ongoing process with several overlapping phases. Although it is true that specific training objectives can be attained with a variety of alternative training procedures, the purpose here will be to focus on the process of training. These can be separated into the four following phases: (1) description and rationale; (2) demonstration; (3) practice; and (4) feedback.

Description and Rationale. The initial emphasis is to provide the client with a description of the new social behaviors that he has agreed to learn. Equally important we must provide him with some rationale for performing the described behaviors so that he can readily grasp our purposes in having him learn them. For example, in training a client to be more assertive, we must specify the behaviors he needs to perform more effectively, and at the same time explain why these changes are important. The trainer may suggest that the client state his or her position more clearly so that others will have a better understanding of what is expected. Additionally, the trainer may suggest that the client speak more forcefully, so that others will believe that he or she means what he or she says. During this phase, the trainer acts like a knowledgeable coach whose task is to help the client develop more effective alternative responses by suggesting alternatives.

Demonstration. Although coaching through verbal descriptions is often effective by itself, a second step in the process is often required. Sometimes it is useful to have a "model" demonstrate the desired response so that the client is shown how to perform as vividly as possible. In situations where social consequences to the model are delivered by another person, the client can obtain a better picture of what to expect when he or she exhibits the behavior by him- or herself. Modeling, based on principles of immitative learning, may be presented live by the trainer, an assistant, or by another client in a group-training situation. An alternative to actual presentations may be the use of prerecorded audiovsual material whereby models demonstrate socially skilled behavior. The advantage of prerecorded models is that they can be used repeatedly.

Practice. It is important that the client have ample opportunity to practice novel social behaviors which are being learned. Repeated performances will allow the client to feel more comfortable in modifying his or her behavior and allow both he and she and the trainer to make delicate adjustments in the delivery of socially skilled behaviors.

The basic vehicle for response practice is through *role-playing* enactments similar to those used during the initial assessment of the client's deficits. Role-playing is one of the most innocuous forms of practice in that potentially threatening consequences which might occur in the natural environment are absent. In addition to overt practice it is possible to have the client covertly practice specific thoughts which he or she has learned during training. Later stages of practice require the client to carry out assignments in the natural environment which require the use of the improved social behavior.

Feedback. Further improvements in performance are shaped using "feedback." Praise and encouragement are offered by the trainer when the client performs well. Corrective feedback is delivered to ameliorate continuing deficiencies along with suggestions for additional improvements. Videotape feedback of performances are also useful in that they allow the client to see how he or she is performing more objectively. Of course, the most important feedback will occur in the natural environment in the form of consequences delivered to the client's newly acquired social behavior.

At the present time, research evidence as to which training techniques are most efficacious with which kinds of trainees for which kinds of interpersonal problems is lacking or sometimes contradictory. The relative effectiveness of coaching and modeling overtly or covertly for different social problems has not been clearly established. Therefore, the trainer has some latitude in trying different training methods to see what works best with his particular client. As long as the trainer is in a position to assess the results, techniques can be changed until the client has learned the most adaptive responses.

Maintaining Therapeutic Gains

Maintenance of therapeutic gains and transfer of learned social repertoires to novel social situations is a problem common to all skills-training procedures. Following completion of the social-competence training which we have just outlined, we may be relatively confident that the client has the *capability* of performing more functional social behavior, but, at the same time, having little assurance that he will therefore perform adequately in actual life situations. This is especially true if the social situations encountered are somewhat different from those in which he or she received training. The solution requires an understanding of what issues are involved in the maintenance of acquired social behaviors.

Some trainers do not fully grasp the fact that appropriate social performance is a continuing process. Behaviors learned by the client one day may be lost or inaccessible subsequent to training. Since we are involved in training complex and interrelated social behaviors, we may expect training to proceed at an uneven pace whereby some aspects of the skill are well trained and others require further improvement. Additionally, the client may appear to have mastered the trained skill in one situation, but fail to exhibit those skills in others which are only slightly different from the first. One way to maintain training effects over time and obtain transfer to different social situations is to increase the amount of response practice the client receives, and then diversify various aspects of the interpersonal training situations so that the skills are, in a sense, overlearned. Continued exercise of newly developed repertoires is essential for maximizing the client's ability to overcome previous habits of less functional social behavior. In addition to repeated practice which the client may be urged to perform on his or her own, the trainer can schedule increasingly dissimilar training situations so that the client becomes prepared to handle variations in social situations with improvisations of his or her responses.

Another problem which is often related to the failure of a client to maintain newly acquired behaviors stems from personal attitudes and feelings about the performance of behavior which has just been learned. In some cases, the client may have agreed with the trainer's rationale for learning new responses to certain social situations, but still feel uncomfortable about responding in a different manner. For example, a client may be taught to express more skillfully his or her opinions in various situations. However, the client still fears that he or she will be disliked or disapproved of for expressing these views. These doubts may result in the failure of some clients to express their opinions in certain critical situations, or abandonment of what they have learned in training so that their expressions are timid and ineffective.

To some extent, a client's expectations of negative consequences can be overcome through repeated practice and by allowing them to experience favorable consequences. However, it is often useful to help clients become more aware of how their feelings may interfere with what they have been trained to do. In addition, the trainer should help clients "cognitively restructure" the rationale for employing different social behavior and prepare them for the fact that their efforts will not be successful on all occasions. Maintenance of skill thus includes helping clients reaffirm the potential utility of their new behavior, and helping them generate sufficient morale to continue efforts at mastery.

Despite the fact that a client may have had sufficient practice and hold positive attitudes toward employing the trained skills, the lack of positive responses from others may inhibit his or her performance. For example, suppose we have trained a man to behave more assertively with his wife. The wife may have had little experience in dealing with someone who "speaks his mind" directly. She may either withdraw from him or begin unwarranted attacks on his assertive behavior. It is important for trainers to be fully aware of the actual environmental consequences of training clients to act in a particular fashion. In this case it might be necessary to enlist the wife's cooperation in the training by advising her what changes to expect in her husband's behavior. It might also be possible to match training with behaviors that the wife will find acceptable. This issue also points to the fact that when training is directed toward helping a person deal more skillfully with another with whom he or she has continued interaction, it is desirable to bring the other person into the training situation to ensure more rewarding consequences to the client.

Another solution to the lack of positive environmental consequences involves helping the client realize that new performances do not automatically ensure success. In some cases, he or she will have to learn further discriminations (such as under which circumstances new social responses should be displayed). Also, the client and the trainer will have to anticipate the possibility that some individuals will require a period of time before changing their expectations regarding the client's behavior.

In summary, trainers have the responsibility of minimizing negative consequences to their clients' changed behavior by anticipating which situations will most likely produce favorable consequences and which situations are likely to evoke less reinforcing or potentially adverse consequences. Second, trainers should help clients tolerate some possible short-term negative consequences by emphasizing the long-term value of maintaining new social behavior. Sometimes it is possible for the trainer to intervene in the client's natural environment, for example, with his or her spouse, so that others will be more favorably predisposed to the client's changed behavior. Finally, to ensure maintenance of behavior, trainers should become involved in helping their clients make adjustments in their approach to a variety of social situations, to ensure that they will have adaptive consequences.

Evaluation of Outcome

The assessment of outcome in social-skills training should be viewed as a continuing process. Evaluation of social competence, of course, begins with the initial assessment of the client's deficits. Progress throughout training is assessed by monitoring performance during successive rehearsal sessions. In addition, progress outside training is evaluated by having the client report on the social behavior he or she engages in at home, or at work, or in novel social situations. Toward the completion of training, greater emphasis is placed on the evaluation of the client's ability to handle more difficult problems during response practice without further assistance from the trainer.

In order to evaluate ongoing progress following coaching and simulated interactions, both trainer and client compare the amount of comfort and skill presently displayed with earlier performances. It is often useful for the trainer to modify some aspects of the situations presented to the client in order to provide novel elements not included during the earlier stages of training. For example, in evaluating changes in assertive performance with strangers, the trainer may present himself as a very persistent salesperson who simply won't "take no" for an answer. Variations in role-playing situations test the client's ability to persevere in the responses he has learned under more stressful conditions, and help determine whether he can modify his repertoire appropriately to handle a greater diversity of related problems.

In addition to role-playing simulations, the trainer and client may jointly formulate plans to test the improved social behavior in more realistic social situations. Let us suppose that a male client has received training in how to interact more successfully with members of the opposite sex. The trainer may suggest that he initiate conversations with women who know him in class or at work. Then the trainer may suggest that he initiate meetings, in a variety of social situations, with women whom he does not know. These assignments would help the client evaluate his performance in natural-environment circumstances. Successful performance with desirable outcomes increases the client's self-confidence, and serves to motivate him to employ his skills in an increasing variety of social situations. In addition to descriptions of performance, the trainer will also want to know how much satisfaction the client perceives himself to be receiving in the performance tests. If possible, it is highly desirable to obtain the opinions of others as to how the client is interacting with them. This may involve informal reports from the client's spouse, friends, or employers.

In summary, the evaluation of outcome converges on the opinions of the trainer, the client, and other informants who have knowledge of the individual's accomplishments in natural life situations. Since the objectives of training have been clearly specified in advance, measures of change should be available for scrutiny on both a gross impressionistic level and along precise quantifiable dimensions of behavior which will be discussed in subsequent chapters. Thus, assessment of outcome following training is consistent with, and in many ways similar to, procedures used during the initial assessment of social skill.

Summary

An individual's mastery over many of life's challenges at home, at work, and in the larger social community depends, to a large extent, on his or her interpersonal effectiveness. Failures in relationships with one's fellows often lead to patterns of social anxiety, depression, or even antisocial behavior. Should these interpersonal failures become chronic or be of a serious dysfunctional nature, the individual is typically referred to our mental-health or correctional facilities for remedial attention. Less seriously impaired individuals often seek assistance from a wide range of mental-health practitioners who offer an infinite variety of psycho-therapies or personal-growth experiences.

Rather than looking upon the outcomes of social dysfunction as indicative of mental illness or flawed personalities, we have proposed that these maladaptive social-behavior patterns be viewed as a lack of interpersonal skill. Conceptualized in this manner, problems with others can be remediated through structured training in social skills.

An overview of the social-learning perspective was then presented. The basic tenets of this view are that both effective and ineffective social-behavior patterns are learned throughout one's life. We learn much of our social behavior through the consequences that our acts elicit from others or by observing and imitating behavior. The social behaviors which become permanent aspects of our repertoirs, some would say incorporated into our personalities, are those which are socially reinforced. Individuals who have been exposed to inadequate models or who are reinforced for inappropriate social behavior typically do not develop the social skills to be successful in their interpersonal relationships.

Although most people intuitively "know" what social skills are, it is hard to develop any single definition which will encompass skilled behavior in all social situations. An alternative is to look at various dimensions of social abilities. One dimension is the behavioral aspect, including the ability to speak and respond to others in a convincing and effective manner. There is also a cognitive dimension of social skills. This includes such abilities as knowing what is the appropriate thing to say, the ability to perceive the other person's intentions, and the ability to predict the likely consequences of one's behavior. Further, an individual's thoughts and behaviors cannot be analyzed apart from the particular social situation. Social behaviors that are typically effective in one situation may not be very useful in another. The implications of this are that when we are evaluating a person for social-skills training, we must also assess the nature of the social situations in which the skills will be used.

Finally, ways in which assessment and training procedures will be employed in fulfilling training objectives were presented. Also discussed were some notions about procedures which might be used to maintain acquired skills, as well as possible methods for evaluating the effects of training. In the next chapter, we will discuss some of the research findings on social-skills training which will provide us with a solid foundation upon which to build successful assessment and training strategies.

From Research to Application

Overview

- The implications of psychological theory and research for practical applications are discussed.
- Development in social-skills training has had its roots in early research on the social competence of psychiatric patients, and more recent notions of the importance of assertiveness in interpersonal relationships.
- Two models explaining social ineffectiveness are presented. In one model, social anxiety is seen as inhibiting the expression of inter-personal competence. In the alternative model, skill deficits are seen as the result of inadequate learning experiences.
- Research on the efficacy of the various skills training components is presented. The techniques are discussed under the categories of response acquisition procedures, response practice procedures, shaping procedures, and cognitive restructuring techniques.

Despite the fact that much of the research on the applications of social-skills training is little more than a decade old, an exhaustive review of the available literature could easily fill several volumes. Consequently, we will narrow our perspective somewhat, and focus only on theory and research results which are most closely related to our presentation for this book.

Before we begin our discussion of the research literature, a few paragraphs are in order about the relationships among research, theory, and actual practice. When we speak about research, basically we are talking about the fact that we are using scientifically sound methods for making systematic observations under specified conditions. The process of conducting research on social behavior invariably changes the social behavior. That is, the presence of the observer, observing what people do, changes to some degree what they do. Thus, all research on social skills which involves direct observation of people takes place under conditions which are to some extent artificial. Sometimes the "facts" obtained about interpersonal behavior obtained through research hold up in the real world, and sometimes they do not. The expectation is that principles governing social behavior which are discovered under experimental conditions necessary to meet the requirements for research will be valid in the natural environment. We do, however, have to be somewhat cautious about drawing conclusions from only one or two research studies.

As we have mentioned, research involves the use of specified observational methods to test ideas which we hope will be relevant to practice. These ideas may originate from certain theoretical notions, for example, "people learn much of their social behavior by watching and imitating how others behave in similar circumstances." Alternatively, some notions which we want to test through systematic research come from casual observations, for example, "people seem to do what you expect more frequently when you praise them for what they have already done." Whether from theoretical models or from casual observations, the ideas linking psychological events must be subjected to research scrutiny through repeated observations under specified conditions. Often the information which results from the research procedures partially confirms our original notions, while indicating that some adjustments in our thinking may need to be made. Sometimes we will learn that our original ideas are really true only under a very few circumstances, and perhaps we would be better off without them altogether. The point to be made is that there needs to be an interplay between our original notions made from theory or from casual observations, and the more systematic observations made from our research procedures. Principles obtained through research need to be tested in practice over a period of time. The results of such application can in turn generate more provocative ideas for research.

Unfortunately, some individuals engaged in psychological research become so intrigued with conceptual and methodological issues that they tend to lose sight of the practical implications of their work. Such researchers become so enamored of their theoretical models that they forget to look at events in the real world which bear on the relative truth or falsity of their model of "what should happen." On the other hand, practitioners often have to produce results in the real world. Frequently the things they do may make intuitive sense to them in the absence of scientifically established principles. There is nothing wrong with this, unless the practitioner should become so convinced that there are no better alternatives that he or she forgets to keep looking for them.

In summary, then, psychological research is based on established methods of making systematic observations under carefully specified conditions. The scientific method often allows one to draw conclusions about the observations. Research, particularly in the area of social behavior, sometimes has the unwanted side effect of changing social behaviors so that they are not the same as they would be in the natural environment. The real world is a source of observations which should temper the conclusions made from research activity. A practitioner applying principles obtained through psychological research must be free to modify what he or she does, in order to meet the requirements of clients in the real world. However, the practitioner is not free of the obligation to question his or her improvisations in the real world before rigidly adhering to them.

Historical Perspective

The relationship between deficits in social functioning and a variety of behavior disorders was empirically documented in the early sixties by two investigators, Edward Zigler and Leslie Phillips. These researchers compared psychiatric hospital patients with each other and with groups of psychiatrically normal persons on global indicators of education, and vocational and marital adjustment (Phillips & Zigler, 1961, 1964; Zigler & Phillips, 1960). The research showed that a person's level of social competence was related to the degree of his or her psychiatric impairment. In general, less social competence was associated with more severe psychiatric symptomology, while greater social competence was associated with normal psychological functioning. In studying the outcome of psychiatric treatment with this population, Zigler and Phillips (1960) found that the person's interpersonal competence prior to hospitalization predicted (better than the type of treatment received) whether or not he or she would make a satisfactory life adjustment following the discharge from the hospital. Persons who possessed relatively good social skills prior to hospitalization required shorter periods of hospitalization and less rehospitalization following discharge than those with relatively inadequate social skills. Unfortunately, these rather impressive results did not quickly give rise to the widespread use of social-skills training to improve the interpersonal behavior of psychiatric patients. At the time these findings were published, there was more emphasis being placed on the assessment and treatment of the patients' symptoms (e.g., depression, anxiety) than on the assessment of social skills. Moreover, there were few methods available to provide social-skills training in remediating the interpersonal problems of severely disturbed psychiatric patients. Recently, such training has been explored with considerable success (Eisler, Blanchard, Fitts, & Williams, 1978; Goldsmith & McFall, 1975; Hersen & Bellack, 1976; Hersen & Eisler, 1976).

Assertion as a Social Skill

Although the investigations of the social competence of psychiatric patients by Zigler and Phillips did not have any immediately observable impact on social-skills research, the predilictions of two scientist practitioners did. Joseph Wolpe and Arnold Lazarus (1966) were among the first to articulate a training paradigm for teaching an important cluster of social skills which they referred to as assertiveness.

Wolpe and Lazarus described assertiveness training as a means of helping people overcome social anxiety which was felt to inhibit their effective performance in interpersonal encounters. The emphasis of the training was initially on teaching individuals how to release feelings of pent-up resentment and anger when they allowed themselves to be intimidated by others in social encounters. The theoretical rationale for the training was that by showing an individual how to express anger appropriately in interpersonal encounters, the disabling effects of anxiety would gradually be overcome by a process called reciprocal inhibition. Moreover, it was assumed that the reductions in anxiety would result in more effective interpersonal behavior.

In subsequent writings, Lazarus (1971, 1973) included the expressions of positive emotions, such as warmth, compassion, and love as also being assertive. In fact, Lazarus (1973) proposed that assertive behavior be divided into four different response competencies: (1) the ability to say no, (2) the ability to ask favors or make requests, (3) the ability to express both positive and negative feelings, and (4) the ability to initiate, continue, and terminate general conversations. Unfortunately, research on the effectiveness of assertion-training procedures has been marked by a diversity of such definitions of assertive skills with little agreement on the response categories which should be called assertive. In addition, the ability to express oneself assertively has been confused with the expression of aggression. This has made it difficult to compare the results of different studies purporting to investigate assertion skills. Nonetheless, the pioneering work on assertiveness has had an important impact on the study of social skill.

Assertion Training and Clinical Problems

The theoretical framework proposed by Wolpe and Lazarus linking debilitating anxiety in interpersonal situations to lack of assertion skills rapidly gave rise to the application of assertiveness training to a diversity of clinical problems. Assertion training was employed to remediate problems ranging from the severe interpersonal handicaps of socially inadequate mental-hospital patients (Eisler, Hersen, & Miller, 1974; Gutride, Goldstein, & Hunter, 1973) to the dating problems of relatively well-adjusted college students (Martinson & Zerface, 1970). Between these extremes of adjustment, interpersonal skills training was used as a treatment approach for depressed individuals (Libet & Lewinsohn, 1973), couples with marital problems (Fensterheim, 1972), and individuals with deviant sexual preferences (Edwards, 1972; Stevenson & Wolpe, 1960). Later, variations of assertion training were applied to individuals with alcohol and drug problems (Foy, Miller, Eisler, & O'toole, 1976; Van Hasselt, Hersen, & Milliones, 1978), and those who exhibited excessive interpersonal aggression (Frederiksen, Jenkins, Foy, & Eisler, 1976; Matson & Stephans, 1978). In the last several years, social-skills training based on the early assertion-training work has been used with children who evidence poor social skills (Bornstein, Bellack, & Hersen, 1977; Michelson & Wood, 1980).

Research Issues

The early clinical reports on the effects of assertion training were almost uniformly positive in terms of beneficial results obtained with a wide variety of cases. Very often the introduction of novel techniques in clinical psychology and psychiatry has met with initial success because of the vigor and enthusiasm with which it has been applied. Before assertion training and variations of it known as social-skills training could be accepted by the professions, serious questions about the techniques employed, their range of applications, and their efficacy needed to be answered through systematic research. For example, some of the questions posed by the early clinical applications were: What are the differences between those who are socially skilled and those who are socially unskilled? Why do unskilled individuals behave differently—is it because they are anxious and inhibited in social situations, or is it because they have never learned how to respond effectively? Why do the same individuals act socially skilled in some situations, but not in others? What are the best techniques to use in social-skills training? How can we assess the effectiveness of training? For the remainder of this Chapter we will focus on the research literature which has attempted to answer some of these questions. It should be noted that much of the work has been conducted in clinical settings. Although it is our contention that social-skills training is broadly applicable, the limitation of this research base must be acknowledged.

Characteristics of Social Skill

The early research studies on the nature of social skills attempted to delineate some of the behavioral differences between those who were judged socially skillful and those who were rated as unskillful. In the first of a series of studies with psychiatric patients, Eisler, Miller, and Hersen (1973) attempted operationally to define assertive skills by comparing the verbal and nonverbal speech behaviors of mental patients who were rated on global impressionistic measures as being either assertive or nonassertive. The ratings were obtained during the presentation of standardized interpersonal situations through role-playing. The results indicated that those who were perceived as assertive, evidenced more pronounced emotional expression, lengthier replies, more forceful speech, shorter response latencies, and were more likely to make a request of their interpersonal partner than those who were judged to be relatively unassertive.

A different approach to examining the nature of social skills was pursued by Peter Lewinsohn and his colleagues at the University of Oregon (Lewinsohn & Schaffer, 1971; Lewinsohn, Weinstein, & Alper, 1970; Libet & Lewinsohn, 1973). In theorizing about the causes of depression, Lewinsohn observed that depressed individuals seemed to derive little reward, satisfaction, or gratification from their interpersonal relationships. Further, he guessed that depressed individuals failed to receive much in the way of positive consequences from their relationships *because* they lacked important social skills. In Lewinsohn's model, social skill was seen as the ability of the individual to behave in ways which would elicit positive consequences (reinforcement) from others. In order to test the notion that depressed individuals had relative deficits in social skills, Libet and Lewinsohn (1973) compared the behavior of depressed and nondepressed individuals who participated in group-therapy discussions on measures of social skill. The results indicated that the depressed, socially unskilled individuals, relative to the socially skilled, nondepressed individuals, (1) initiated conversations less frequently, (2) spoke to fewer people in the group; (3) took a longer time to respond to other people, (4) gave much briefer replies, and (5) failed to show agreement, approval, or interest in others during conversations.

Thus, there were some similarities and some differences between the findings of Eisler *et al.* (1973) and Libet and Lewisohn (1973) on the nature of social skills. In both studies, unskilled individuals tended to give very brief, uninformative replies with long latencies of response, compared to the socially skilled individuals. However, Lewinsohn and Libet found that the socially skilled individuals were more "reinforcing" to their interpersonal partners than the unskilled. On the other hand, Eisler *et al.* found that socially skilled individuals were more apt to make assertive requests of their interpersonal partners than their unskilled counterparts. The differences between the findings could have resulted from the fact that different client populations were studied, behavioral observations of skill were experimentally conducted in different sorts of interpersonal situations, or that different measures of skill were employed.

More recently, a study by Arkowitz, Lichtenstein, McGovern, and Hines (1975) attempted to isolate behavioral differences in social skills exhibited by college men who dated frequently, compared with "shy" men who rarely dated. Comparisons between the high- and low-frequency daters of simulated dates with female confederates yielded few specific behavioral differences between groups, although global ratings of social skill were higher for the frequent daters than the infrequent daters. The investigators were surprised by the lack of differences on the specific behavioral measures of social skill similar to those used by Eisler *et al.* (1973). They concluded that skill differences might be more complex than the observation of specific individual behaviors, and that measures of reciprocal exchanges between interpersonal partners might capture true differences in skill. The differences between groups of impressionistic ratings of social skill between daters and nondaters found by Arkowitz *et al.* (1975) was confirmed by Twentyman and McFall (1975), although the specific nature of the differences was difficult to determine.

In summarizing some of the research on the behavioral differences between socially skilled and socially unskilled individuals, the results have shown that skilled versus unskilled individuals can be consistently differentiated on the more global impressionistic ratings by trained observers. The specific nature of the behavioral differences has not been so clear. The results seem to vary depending on the nature of the definition of social skill employed, the nature of the population studied, the interpersonal situations studied, and the kind of measure employed. Once again, we must conclude that the behavioral differences between socially skilled and socially unskilled individuals are not likely to fit any single definition. For the practitioner, this means that global impressionistic ratings will continue to be a good bet in assessing social skills, and that specific behavioral measures will depend on a good deal of the nature of his or her clients, and the characteristics of the skills being trained.

Social Anxiety versus Skill Deficit

There has been considerable controversy in the literature as to whether the observed failure of an individual to exhibit socially skilled behavior results from the skills' never having been learned, or whether interpersonal anxiety prevents the individual from behaving effectively. There are some theorists, most notably Wolpe and Lazarus (1966) who have argued that interpersonal relationships which evoke anxiety may inhibit the performance of socially adaptive behavior. In contrast to the anxiety-inhibition hypothesis, McFall and Twentyman (1973) have expressed the view that appropriate responses may never have been learned. According to this model, anxiety may arise during interpersonal encounters because the person does not know how to behave effectively.

These two models explaining the lack of effective social behavior could theoretically have different implications for training. If Wolpe and Lazarus are correct, training should focus on the reduction of anxiety in interpersonal situations. Possibly cognitive restructuring would be emphasized here, so that the individual would no longer fear the social consequences of behaving in different ways. On the other hand, should McFall and Twentyman be correct, then the focus should be on training the person to acquire those skills in which he or she is deficient.

The present authors feel that both of these theoretical positions have merit. In some instances, individuals have never learned behavior appropriate to certain social situations, and training should focus on teaching the requisite skills. In other instances, social anxiety, stemming from a poor self-concept or fear of untoward social consequences, may motivate the individual to avoid important social contacts. Although individuals in this category have some social skills, they are not well developed because the individual is prevented by anxiety from social experiences which would strengthen those skills. In such circumstances, training could be oreinted toward both anxiety reduction and skill acquisition. In any case, the outcome of this debate may have few practical implications since the training techniques described below would be useful in both instances.

In support of the skill-deficit model, Eisler and his colleagues (Eisler, Miller, & Hersen, 1973; Eisler, Hersen, Miller, & Blanchard, 1975) have consistently noticed behavioral differences in the social skills of psychiatric patients who were judged to be "very assertive" compared with those who were rated as "very unassertive." Further, ratings of the social skillfulness of the unskilled patients could be greatly improved following training procedures which emphasized the learning of new social behaviors (Edelstein & Eisler, 1976; Eisler, Blanchard, Fitts, & Williams, 1978; Herson & Bellack, 1976).

Additional studies with psychiatric patients have provided support for the skill-deficit model. Weinman, Gelbart, Wallace, and Post (1972) compared the effects of a behavioral-training approach with anxiety-reduction (systematic desensitization) methods in an attempt to increase the interpersonal skills of schizophrenic patients. The results indicated that although both skill-acquisition and anxiety-reduction techniques reduced interpersonal anxiety, only the behavioral-development approach produced improvements in the interpersonal behavior of the patients. Similar results were reported by Goldsmith and McFall (1975) in a very sophisticated skills-acquisition program for psychiatric hospital patients which emphasized learning and practicing socially skillful responses to social situations which posed the most difficulty for them.

Studies which have tended to support the anxiety-inhibition hypothesis of skill deficits have generally been performed with college students who date infrequently. For example, Arkowitz et al. (1975) compared high- and low-frequency daters on numerous measures of social anxiety and social behaviors. Although the self-reported and peer ratings of anxiety distinguished between the two groups, the behavioral ratings did not. In order to compare the anxiety levels of dating and nondating college students, Twentyman and McFall (1975) compared the pulse rates of the two groups during simulated dating interactions. It was found that the pulse rate increased only for the nondaters during role-played interactions, and decreased when they avoided interactions.

Finally, two studies by Curran (Curran, 1975; Curran & Gilbert, 1975) compared the efficacy of anxiety-reduction procedures with skill-acquisition training for nondating college students. The results indicated that both procedures were about equally effective in improving dating skills in the short term; however, the skills-acquisition procedures were found to be superior to the anxiety-reduction methods when both groups were compared during a six-month follow-up.

In summary then, what has the literature told us about the causes of socially unskilled behavior? At the present time, it appears that investigators working with the more severely impaired psychiatric populations have obtained results which favor the hypothesis that appropriate skills have never been learned. On the other hand, studies which have investigated the minimal dating patterns of college students have found results which seem to favor the anxiety–inhibition hypothesis. Based on these research results, we might conclude that individuals show generalized interpersonal incompetencies, that is, some patients have never learned appropriate social behaviors. Conversely, other individuals evidence more specific response deficits, for example, college students may suffer from excessive anxiety in certain interpersonal situations which inhibits their performance. Between these two types of clients, most socially unskilled individuals are probably not effective in social situations because of the combined effects of interpersonal anxiety and lack of polished skills appropriate to those situations. Therefore, effective training programs must be based on an appreciation of both these factors. Fortunately, the training techniques described in this volume may be sufficient to improve interpersonal functioning independent of the original cause of the difficulty. In the next section we will devote considerable attention to the various techniques which have been utilized in social-skill training, and present some of the studies which have attempted to evaluate their effectiveness.

Research on Training Techniques

Social-skills training programs have been developed under a variety of rubrics, including "Structured Learning Therapy" (Goldstein, 1973), "Behavioral Replication Techniques" (Kanfer & Phillips, 1970), and "Behavioral Training" (McFall & Twentyman, 1973). Essentially similar training procedures are used in all training programs, although differences in the emphasis of the various training techniques are common. In general, training programs have included a number of integrated training components or elements which are utilized during different operations in training. These operations may be categorized as (1) response acquisition, (2) response practice, (3) response shaping, and (4) cognitive restructuring.

Let us now turn to the research literature to help us evaluate the effectiveness of the training components listed in the four categories above. In some cases we will find clear-cut answers to our questions about the utility of various techniques. In other instances, further research is needed to evaluate fully the pros and cons of using them in practice. In either case, suggestions will be offered concerning the use of the techniques based on our conclusions from the literature.

Response Acquisition

Training techniques used during acquisition operations usually consist of giving the client information about desirable social-response patterns. Two procedures frequently employed during response acquisition are *instructions* describing the behavior to be performed, and giving the client the opportunity to observe *models* performing the desired behavior patterns. When instructions and modeling are used in combination, the client is typically instructed to focus his or her attention on specific aspects of the model's performance, for example, "Notice how the model gets her point across by appropriate eye contact while clearly stating her position."

Instructions. Instructions are used to coach the client in the utilization of specific responses or patterns of response primarily but not exclusively during the response-acquisition phase. Additional instructions to the client can also be given during the corrective-feedback phase by the trainer or by group members in a group training program.

A number of research studies comparing instructions with other response-acquisition methods have found that instructional coaching is extremely effective in generating new social-response patterns (Eisler *et al.*, 1974; Goldsmith & McFall, 1975; Hersen, Eisler, Miller, Johnson, & Pinkston, 1973; McFall & Twentyman, 1973). The Hersen *et al.* (1973) study, however, showed that instructions seemed to have the most powerful effects when teaching specific behaviors which could be easily described, such as eye contact or voice volume. When the behavior to be taught was more complex or difficult to describe, for example, how to make a socially appropriate request, or how to improve one's emotional expression, training was made more effective by combining instructions with a modeling display. McFall and Lillesand (1971) found that instructions combined with rehearsals or practice was effective in increasing the subjects' use of assertive skills.

In summary, the effectiveness of direct instructions or coaching clients on how to behave has unambiguous support in the research literature. There are some hints, however, that instructions should be supplemented with additional techniques when teaching complex patterns of behavior or behaviors which are difficult to describe verbally through instructions.

Modeling. In a review of the social-skills-research literature, Twentyman and Zimmering (1979) found that models portraying competent interpersonal responses were employed in over 70% of the studies surveyed. One interesting aspect of the review was that modeling displays were presented to clients in a variety of ways. For example, Lazarus (1966) employed the trainer as a model; McFall and Lillesand (1971) used audiotaped models; Eisler, Hersen, and Miller (1973) used videotaped models; and O'Conner (1972) employed models on film. Kazdin (1974) has described a novel approach to modeling whereby the client is asked to imagine a model responding competently to hypothetical social interactions in a technique called covert modeling.

Modeling has generally been found to be effective by itself or in combination with other techniques. However, certain attributes of modeling procedures appear to be critically important. For example, modeling appears to be more effective when the characteristics of the model are highly similar to those of the client (Friedrich & Stein, 1975; Nietzel, Martorano, & Melnick, 1977). Exposure time to the model also appears to be important. McFall and Twentyman (1973) found little beneficial effects from modeling using brief client exposures to audiotaped models. On the other hand, Eisler, Blanchard, Fitts, and Williams (1978), and Goldstein (1973) employed models in longer interpersonal interactions with positive acquisition effects.

It has been well established that the consequences delivered to the model by the interpersonal partner in the modeled scene are important. When the model's social behaviors produce positive consequences, the model is more likely to be emulated than when the model's behavior produces unfavorable consequences, such as punishment (Bandura, 1969; Goldstein, 1973).

Modeling has also been differentially effective with clients who differ in major characteristics. For example, Eisler, Hersen, and Miller (1973) found that psychiatric patients exposed to an assertive model learned appropriate behaviors, whereas McFall and Twentyman (1973) in training college students did not find acquisition of response through modeling. Further evidence that modeling may have differential utility with different kinds of clients was provided in the aforementioned Eisler et al. (1978) study. These authors trained equally unskilled schizophrenic and nonpsychotic psychiatric patients in interpersonal skills using coaching techniques both with and without exposure to a socially competent model. Although both types of training program were found to be effective, the results indicated that modeling was *essential* to producing skill improvements in the schizophrenics, but not necessary to increasing the skills of the nonpsychotic individuals.

In summary, it is clear that the use of modeling displays can contribute substantially to the response-acquisition process. Although the evidence is not entirely clear on this point, it does appear that modeling has additive benefits in situations where the behaviors to be learned are relatively complex (Hersen et al., 1973) and cannot easily be explained through instructions alone. In order to be effective in training, models should be employed who have characteristics similar to those of the client. Exposure to the model should also be sufficient in duration to produce changes in the client's behavior. At this time, it appears that modeling may be more or less effective with certain types of clients, although the nature of this relationship is not known with any certainty. In deciding whether or not to employ modeling techniques, the trainer should weigh the extra cost in time and effort needed to develop modeling displays against the results which might be obtained with practice and instructional techniques alone. Using the trainer or other training-group members as models is certainly the simplest and least costly approach to modeling, and it has been found to be effective.

Response Practice

Response practice is an integral training component common to virtually all social-skills training programs. In response practice, the client's recently acquired behavior patterns are strengthened to the point where the client feels comfortable with them, and they are available for use almost without thinking. Most commonly, response practice is employed in combination with other procedures such as instructions, modeling, and feedback. Repeated practice increases the chances that acquired behaviors will be actually used in appropriate social situations.

Response practice can be used as an overt practice technique, called behavior rehearsal, whereby observable social behaviors are produced through role-playing (Lazarus, 1966; Schinke & Rose, 1976). Another practice method, called covert rehearsal, is a technique whereby interpersonal responses can be rehearsed in imagination prior to actually performing them (Kazdin, 1974, 1975; Nietzel et al., 1977).

Behavior Rehearsal. Ever since behavior rehearsal was found to be effective (Lazarus, 1966; McFall & Marston, 1970), it has been examined in most studies of social skill. However, since behavior rehearsal has usually been evaluated in combination with other skill-acquisition techniques, the utility of practice alone has been difficult to assess. McFall and Twentyman (1973) found that behavior rehearsal alone produced increases in social skills of college students. Using a population which was generally more socially deficient, Eisler, Hersen, and Miller (1973) found that overt rehearsal alone did not produce behavioral improvements. The discrepant findings may, in part, be accounted for by the fact that McFall and Twentyman (1973) gave their trainees a rationale for rehearsing the skills, whereas Eisler, Hersen, and Miller (1973) did not. It seems likely that the rationale given to those in the McFall and Twentyman study acted like coaching, and the trainees, being college students, were more able to call on responses already in their repertoires than the socially deficient clients in the Eisler et al. study.

Covert Rehearsal. Covert rehearsal, whereby the client practices social responses in imagination, has been almost impossible to evaluate independently from other training components. For example, Kazdin (1974, 1975) has consistently obtained positive results from training components incorporating covert rehearsal. However, it must be noted that in these studies the trainees received some instructions from the trainer as to what they should rehearse mentally (covert modeling). Studies comparing covert with overt rehearsal have found few differences between the two forms of practice, with both types of rehearsal producing improvements in performance (McFall & Lillesand, 1971; McFall & Twentyman, 1973).

In summary, the advantage of covert rehearsal over overt rehearsal appears to be that the client can practice social responses in imagination wherever and whenever he or she pleases, which probably can contribute to the transfer of training. The primary disadvantage of covert rehearsal would appear to be that the trainer has no direct way of assessing the adequacy of the imagined rehearsals. In overt behavior rehearsal, the trainer can observe the client's practice and make suggestions for further improvements. Based on the research literature, it would appear that both types of rehearsal can be effective. Overt rehearsals are useful in the earlier stages of training when corrective feedback can be employed to improve and refine actual behavior sequences. Covert rehearsal can be employed in the latter stages of training when practice is required closer in time to the actual employment of the skills in the natural environment.

Response Shaping

During the response-shaping phase of training, the client's newly acquired social behaviors are further refined and improved through *corrective feedback* and *reinforcement*. The shaping procedures are necessary because the client is seldom able to attain the desired degree of proficiency by practice with the initially administered instructions and/or modeling alone. Feedback from the trainer or members of a training group, or through playback of audiovisual recordings, are useful in that they help the client make important changes in his or her social performances. Usually feedback is based on the evaluations of the client's previous attempts to add to his or her behavioral repertoires, or to change existing patterns of response. Reinforcement in the form of trainer praise or approval rendered by training-group members serves to motivate the client to continue to make further corrections and improvement.

Corrective Feedback. The use of feedback to shape and refine learned social responses can take several forms. Following a client's performances, evaluative feedback can be administered by the trainer or members of a training group. Information is thus given to the client about what was effective about his or her performance and what aspects need further changes. Another method of feedback involves presenting the client with audio or visual recordings of his or her behavior rehearsals. In fact, it is not unusual for the client and trainer to observe tape recordings of the behavior rehearsals together. Finally, the client can provide self-corrective feedback by critically evaluating subsequent performances following social interactions in the natural environment.

Research evaluations of the effects of various forms of feedback techniques are mixed as feedback appears to be effective under some conditions but not others. For example, Eisler, Hersen, and Agras (1973) administered audiovisual feedback to marital couples on their nonverbal behaviors (smiling and eye contact). The feedback was administered under two conditions, both with and without instructions to the couples to focus their attention on their nonverbal behaviors. It was found that videotape feedback produced no changes in behavior when administered alone, but when feedback was combined with instructions to focus on eye contact and smiling, significant increases in the frequency of these nonverbal behaviors did occur.

In a similar study, Barbee and Keil (1973) assessed the effects of videotape feedback in training disadvantaged individuals in employment interview skills. Some individuals received videotape feedback alone, some received videotape feedback in combination with coaching and reinforcement, and some received no training. The results indicated that those in the videotape-feedback-alone group performed no better than those in an untrained control group. On the other hand, those individuals receiving videotape feedback in combination with coaching improved on measures of behavioral skill, and were rated as more likely to get a job than the videotape-feedback-alone and no-training control groups.

Other studies which have combined corrective feedback with supplementary training techniques have generally found that feedback facilitates other techniques. Edelstein and Eisler (1976) trained a socially withdrawn client to be more skillful in dealing with his supervisor at work and with women in heterosocial situations using a combination of coaching, modeling, and videotape feedback. Frederiksen et al. (1976) found that verbal feedback was effective in reducing the expression of excessively aggressive comments in hostile-explosive clients when combined with the coaching and modeling of more socially appropriate responses. Melnick (1973) compared the effectiveness of videotape feedback combined with behavior rehearsal with the effects of modeling and rehearsal alone. The results indicated that the combination of rehearsal with feedback was superior to either modeling or rehearsal alone.

In summary, a review of the results obtained with the use of feedback in social-skills training would appear to indicate that it is of little use unless combined with other techniques which help the client acquire new social behaviors. However, verbal and videotape feedback has been demonstrated to facilitate the effectiveness of coaching, modeling, and rehearsal when incorporated as *one* of the training components.

Reinforcement. Positive reinforcement, such as praise and approval, is usually given to clients when they have demonstrated proficiency of response during behavior rehearsals and in natural-environment situations. Reinforcing comments by the trainer, group-member trainees, and interpersonal partners in the natural environment are felt to increase the client's motivation to improve his social performance, and also to maintain the improvements that he or she has already made. Although few studies have investigated the effects of social reinforcement as a single treatment component in the context of social-skills training, literally hundreds of studies cited in most introductory psychology texts have demonstrated the successful application of positive reinforcement in increasing desirable human behaviors (Redd, Porterfield, & Anderson, 1979).

In studies using training-group members to monitor and reinforce the utilization of trained skills in each other's performance in the natural environment, Azrin, Flores, and Kaplan (1975) and Rose (1975) found group-member pairs to be effective in the utilization of social-reinforcement techniques. Schinke and Rose (1976) used interpersonal behavior contracts between group members in order to provide reinforcement for the performance of role-played skills in the natural environment. After role-playing social behaviors to specified criteria in training sessions, group trainees agreed via contracts to perform the newly acquired skills in natural-environment situations. Clients who were in the rehearsal-reinforcement groups performed better than groups who merely discussed what they would do in interpersonal situations.

In summary, the bulk of the evidence shows that social reinforcement in the form of praise and delivery of positive consequences to a person's behavior is extremely effective in increasing and maintaining those reinforced behaviors. These reinforcement principles also seem to apply to the development and maintenance of social behaviors acquired during interpersonal-skills training, although not many studies have examined the effects of social reinforcement alone. The most recent studies seem to show that when group training methods are employed, social reinforcement delivered by group members can be effective in promoting transfer of training to the natural environment.

Cognitive Restructuring

Following the acquisition, practice, and shaping phases of training, clients need to learn how to utilize their newly developed skills in actual environmental encounters. Some studies which have not found transfer of acquired-skill patterns to natural-environment encounters have suggested that cognitive restructuring techniques are probably required to ensure transfer of training (Hersen, Eisler, & Miller, 1974; McFall & Lillesand, 1971). Cognitive-restructuring techniques generally refer to procedures which modify the client's faulty beliefs about him- or herself and change expectations of negative consequences when he or she begins to behave differently in social situations. For example, in assertiveness training, clients must strongly believe that they "have the right" to express their opinions and feelings, or they will fail to do so (Alberti & Emmons, 1974).

One of the leading proponents of cognitive restructuring has been Donald Meichenbaum, at the University of Waterloo, who has noted that most behavioral training programs have overemphasized the importance of environmental events and underemphasized how a client perceives and evaluates those events:

> Our research on cognitive factors in behavior therapy techniques has highlighted the fact that environmental events per se although important are not of primary importance; rather what the client says to himself about those events influences his behavior. (Meichenbaum, 1977, p. 108)

Evidence from several research programs has suggested that teaching clients to restructure their thoughts about themselves in a more positive and confident manner during social encounters tends to reduce their anxiety and facilitate transfer of training (Meichenbaum, 1977; Spivack & Shure, 1974). More specifically, Glass, Gottman, and Shmurak (1976) compared the relative effectiveness of response-acquisition training alone with cognitive restructuring of self-statements in enhancing the dating skills of shy males. Trainees exposed to the cognitive-restructuring procedures made a greater number of phone calls to potential dates, and were rated as more socially skillful by the female recipients of the calls than those in the skill-acquisition-alone group.

A study by Eisler, Frederiksen, and Peterson (1978) explored the differences in the cognitive choices of clients who had demonstrated highly assertive behavior compared with those who were behaviorally unassertive. When presented with a number of response choices to a list of interpersonal situations, the highly assertive individuals tended to choose descriptions of socially effective responses more frequently than the unassertive individuals who chose a higher proportion of passive-ineffective alternatives. In addition, the assertive individuals generally expected more favorable or reinforcing consequences from their social behaviors than the unassertives. The authors concluded that limited transfer of training observed in previous studies on assertion training might have been due to inadequate assessment of the socially unskilled individual's negative expectations about behaving assertively.

Finally, some studies have employed cognitive-restructuring techniques which enable clients to assess more realistically the probable consequences of their social behavior. Preliminary results with this technique known as projected consequences has generally shown positive effects. It appears that having clients anticipate the likely consequences of new social behaviors facilitates acquisition of a greater range of social skills and increases the likelihood of transfer of training (Kazdin, 1974, 1975; Nietzel *et al.*, 1977).

In summary, it appears that some social-skills training programs have not promoted transfer of training because they have failed to assess adequately the client's faulty attitudes and beliefs concerning the use of certain categories of trained behavior, such as assertion. Moreover, some trained behaviors do not transfer to natural environment situations because clients have unrealistic expectations that negative consequences might result from their exhibition of certain kinds of behavior. Cognitive-restructuring techniques, which help the client accept more realistic beliefs about him- or herself, and provide more accurate expectations of consequences from others, have been found to be effective training components in promoting transfer of training.

Summary

In this chapter we have discussed the important roles that theory and research play in the development of principles and procedures utilized in practice. We have noted how theoretical notions and casual observations are more carefully scrutinized through systematic research. Although research does not always provide unequivocal answers to practical problems, it does serve as a guide on what factors and principles we should focus our attention.

Historically, social-skills training arose from early observations on the social inadequacies accompanying the problems of mental patients. Some of the original techniques used in social-skills training had their origins in the theroetical notions Wolpe and Lazarus had about the importance of assertiveness in interpersonal problems.

One of the first research questions raised about social-skills training was about the behavioral nature of interpersonal skills. The answers to this question have been diverse in that though there is some broad agreement about the function of social skills generally, there has been no single list of behaviors that defines "social skill" in all situations. The characteristics of the client, and the nature of the interpersonal situations in which the skills are to be used, are also important considerations.

In looking at the antecedent causes of socially unskilled behavior, we have uncovered two rival but not necessarily mutually exclusive hypotheses. Some theorists and practitioners feel that social anxiety inhibits the execution of socially competent behavior, and that training techniques should be aimed at anxiety reduction. Those advocating the alternative position feel that the skills have never been learned, and that remediation should be based primarily on response-acquisition techniques. Our feeling is that the evidence does not clearly support either position. Further, this controversy may have little practical significance since the training techniques discussed in this book may serve simultaneously to reduce anxiety and to develop new skills.

Finally, we reviewed research which supports the practical utility of a variety of training techniques. In the area of response acquisition, instructions and modeling were found to be effective, with modeling probably being more important to the learning of more complex social behaviors. In the area of response practice, both overt-behavior rehearsal through role-playing, and covert rehearsal through imagery were found to be useful techniques. The overt rehearsal is probably more useful during the initial acquisition of the response, whereas imagery is probably useful during the later stages of practice when the client is ready to try out new responses in the natural environment. In response shaping, both corrective feedback and reinforcement were discussed as techniques designed to maintain the client's motivation, and help in the refinement of learned responses. Cognitive-restructuring techniques were presented as potentially critical in motivating the client to use newly acquired responses in the natural environment and facilitate transfer of training.

II

Developing Social Skills

The purpose of this section is to provide the reader with information on how actually to conduct social-skills assessment and training. Building on the conceptual and research base established in Part I, we move from the "why" of skills training to the "how."

The first chapter in this section (Chapter 3) focuses on the strategy of social-skills assessment. What kind of information about the client's social functioning must the trainer have? What are the strategies that can be used for obtaining this sort of information? Put another way, what must we assess and why?

In Chapter 4 the discussion moves to the actual techniques or tactics of social-skills assessment. What specific kinds of procedure can be used to obtain this needed information? How is this information combined to yield both a comprehensive and a specific view of the client's social functioning?

The process of training (Chapter 5) is closely linked to assessment. Based on our understanding of the client's functioning, the trainer must first agree on the goals of training and establish a good working relationship with the client. The actual techniques used in the training session are then reviewed and illustrated. Throughout this review, special attention is payed to alternative procedures which allow the trainer to tailor the session to the needs of the client and practical constraints.

As important as the training session may be, the ultimate goal is to get the client to use his or her skills productively in his or her natural environment. Strategies for promoting the transfer of training to the client's natural environment are reviewed in Chapter 6. Four of these strategies revolve around the training sessions themselves. How does the trainer structure the sessions to maximize the possibility of transfer? The remaining four strategies are centered in the person's natural environment. What can be done outside training to aid in transfer?

3

What to Assess and Why

Overview

- Assessment is basic to social-skills training. It should result in general impressions of deficit areas as well as specific behavioral objectives.
- To be maximally useful, assessment information should be both accurate and representative of the client's actual functioning.
- Comprehensive assessment should include considerations of (1) verbal and nonverbal behaviors, (2) cognitive activity, such as knowledge of appropriate responses. Beliefs and attitudes, perceptions of others, and expectations regarding social consequences, and (3) the situational specificity of skill deficits.

Accurate assessment of specific social behaviors which are representative of the client's interpersonal difficulties is the hallmark of the social-skills-training approach to interpersonal competence. Social-skills training is distinguished from more traditional forms of counseling by its emphasis on comprehensive assessment procedures which are directly linked to the training procedures. To the extent that the assessment provides us with accurate samples of the client's thoughts and behaviors in critical interpersonal situations, training can be maximally effective. To the extent that assessment is only partially complete or aimed at situations which are atypical for a particular client, the training will be misguided and ineffective. The point we wish to make is that social-skills training depends on a highly *individualized* assessment approach which is carefully tailored to each client. This requirement is true whether the trainer is working with one individual at a time or with several clients simultaneously in a group-training situation. Therefore, in order to obtain assessment information which reflects the uniqueness of the individual, the assessment procedures must focus on that person's particular pattern of social responses to the specific situations that are encountered.

One additional consideration should be highlighted. Assessment for social-skills training should be regarded as a *continuous* process rather than an isolated procedure prior to the initiation of training. As we shall see in subsequent chapters, there is a continual interplay between the effects of training and updated assessments which serve to guide the training process toward its goals.

In this chapter we will introduce the reader to some considerations regarding the general objectives of assessment. Next we will present the reader with some guidelines about the sorts of thing which should be assessed at different points in time. These considerations should guide the use of specific assessment procedures described in the next chapter.

Assessment Objectives

Level of Understanding

One of the major goals of the assessment procedures is to provide the client and the trainer with a mutual understanding of the client's current social-behavior patterns from two perspectives. These two perspectives are labeled, for convenience, a general impressionistic perspective and a specific behavioral perspective.

General Impressionistic. The general perspective relates to typical modes of response that a client may exhibit in a variety of situations. For example, a young man named Jack may typically have difficulty in initiating conversations with others whom he encounters. Upon interview we may discover that Jack has difficulty in initiating conversations with others on the commuter bus he rides to work, or with a girl he has been dating, or with his peers at the office. In all of these situations he appears awkward, unsure of himself, hesitant, and tends to make the other person feel uncomfortable although he is genuinely interested in social contact. Therefore, one of the tasks of assessment is to isolate similar repetitive patterns of social behavior which seem to recur in many different social situations. The idea is to obtain a general impression of what these patterns are like and to define the common elements. In the example with Jack, casual observers might label the behavior pattern as shyness or passivity. This general impression identifies the areas that require detailed behavioral specification.

Specific Behavioral. The specific behavioral perspective refers to all the cognitive and behavioral components of the general behavior pattern that we have noted. In the above illustration with Jack, we have observed that he generally fails to initiate social conversation, although he is motivated to do so. On closer examination of this social-response pattern, we discover that Jack typically avoids eye contact with others in close proximity to him, or averts the gaze of others when they casually look toward him. He also fails to smile at others in these situations. And as most of us are aware, smiling is often viewed as a nonverbal cue that someone wants to attract your attention or begin a conversation with you. Further, in our analysis of Jack's problem, we become aware of the fact that Jack has persistent thoughts that should he actually speak to someone, they will probably not respond to what he says, or ignore him completely. Jack's response to these thoughts is to feel foolish and embarassed every time he *thinks about* initiating a conversation.

Thus, the general pattern of noninitiation of social behavior, impressionistically labeled "shyness," is broken down further into specific behavioral components which further identify Jack's problem. The specific behavioral components in this case are avoiding eye contact and failing to smile appropriately, which are the typical precursors to conversation initiation. Further, Jack has thoughts of being embarrassed should his overtures be ignored, which also discourages his attempts to initiate conversation.

Although we will have more to say about training in subsequent chapters, it should be pointed out here how assessment of the general behavior pattern with its specific components can lead to remedial procedures. In this situation, it would be necessary to give Jack training in how and when to look and smile at people appropriately when he desires to initiate conversation. In order to overcome his fear of people's not responding appropriately when he speaks, it may only be necessary to encourage him to practice speaking first, no matter how he thinks others will respond. Failing this, we could coach him in various alternatives about what he might say in different social situations.

Reliability

A major concern of social-skills assessment is reliability. In a general way, reliability refers to the degree of agreement among observers that they are witnessing and labeling events in a similar fashion. Obtaining reliable assessment information regarding social behavior may not always be as simple and straightforward as it seems. Let us take the hypothetical example of Betty, a student of history, in a class with fifty other students. In response to the history professor's question posed in a class discussion, Betty stands up and gives her answer. All fifty students agree that Betty has verbally responded to the professor's question. Therefore, we have a reliable assessment of that fact. However, should we pose the question, did Betty "sound sure of herself" when she answered the question, we might get some differences of opinion. Should one student feel that she was hesitant, and another venture an undecided opinion, we would not have confidence in the reliability of that assessment.

It becomes clear from the above illustration that the reliability of assessment of social behaviors sometimes present problems which must be overcome. This becomes increasingly true when we are attempting to assess complex social behaviors in a general impressionistic way, that is, for example, did Betty sound sure of herself in class? To increase the reliability of the assessment it is often possible to break down the general assessment question into component parts upon which it is easier to obtain agreement. For example, we could inform Betty's classmates that, in order to sound confident of your statements, you need to (1) look at the person whom you are responding to; (2) speak in a loud and clear voice; and (3) give a thorough and comprehensive answer. Hopefully, now that we have defined "sounding sure of oneself" in terms of its three component parts, the assessment observers will be more likely to come to an agreement about what they have observed. If Betty had looked at the professor when she spoke, given her answer in a strong clear voice, and had given a thorough answer, theoretically we would obtain consensus that Betty had "appeared confident."

The point of all this is that typically in routine assessment of social behavior there will be some discrepancies between what a client may observe when reporting about his or her own behavior and what others may observe. It is likewise possible that outside observers will have discrepant opinions among themselves about what they observe. The implications of this are that when most individuals assess the social behavior of themselves or others, they rely on general impressionistic terms such as shy, aggressive, confident, etc., which lack sufficient precision for purposes of accurate assessment. In order to increase the reliability of the assessment procedures, it is necessary to designate the specific behavioral components of the response pattern, as we have discussed previously, so that the attention of the observers is focused on the relevant elements of the response pattern.

Representativeness

The remaining general-assessment issue to be discussed in this section is the representativeness of the assessment, which is often described in psychology texts as the question of validity. In simple terms, the assessor wants to be sure that the assessment information collected adequately reflects, or is representative of how the client behaves in actual or real-life social situations. In social-skills assessment we are usually concerned with two aspects of representativeness, the *sampling* and *predictive* aspects.

Sampling Representativeness. The sample aspect of representativeness relates to our concern that the assessment measures produce samples of the client's problematic social behavior which adequately reflect all of the situations which elicit it. Since social behavior is by definition a product of the client's interaction with others in various social contexts, we must know about as many of the characteristics of the behavior of others and the social situations themselves which elicit the problems. In performing the actual assessment, the emphasis is on relevant samples because we cannot possibly assess in detail how the client behaves, or will behave, with every individual in every situation. However, we can usually determine the distinguishing features of the behavior of others which elicit the client's problems. Then, the task of assessment is to obtain a detailed picture of a representative sample of these other-person behaviors and social contexts which lead to the display of the client's social problems. Perhaps a brief example will clarify the issue of representative sampling of social situations. Suppose a young woman, Mrs. Faye, presents herself with problems which we impressionistically label as difficulties in assertion. Mrs. Faye is a married woman with two children who works as a manager of a clothing store. Upon initial interview we form a general opinion that Mrs. Faye's lack of assertiveness is confined to some of her interactions with her husband and employees of the clothing store whom she supervises. She has no apparent assertion problems in dealing with her children, her in-laws, members of the school board, etc. Note that Mrs. Faye has assertion difficulties with individuals with whom she has daily contact and on whom she frequently has to depend.

So far it is clear that we need to obtain samples of Mrs. Faye's interactions with her husband and some of the employees who work for her. However, we need to delineate further the characteristics of these interactions which are relevant since it is clear that not all of Mrs. Faye's interactions with her husband and the clothing-store employees present problems for her. What are the situational characteristics of the interactions with her husband and the employees at work which elicit her lack of assertion?

On further detailed interviewing, we discover that there are two categories of interaction that Mrs. Faye has with her husband and the employees which make it difficult for her to express herself assertively.

Note that once we begin to examine the details of the problem interactions, the general assertion problem resolves itself into a more specific behavioral focus. One type of problem situation arises when Mrs. Faye needs help from her social partner, but isn't sure she has a legitimate right to make the request. The other category of situation occurs when she receives criticism from her social partner which she feels is unjust. Without going into details about how to select sample situations, the following are brief descriptions of problem interactions Mrs. Faye has with her husband and her employees which could be a *representative* sample of interpersonal situations which describe her problem in assertion.

1. She has worked hard to prepare dinner, and her husband complains about the quality of her cooking.
2. A female employee accuses her of always trying to get ahead at the expense of the employees.
3. She needs to ask her husband to take care of the children because she unexpectedly has to work late one night.
4. She has to ask a male employee to send back some merchandise that she ordered by mistake.
5. Her husband expresses displeasure at her new short hair style which he says makes her look like the man in the family.
6. A male employee criticizes her selection of new suits for sale at the store.

Clearly, there are many more interpersonal situations which we could have selected which pose assertion problems for Mrs. Faye. We have, however, selected situations which we believe to constitute a representative sample of the person(s), and the behaviors of the person(s), which elicit problems. In this case, the individuals she usually depends on, that is, husband and employees, are the relevant persons. The other two dimensions of Mrs. Faye's social problem which we have sampled are having to ask for help when she is not sure that the request would be legitimate, and her inability to respond when she receives unjust criticism from these social partners. The next task of assessment is to evaluate the interactions we have sampled in greater detail in order to pinpoint areas for remediation.

Prediction. The second question regarding the representativeness of the assessment is, will the assessment data we have obtained be sufficient to predict how the individual will behave in real-life interactions? Very few assessments of interpersonal behavior can be made in the client's natural environment. We usually have to rely on other response formats, for example, interviews, self-report questionnaires, and hypothetical role-playing situations to obtain information. Obviously we have little interest in how a client responds to an interpersonal-behavior question-naire, unless it is representative of how the person behaves in actual social situations when there are no assessors around to observe the client's behavior. Therefore, we are concerned that the assessment in-formation, whether obtained through interview or from other observers, will, in fact, be predictive of how the client behaves in real-life situations.

Let us use the hypothetical assessment problem concerning Mrs. Faye just presented above to illustrate the issue. Suppose we want to assess in detail Mrs. Faye's interactions with one of her employees. We have decided to assess the interaction by having Mrs. Faye and the trainer role-play a sample interaction where the employee is critical of Mrs. Faye's selection of men's clothing. We have chosen role-playing as rep-resentative of the real interaction because it is not feasible to perform the assessment in the store or bring the employee into the assessment situa-tion. The representative question is, will a role-played interaction be-tween the trainer and Mrs. Faye predict how she will actually interact with the employee at work? If it does, we have satisfied the predictive-validity requirement of the assessment. If the role-played interaction is not predictive of the actual interactions with the employee, then we would have to find some other means of assessing the interaction, such as, asking Mrs. Faye's supervisor to provide us with the information.

What to Assess

As we have pointed out in Chapter 1, social skills are reflected in relatively complex patterns of behavior which are displayed in a great diversity of interpersonal situations. From our earlier discussion, it was also quite apparent that no single definition of social skill would be likely to be sufficiently comprehensive to suit our needs in the range of social situations to be considered in this book. However, there are several interrelated areas that need to be considered.

Behaviors. Social behavior is comprised of an observable series of discrete verbal and nonverbal speech behaviors and motoric gestures which are displayed by the individual to convey a variety of messages to another person or group of individuals. The "verbal attributes" of speech refers to the content of the message, or *what* is said. The "nonverbal aspects" of speech refers to all the paralinguistic qualities of speech, such ad loudness, tone of voice, tempo of phrasing, etc. These nonverbal components of speech combined with facial expressions and gestures refer to the stylistic aspects of the message, or *how* it is said. What is said, and how it is spoken, constitute the overt *behavior components* of social response patterns which can be assessed independently by any number of observers.

Cognitions. Another consideration regarding social behavior involves the notion that overt behavioral signals are directed by the thought processes or cognitions of the individual. Although not directly observable, covert thought processes are potentially measurable through the individual's self-report. Furthermore, the overt behavioral expressions may be either enhanced or inhibited by changes in the person's level of emotional arousal which can also be assessed through self-report.

Situations. It is important to realize that behavioral, cognitive, and emotional reponse dimensions of social behavior are learned responses which are intended by the individual to have quite specific effects in particular social situations. Therefore, an attribute of social behaviors which have implications for the assessment of social skill is the adequacy of those behaviors to convey the individual's intentions which may vary from situation to situation. A socially skilled individual is one who has learned when and where to exhibit a particular pattern of social behavior for some purpose.

Assessing the Behavioral Components of Skill

The behavioral components of social skill refer to all observable behaviors that an individual exhibits when engaged in social behavior. For convenience in our assessment we can categorize the overt behavioral components as (1) the verbal-content dimension of speech; (2) the nonverbal-expressive dimension of speech, and (3) motoric behaviors which accompany speech, such as facial expressions and gestures.

Verbal Behavior. The verbal content, or what is said in social situations, is of paramount importance in assessing the social skill of the actor. The content of speech behavior transmits the intent of the individual more directly than any other aspect of social behavior. However, it is possible that the same intent may be communicated more or less effectively depending upon the selection of content.

Table I lists a number of verbal-content components of social skills. Each of these components is defined by a particular kind of statement or request. For example, *refusing a request* is defined as a "direct and unambiguous statement declining the request, often including a reason for the refusal." An example of each content component is given in the last column. It should be remembered that there are only examples of verbal content. None is "skillful" by definition.

When evaluating the skillfulness of the verbal content employed by a client, the assessor must be aware of *both* the client's *intent,* and the *likely*

Table I. Verbal-Content Components of Social Skill

Verbal-content component	Definition	Example
Making an appropriate request	A direct statement of your wishes, without coercing, threatening, or apologizing to the other person.	"I would really appreciate it if you would help me with this problem."
Refusing a request	A direct unambiguous statement declining a request; often giving an honest reason for the refusal.	"I'm sorry I can't go with you tonight, I've already made other plans for this evening."
Giving a compliment	A direct statement clearly indicating your positive feelings about a person, or about what that person has said or done.	"I really liked that meal you prepared; you are a wonderful cook."
Giving negative feedback	A clear statement indicating your displeasure or disapproval about something a person has said or done. Often, a suggestion as to how the other could improve their behavior is included.	"I find your manner very insulting. However, if you speak to me politely, I'll listen."
Making an empathetic statement	A statement expressing your understanding, but not necessarily acceptance, of another person's feelings.	"I can understand why that might make you angry, but my intention was to make a constructive criticism."
Making a request for feedback	An open and honest request for information about how another person views your behavior.	"How do you think I handled the disagreement in the meeting today?"

effectiveness of alternative contents in the same situation. In a very real sense, evaluation of verbal behavior depends on the skill of the assessor in predicting the likely effects or consequences of the verbal behavior used by clients in particular social situations.

One caution should be introduced here when attempting to evaluate what a client has said from his or her verbal report of the events. Typically, most people have difficulty in relaying accurate accounts of what they have said during a particular social occasion. When asked to report what they have said, many clients use a shorthand, third-person terminology which is of very little use in behavioral assessment. For example, one client, reporting her response to her boss's request for her to work late one night, reported that she said, "I told him to forget it," instead of precisely what she did say, "I can't work tonight because I don't feel very well."

Second, most individuals have trouble being objective about what has transpired during social interactions. Should any of our readers doubt this, we would encourage them to try an experiment whereby they ask two people to step into a room to discuss a mutual problem. Then, independently ask each participant in the conversation to recall precisely what he or she said. The point to be made is that asking clients to report on what they have said in a particular social situation carries some risks, in that their interpretation of what transpired may be somewhat different from what actually happened. Later, in the section on how to assess, we will describe some methods for obtaining more precise information on clients' verbal behavior.

Nonverbal Behavior. The nonverbal behavioral attributes of speech, such as voice volume, intonation, pauses, etc., accompany the verbal content of any conversation. The nonverbal attributes of speech behavior often convey messages of an emotional nature which may or may not be congruent with the verbal content. Everyone is familiar with the verbal message, "I love you," which can be transmitted with nonverbal attributes to convey that the person either meant it passionately, or was rather insincere in making the statement.

In evaluating behavioral components of skill, particular attention should be focused on the nonverbal elements accompanying the verbal message. The particular synthesis of verbal and nonverbal speech components may, at the extremes, serve either to intensify the impact of the message, or to *nullify* it completely.

In assessing the nonverbal speech of a client, the following are some of the characteristics that we want to observe. The duration of speech is important. Does the client speak at sufficient length clearly to convey his or her intentions? On the other hand, does he or she pause long enough between thoughts so that the other person has time to respond to the messages? Does he or she listen to the other person? Does he or she speak in a tone of voice which is appropriate for the message, that is, does voice volume increase when expressing strongly felt assertions? Does the client sound confident of what he or she is saying? Does he or she speak too rapidly or too slowly for optimum delivery of the message? How many speech disruptions are present, such as, "ahs, ohs, ums," which might limit effective delivery? Table II lists some common nonverbal components of social skill. Importantly, these can be assessed without any specialized training. Each skill component is described, and ways of measuring it are suggested.

Motoric Behaviors. In addition to the verbal and nonverbal dimen-

Table II. Nonverbal Components of Social Skill

Skill component	Description	Measure
Eye contact	Looks directly at the other person's face when speaking or listening.	Frequency of glances, amount of time spent looking.
Smiles	Shows obvious grin or laugh appropriate to the conversation.	Frequency of smiles.
Voice volume	Speaks neither too loudly nor too softly. Volume appropriate to the conversation.	Rating scale (1–5); 1 being very low to 5 being very loud.
Speech fluency	Speaks without many inappropriate pauses, or "ahs," "ohs," and "ums."	Frequency of speech disruptions per time spent talking.
Emotional tone	Tone of voice full, animated and emotionally expressive.	Rating scale (1–5); 1 being flat and unemotional to 5 being very expressive of emotions.

sions of speech behaviors, other motoric behaviors during conversation, including eye contact, facial expressions, gestures, and posture, should be part of the assessment. During social interaction, head nods, smiles, frowns, hand motions, and change in body posture convey information not necessarily included in the other vocal channels. For example, leaning forward in one's chair and smiling usually signals the social partner that the listener is attending very closely to what the speaker is saying. Whereas, shaking one's head from side to side and frowning typically communicates the listener's disapproval or disagreement with what the speaker is saying. However, it is not entirely clear whether all motoric movements during social conversation have unequivocal meanings. Nevertheless, motoric activity is a part of the interpersonal communication process and should be evaluated for congruence with the content of the message, as well as for its overall impact. Table III lists and describes some of the most commonly observed motoric and gestural components of social skill. Both descriptions and suggestions for rating and motoric components are included.

Assessing the Cognitive Components of Social Skill

In recent years, psychological researchers and practitioners have increasingly advocated the assessment of cognitive processes in the

Table III. Motoric and Gestural Components of Social Skill

Skill component	Description	Measure
Posture	Sits or stands comfortably, body position appears open and relaxed.	Rating scale (1–5); 1 being tense and uncomfortable and 5 being relaxed.
Gestures	Appropriate use of hands and arms when speaking, consistent with speech.	Rating scale (1–5); 1 being absence of appropriate gestures, and 5 being presence of appropriate gestures.
Head nods	Up and down movements of the head when listening, usually indicating the listener's attentiveness or agreement with speech.	Rating scale (1–5); 1 being absence of appropriate head nods, and 5 being presence of appropriate gestures.
Facial expressions	Animated facial expressions consistent with and expressive of verbally stated emotions.	Rating scale (1–5); 1 being absence of appropriate facial expressions and 5 being presence of appropriate facial expressions.

evaluation of social skills. The absence of socially skilled behaviors, in some instances, may be due to faulty or inappropriate thoughts which occur in social situations. For example, a young man has ordered a meal in a fast-food restaurant. The waitress mixes up his order and brings him something else. He looks disappointed at the meal he has received, but says nothing to the waitress. Assuming that he wanted to exchange the meal he received for the one he ordered, he certainly had demonstrated a lack of socially skilled behavior. We cannot be sure, however, that he handled the situation poorly because he didn't know *what* to say, that is, "Please take this back, I ordered such and such". He may have failed to act appropriately because he had anticipatory thoughts that the waitress might refuse to take the order back and therefore embarrass him. He may have had thoughts that others in line behind him might think he was silly, or he may have felt that the waitress was very busy and that it would be unfair of him to trouble her. Although this is a rather simplified example, it does point out how lack of skilled behavior may have its roots in faulty perceptions, attitudes, or expectations.

In the previous section, we have discovered that assessment of the behavioral components of social behavior has helped us to evaluate the adequacy of *what* a person will actually do under a particular set of circumstances. An assessment of a person's thoughts and feelings will help us evaluate *why* he or she will perform certain kinds of behavior. We are very interested in the why elements underlying social responses because it is becoming increasingly clear that certain kinds of thoughts can facilitate the performance of socially skilled behavior, whereas other kinds of thoughts can inhibit or prevent the execution of socially skilled behavior.

In the assessment of the cognitive components of social skills, the following categories of cognitive processes appear to be the most functionally relevant to a comprehensive understanding: (1) knowledge of appropriate response alternatives; (2) beliefs and attitudes about displaying certain kinds of behaviors; (3) perceptions of the social partner's intentions and motivations; (4) expectations regarding the probable consequences of displaying certain kinds of behavior.

Knowledge. The lack of social skill exhibited by some individuals may result almost entirely from deficits in their knowledge of appropriate responses which could be used effectively in various situations. Individuals who are regarded as socially skillful are usually aware of a wider range of response alternatives than those who are not perceived as skillful. The following example should clarify the point:

> Mr. Tuff, foreman of a machine shop, has a problem with one of his employees who is observed taking breaks more often than he is seen on the job. The foreman's typical reactions to this have been either try and ignore what the employee does, or to blow up and threaten to inflict bodily harm. Mr. Tuff has been brought up without knowing how to confront someone about the behavior he disapproves of in a manner likely to produce changes in that person's actions. Certainly, trying to ignore the other person's actions can't alter his behavior, and periodically administered explosive threats do little to engender an attitude conducive to skilled behavior which will produce the changes he wants in the employee's behavior.

Following evaluation of a client's actual behavior through observation or verbal report, the strengths and weaknesses of the client's knowledge of appropriate responses can be assessed by exploring his or her awareness of alternative responses which might have been more effective than the ones used. Some clients clearly do not know how they could have improved their responses to the situation. In other cases, the client can specify in great detail how his or her responses could be improved. Some clients do not perform potentially more effective social behaviors because of competing maladaptive thoughts similar to those described below.

Beliefs and Attitudes. Some people fail to demonstrate socially skilled behavior because they hold faulty or erroneous beliefs about what behavior is required in certain situations. For example, some people believe that it is *never* appropriate under any circumstances to express their displeasure or anger. Self-imposed faulty beliefs such as these constrict a person's behavioral options so that they cannot respond effectively in certain situations.

> Mrs. Sweet believes that a woman should never question the opinion of those whom she believes are more "intelligent" than she. She believes that her husband, who has a Ph.D. in physics, is more intelligent than she. Recently, she stopped working on a job that was a great source of satisfaction to her because her husband didn't think that her working was good for the children. He is planning on buying a new boat which she feels they can't afford, and she knows she won't enjoy. She has complained to her husband about these decisions in a tearful manner, but because she believes that she really has no right to question her husband, she has been socially inept in confronting him.

Albert Ellis (1962) has written about how faulty, irrational, and "self-defeating" thoughts can prevent a client from dealing effectively in many interpersonal situations. For our purposes, assessment of a client's beliefs and attitudes about social behavior can result from the following kind of inquiry. Does the client believe that he or she has the right to express various opinions, beliefs, and ideas? Does he or she have faulty cognitions about the expression of certain kinds of emotion, such as anger, tenderness, pleasure, praise, etc.? How does the client feel about challenging the beliefs, attitudes, and acts of others? Does the client have erroneous beliefs about the rights of others in interpersonal situations, as for example, "Children should do as they're told without question"? The point we want to emphasize here is that no amount of behavioral training can have any lasting effects if the client believes that there is something wrong about behaving in ways most of us would consider appropriate and probably effective.

Perceptions of Others. Another cognitive process relevant to the employment of social skills involves the ability accurately to perceive the intentions and motivations of others in social situations. In some instances clients are generally not sensitive to the cues and signals displayed by others, for example, the guest that does not perceive that the host's yawns, and casual mention of the fact that he has to get up early in the morning, are signals that he should think about going home.

In other cases, clients may have generalized perceptions that all people cannot be trusted, or that most people will try to take advantage of them in some way, so they have distorted perceptions about the *particular* person with whom they are interacting. Assessments should be made to determine whether the client can "read" different social situations accurately, or whether generalized perceptions of others interfere with his or her ability to make discriminations from one situation to the next.

> Mr. Clode has a problem in dating women. He is not a bad fellow, really, but appears to be attracted to women who have signaled him in various ways that they have no romantic interest in him. In attempts to initiate dating relationships, he talks profusely about his mother and his stamp collection without perceiving that his partners have no interest in those topics. Mr. Clode has many faulty perceptions about the effects his behaviors have on women and cannot perceive any of the signals sent by his social partners that the interaction is going poorly until they refuse to go out with him.

Some analysis of the client's perceptions can be made by comparing the client's view of the social situation with whatever objective evidence is available. How does the client interpret the situation? Does he or she have any generalized notions about people which color his or her objectivity about the specific person he or she is interacting with? Does he or she classify certain kinds of people with stereotypes, for example, all men are ruthless, all women are insincere, all insurance salesman are phony, all executives would sell their grandmothers to get to the top? Do his or her perceptions of others seem to be accurate, based on evidence, or does he or she make sweeping conclusions based on little information? In social situations does he or she strive to verify initial impressions? Do his or her perceptions change during social interactions? Accuracy of the client's perceptions of others are important since a great deal of the later training will be based on his or her reports and analyses of a real-world social situation.

Expectations of Consequences. The fourth category of cognition regulating social performance is the client's expectations of the probable consequences resulting from engaging particular social behaviors. Obviously, in most social situations, individuals behave in ways which they believe will maximize positive consequences from the other, and minimize negative ones. What we mean by positive and negative consequences depends, in part, on what the actor in the social situation hopes to derive from the interaction. However, in general, most of us want others to like and respect us. We also want to convince others that our ideas, opinions, and feelings are worthy of consideration. And when social interaction is used to resolve conflict, we generally want to convince others to do things our way. The list of potential positive and negative consequences to social behavior is, of course, endless. The point is that whether we speak to a stranger on a bus to pass the time, or try to convince the boss that we deserve a raise, social interaction is always goal-directed. We believe that what we do in interpersonal situations will elicit responses from the other, and hopefully the responses will fulfill our expectations.

Some of the anticipated consequences are based on our knowledge of social norms which lend a degree of predictability to social situations. If we behave in socially polite ways, we expect others to behave in a similar fashion. Some individuals lack social skill in certain situations, either because they are not aware of the kinds of behavior expected in that situation, or because they intentionally violate those expectations.

Perhaps more germane to our discussion of social skills assessment are predictions of consequences which occur in social situations where it is not entirely clear what results to expect from the other person. Casual observations of the other person and adherence to accepted norms do not always lead to clear predictions of consequences. Perhaps a hypothetical presentation of an employment interview will illustrate this point:

> Ms. Sly is applying for a position as a buyer for a large department store. She has passed the preliminary application process and is now being interviewed by one of the firm's senior vice presidents, a man in his late fifties. Presumably Ms. Sly is aware of the basic norms in operation during an interview of this nature. She is to appear bright, motivated, pleasant, competent, etc. But how is she to convince the vice president that she is the best of all the applicants? Should she appear very serious, or show that she has a sense of humor? Should she let him ask all the questions about her, or should she volunteer information about herself? Would he be pleased or put off should she ask him some serious questions about company policy?

Most clients don't think about their social behavior in terms of expected consequences, although these factors are always in operation. However, it is difficult to assess anyone's social skill unless we have some idea of what their goals and objectives are in interacting with others. Inquiry into the nature of the client's expectations of others often serve to clarify objectives for them in more concrete terms, and, in fact, can facilitate training procedures.

Assessing the Situational Components of Social Skills

By now the reader should be familiar with our thesis that evaluation of social skills is inextricably interwoven with an assessment of the individual's behavior in specific social situations. Moreover, we cannot successfully evaluate social behaviors independently of the situation. Thus far we have discussed the assessment of the behavioral and cognitive components of the individual's behavior leading to an assessment of his or her social skills. Let us now turn more directly to what about social situations should be assessed.

The situational specificity of social skills can be approached in several ways. First it is clear that different social situations have different requirements in terms of the response components deemed necessary for dealing with them skillfully. For example, negotiating with one's spouse as to how to discipline the children effectively probably requires different response components from those useful to a union leader negotiating with management for increased worker salaries. Both situations may require skill in showing recognition of the other's position, the ability to effectively state one's own position, and the ability to compromise on certain issues. However, the skillful use of timing and self-disclosure may be quite different. Some individuals may have difficulty in behaving effectively in one situation and not the other. Other individuals may have trouble in both situations. In the latter instance, we have identified *generalized* skill deficits.

On the other hand, it is possible that a certain kind of skill deficit will manifest itself only in a much more restricted range of situations. For example, a male client may have no problems in expressing his opinions at work with his boss, his co-workers, or even complete strangers, but he cannot stand toe to toe with his wife when she squelches his right to disagree with her. The restriction of the occurrence of response deficits to particular individuals or certain kinds of social situations is known as *specific* response deficits.

One of the major purposes for our assessment of social situations is to differentiate highly specific response deficits, those behavioral problems which occur in particular kinds of encounters, from generalized response deficits, or those which occur in many social situations. In order to accomplish this we first need to identify the kinds of situations in which the client exhibits problems. In accomplishing this we may identify a number of situations which give rise to generalized response deficits. For example, the client may have problems in expressing him- or herself adequately in any situation which involves a group of more than three or four people. He or she may also have problems in a different kind of situation which requires a fairly high degree of self-disclosure or expression of intimacy. The latter problem may be specific to one to one encounters.

The problem of assessing the generality or specificity of the client's problem behavior boils down to attempting some classification of situations which give rise to the response deficits. Does the problem occur with those with whom the client is unfamiliar, does it occur with friends and acquaintances, or does it involve those with whom the client has intimate interpersonal interactions? Does it occur more often with males than females, or those who are younger or older? Does it manifest itself only with those in authority, such as parents or work supervisors? Does it occur in one-to-one situations or in social groups? Is the problem confined to marital interactions, or is it operative in all opposite-sex relationships?

In assessing all the situations where the client exhibits skill deficits, a picture will begin to emerge in which either specific social-behavior problems are related to a specific class of interactions, or generalized deficits are found in the individual's ability to relate successfully to a variety of individuals. There will, however, be several cases where the social-behavior problems appear to include almost all individuals in all social situations. These instances are rare, and usually confined to working with an especially deficit population in mental hospitals or with intellectually retarded individuals.

Summary

Effective social behavior consists of a complex configuration of verbal and nonverbal behavioral components which are exhibited in social situations. The verbal portions of the social message can vary to the limits of language itself, although learned social norms set restrictions on what can be said in any social situation. The nonverbal components of speech, combined with various facial expressions, gestures, and other motoric movements employed during conversation, relate to the stylistic components of the message, frequently described as its emotional tone. The nonverbal behaviors have a profound impact on the overall effectiveness on whatever content is spoken. And though a social partner responds to the total configuration of all the overt verbal and nonverbal responses exhibited during social discourse, examination of the specific components helps us to identify deficits in the client's performance which can lend themselves to remedial training.

We have also stressed the importance of assessing the client's thoughts and feelings which are precursors to social behavior. The client's knowledge of effective responses, perceptions of the other, attitudes and beliefs and his or her expectations of consequences serve to direct and manage the flow of social behavior. Assessment of these covert responses is vital to a thorough understanding of why the client manifests any particular pattern of behavior and helps lay the groundwork for remedial training.

Finally, in addition to assessment of the client's overt social behaviors and the cognitive process underlying them, we have pointed out the necessity of assessing the nature and range of social situations which give rise to the client's problems in social interaction. Some clients exhibit social-skill deficits in a narrow range or class of situations. These deficits are clearly situation-specific. Other individuals exhibit more generalized response deficits, which means that they lack competence in a wide variety of social situations. In order to train clients to cope effectively with social situations relevant to their everyday lives, the situation-specific versus the generalized nature of their social-skill deficits should be evaluated.

4

How to Assess

Overview

- Assessment information can be obtained through client's self-report and through direct observations by others.
- Self-report methods include (1) structured paper and pencil inventories, (2) focused interviews, and (3) self-monitoring techniques.
- Direct observations can be made during (1) interviews, (2) interactions with natural-environment social partners, and (3) role-played or simulated interactions.
- Although each of the individual techniques has its limitations, the combination can provide useful information in forming general impressions and measuring specific target behaviors on an ongoing basis.

In this chapter we will consider a variety of assessment methods which can be used in various combinations to assess the dimensions of social skill. Although a number of complex interpersonal behavior-recording schemes and rating systems exist, the emphasis will be on methods that are relatively economical in terms of equipment costs, and on those which do not require a great deal of observer time.

Basically, there are two sources of data relevant to the assessment of social skill. These are the *self-report* by the client, and *direct observations* of the client's behavior by external observers. A comprehensive evaluation always includes some data from *both* sources, the client and at least one observer. The other observer may be someone in the client's natural environment, for example, spouse, employer, friend, or the person conducting the assessment. There are several formats available for the collection of self-report data, such as paper-and-pencil questionnaires, structured interviews, and self-monitoring procedures whereby the client records his or her behavior as it occurs.

Direct observations of the client's behaviors can also be made in a variety of ways. In some instances, interviews can be conducted with individuals who have observed the client's performance firsthand in the natural environment. In other cases it will be possible for the assessor to observe the client in the natural environment. This is most often feasible with children who can be observed in school. In situations where it is not possible for the assessor to be present, audiotape or videotape recordings can be made "on location," at home or at work. Finally, should all of the aforementioned direct observational techniques prove to be unfeasible, simulated social interactions can be structured in the office through the use of role-playing, or in group-assessment situations.

In terms of our assessment strategy, it is important to bear in mind that we wish to obtain information on *all* aspects of social skill which we have previously discussed. That is, we require information on the behavioral components of the client's behavior, the cognitive and emotional elements of his or her behavior, and the situational dimensions in which the social behavior is embedded. Another general consideration in our strategy is that we first want to obtain general impressionistic data which then can lead to more refined observations on the specific behavioral and cognitive aspects of performances which occur under specific circumstances.

Finally, in terms of our overall strategy, we must remember that assessment is a continuous process. Initially, we may desire to know precisely where the client is in terms of general interpersonal ability prior to training. However, as we begin training, the assessment process continues so that we can monitor changes in social skill and also continue refining our assessments to ensure representativeness of our observations. The latter is important so that we can predict the client's behavior in future situations which are likely to occur.

Self-Report Methods

Let us now turn to specific assessment methods. First we will consider techniques which are used to obtain self-report or self-observational data. These methods give us some ideas as to how the client typically thinks, feels, and behaves when confronted with various interpersonal situations. These include (1) structured paper and pencil inventories, (2) focused interviews, and (3) self-monitoring techniques.

Structured Inventories

A number of self-report inventories are available to assist individuals in reporting their responses to social situations. Most of these questionnaires have been developed for research purposes on fairly homogeneous populations—college students, neurotic adults, etc.—so that their application to any particular client who does not have the characteristics of college students or neurotic adults needs to be made carefully.

Most of the self-report questionnaires which have been developed to date assess only a few facets of social skills, such as "assertiveness," "heterosexual skill," or general "social anxiety," so that no single questionnaire or group of questionnaires can possibly assess all of the relevant dimensions of a particular client's social competence. Despite these limitations, the measures which have been developed thus far can provide the assessor with hypotheses about the client's general areas of difficulty. These tentative ideas of general areas of difficulty can then be amplified through interviews, and the attainment of observational evidence.

How do these self-report questionnaires operate? Most of the instruments sample a universe of interpersonal situations which typically elicit reponses of interest, for example, how does the client perform in situations which typically require assertive responses, or how much anxiety does the client feel in various social situations? The client is asked to indicate how true the statement is of him or her, or how typical the behavior described in the statement is of him or her.

For example, the Rathus Assertive Schedule (RAS) was designed to assess assertive behavior. The RAS is a 30-item inventory in which the respondent is asked how "characteristic" the following statements are of his or her behavior: "I often have a hard time saying no," or "When I am given a compliment, I just don't know what to say." Two popularly employed self-report measures of social anxiety have been developed by Watson and Friend (1969). The Social Avoidance and Distress Scale was designed to assess the client's experience of discomfort and anxiety in social situations. The other measure, known as the Fear of Negative Evaluation Scale, was designed to evaluate the degree to which the client affirmed statements indicating a fear of social disapproval in interpersonal situations.

What are some of the uses of self-report questionnaires such as these in our overall assessment strategy? In the first place, they are economical of time, in that the assessor need not be present when the client responds to them. In addition, they do not take the client more than a few minutes to complete, and they help him or her begin to think about how he or she responds to various kinds of social events. Second, most of the questionnaires can be scored objectively so that comparisons can be made between a particular individual's score and those of similar individuals. As we alluded to earlier, the questionnaires may help in identifying broad problem areas which can be scrutinized more carefully later on in the evaluation. Also, the questionnaires can be administered two or three times to provide some general indications of the client's progress following training.

Self-report questionnaires do have some important limitations which readers should be aware of. Assuming that the client is motivated to respond frankly, he or she may have problems remembering precisely how he or she behaved in previous social encounters, and thereby bias the results. It also may be difficult for clients to make accurate judgments about certain aspects of their behavior. For example, some clients may not know whether their actions in certain kinds of social situations would be regarded as appropriately assertive or inappropriately aggressive. A final problem with self-report inventories is that the items are usually phrased in general terms, that is, do you "usually," "sometimes," or "never" do thus and so? This poses a problem for clients in that they are forced to "average" their social behavior over many social situations without being able to report how they typically behave in certain type of situation. Thus, an individual may always "be able to assertively say no" to his wife, but frequently be unable to "say no" to his employer.

In summary, self-report questionnaires can be used relatively economically to obtain a general view of how the client perceives certain aspects of his or her social behavior. They can be scored objectively so that comparisons can be made among individuals completing them. The major drawback is that self-report measures currently available do not assess many aspects of social skill which we have outlined in this book.

Focused Interview

Interviewing is probably the most frequently used and most convenient method of evaluating a client's social behavior. However, all interviews are subject to biases in reporting which limit the accuracy of some of the information obtained. In one sense, the client knows more about his or her behavior in social situations than anyone else. The apparent paradox of this situation is that though the individual is "always there" in every social situation, he or she is not necessarily the most accurate observer of his or her social behavior.

Nevertheless, many clients can report on their behavior and the behavior of others with reasonable accuracy, and most clients can learn, with practice, to increase the accuracy of their self-observation. Another advantage of interviews is that the client is the absolute expert on the cognitive components of his or her social behavior. In other words, the best source of information on the client's behavior is the client. The client's biases, distortions, or misconceptions can be important sources of data in assessing social-skill deficits.

Focused interviewing can be conceptualized as consisting of several overlapping phases, each phase having one or more objectives. In addition, interviews can be conducted over several sessions to help clarify data from other sources, or even during training to assess progress. Let us review some of the objectives of the initital interviews.

During the first phase of the assessment interview, it is obviously necessary to establish a good working relationship with the client so that he or she will have confidence in revealing some very personal information to the interviewer. It is usually possible to accomplish this by listening attentively to the client and demonstrating a sincere concern for his or her problems. It is also important at this stage to avoid asking penetrating questions, or offering definite opinions. Therefore, the first step in the interview is listening in a nonjudgmental way, and communicating an empathetic understanding of the client's situation.

Once a working relationship with the client has begun, the second step is to begin a survey of the client's problems in social interaction. The objectives are to obtain a thorough history of the client's difficulties in dealing with people and a general picture of the client's difficulties over time. Most clients will begin discussing their problems in the vague terminology of personality, such as always having been excessively "shy," or "anxious," or having an inability to make "small talk." In order to begin helping the client to specify the history of his or her social problems in behavioral terms, some direct questions can be asked regarding who the problems were with and what he or she did in those situations. For example, has the client had pervasive problems with many relationships, or were they confined to just a few people? How did the client get along with members of his or her family? Did he or she have many friends? What were these relationships like? Did he or she have any problems in dating? When did he or she first show signs of being anxious, or belligerent around others? What does he or she do when he or she feels anxious in social situations? How does he or she react to criticism or to praise? How does he or she deal with others when they cause him or her to feel frustrated or angry? Toward the termination of this phase the assessor should have some general picture of how the client has dealt with social relationships in the past and whether the difficulties remain in the present.

At the beginning of the third phase of the interview, the focus should shift more directly to the client's current interpersonal relationships with friends, teachers, spouse, employers—in short, anyone the client has recurrent interactions with on a day-to-day basis. A partial list of areas to be explored might look like this:

1. How does the client express opinions to others, which others, how successful is he or she?
2. Can the client, without difficulty, ask favors of others, are there some situations in which he or she cannot ask favors?
3. How does the client initiate conversations with peers, with members of the opposite sex?
4. Can the client refuse unreasonable requests from friends, from strangers?
5. Does the client have any problem offering compliments to another person or showing appreciation for what someone has done for him or her?
6. How does the client negotiate in give-and-take with members of his or her family, friends, work relationships?
7. How does the client present him- or herself for a job? What are his or her expectations in this situation?
8. How does the client ask for help when he or she needs it? Are the client's requests generally successful?
9. Can the client resist pressure from others to behave in a manner contrary to his or her beliefs? How effective is it?
10. Does the client typically express his or her angry feelings toward others? What does he or she usually say, what happens?

Toward the conclusion of the third phase, the interviewer should have some very concrete ideas regarding with whom the client is currently having difficulties, and over what sorts of issues. In addition, the interviewer should have specific information on precisely what the client does in these difficult situations which is described in specific behavioral terms. The cognitive style, or how the client approaches people, should also be apparent. And, finally, the interviewer should have formed some opinion as to whether the social-skills deficits seems limited to one or two types of situation, or whether the skill deficits are general to a large number of social situations.

During the fourth and final phase of the interview, the assessor may want to give the client some general feedback about what he or she has learned. The feedback should be direct and given within a framework of hypotheses rather than firm conclusions. Thus, in this place, the interviewer is beginning to draw some tentative conclusions, and should present a posture of seeking confirming or disconfirming evidence from the client. There is also the goal of sharing impressions with the client during this phase which should serve to strengthen the working relationship. Finally, at the conclusion of the interview, the client should be informed about next steps, and whether further assessments will be necessary or whether the training procedures will begin soon.

Self-Monitoring

Self-monitoring (SM) is an extremely useful technique in social-skills assessment. It enables clients to observe, record, and report on their interpersonal encounters in a more detailed and systematic fashion than could be achieved by either self-report questionnaires or interviews. Kazdin (1974) has pointed out that self-monitoring is a means of reporting on *both* one's observable (public) behavior and one's thoughts (private) behaviors. Thus SM can be used to assess both the client's overt social behaviors, and his or her thoughts in social interactions. The self-monitoring procedures require the client to learn *what* to observe during social interaction, and then to systematically record *when* it occurs and under what circumstances it occurs.

One of self-monitoring's major advantages is that it helps clients to focus on the specific rather than the general aspects of their social behavior. As we have previously noted, data on the specific components of skill can be more useful than impressionistic data when it comes to defining social behaviors for purposes of remedial training.

For example, in carrying out an SM assignment, clients may be asked to record specific social situations in which they feel anxious (that is, when their social ability is inhibited). In order to accomplish this, clients must note how often they find themselves in social situations which make them anxious. In addition, they must also take note of the characteristics of the social situation which makes them uncomfortable. Is it the particular person with whom they are interacting? Is it when they have to make a difficult decision? Is it when they have to confront someone *about* being angry? They are also asked to record specifically what they did to cope with the situation. Did they put off making the decision? Did they express anger at the other person? How did they do it? Did they leave the situation without doing anything? Could they have done anything which might have made the outcome or consequences more favorable? You can see that assessment information obtained in this manner is rather comprehensive. We have assessed what social situations prompted the behavior, how frequently these situations have occurred, what were the specific characteristics of these situations, and how the client responded to these critical events. Moreover, using information from self-monitoring, we can begin to evaluate how effective the client's responses have been to important social situations.

Figure 1 indicates how a self-monitoring recording form might look from a hypothetical client, Ms. Smith, who had been asked to collect data on social situations which were relevant to her difficulty in initiating conversations. From these monitoring data we can observe that Ms. Smith had at least five opportunities to initiate social encounters on July 15, 1979. From her rating of anxiety in the different situations, we learn that she was more anxious with individuals she didn't know very well. From the column on self-monitored thoughts, we find that Ms. Smith had thoughts or anticipations of personal rejection prior to the initiation of conversations with unfamiliar persons. In addition, the thoughts of rejection sometimes prevented her from initiating the conversation. Looking across the table, there appears to be some evidence that there is a relationship between higher levels of tension and her lack of satisfaction with her performance. This illustration points to the fact that self-monitored data can yield an abundance of relatively specific information which can be used to pinpoint a client's interpersonal strengths and weaknesses.

Another feature of self-monitoring procedures is that they can be used repeatedly throughout assessment and training. This is consistent with our notion that assessment should be a continuous process. The pinpointing of the behavioral and cognitive components of social skill should lead to an evaluation of the client's deficits in certain kinds of situations which then can be targeted for training. Deficits which are assessed prior to training can and should be reassessed during and following training. Thus, self-monitoring techniques which are employed to establish a client's specific skill deficits can be utilized during training to assess improvements in social behavior.

The following are some suggestions to aid in the development and use of self-monitoring procedures.

1. From our experience it is apparent that some clients provide more useful data from self-monitoring than others. Those clients who are highly motivated to improve their social skills and who have some basic understanding of their skill deficits are likely to provide the most accurate information through the use of SM procedures. Therefore, some preliminary training in how to self-monitor with very simple behaviors is often useful in training the client on how to observe his or her own behavior.

2. Self-monitoring can begin once the client and the assessor have decided upon the specific skill components to be assessed, and have some awareness of the social situations likely to elicit the skill deficit. Target behaviors to be monitored should be defined as unambiguously as possible with several examples described to the client. For example, some

Self-Monitoring Form
Social Behavior Situations

Name: Nancy Smith
Date: July 15, 1979

When occurred	Situation	Anxiety Rating Low 1–5 High	Thoughts	Social behavior observed	Others' response	Satisfaction with outcome (1–5)
8:30	On bus, saw girl who is in my accounting class.	3	I have to ask her how she liked class. Afraid she wouldn't recognize me.	Sat down next to her and smiled but didn't say anything.	After 10 minutes she ask me how I like professor.	(2) I wish I had started conversation.
10:00 A.M.	Went to cafeteria for coffee; saw group of people in my class at table.	5	Wanted to ask if I could join them; afraid they might say no.	Looked over at their table, but did not go over.	They did not notice me.	(1) Felt they should have asked me to join them, but maybe they didn't see me.
12:00	After economics class, professor packing up lecture notes.	3	I wanted to tell him how much I enjoyed class. I thought he might want to leave rather than talk to me.	I went over to professor and told him I enjoyed class.	He smiled and thanked me; said I was a good student.	(5) Felt I overcame my anxiety this time and was pleased with his response.
3:00 P.M.	Going home with girlfriend.	1	Wanted to invite her to my house to study.	I had no trouble asking her to come over tonight.	She couldn't make it tonight; will come over tomorrow.	(4) Comfortable with her refusal because I know her well
5:00 P.M.	At department store to buy gift for my father; salesman at counter.	4	Wanted help with selection of gift; felt salesman would think I was stupid; felt awkward.	Selected tie and told salesman I wanted to pay for it.	He wrapped it up; said he thought tie would look good on me.	(1) I wish I had asked his opinion about tie; just wanted to get it over with.

Figure 1. Example of self-monitoring data.

individuals with problems in public speaking might be asked to monitor their thoughts prior to public-speaking situations in classrooms, school-board meetings, etc. Others might be asked to monitor their responses to unreasonable requests from employers, friends, strangers, etc.

3. Clients can be prepared for self-assessment observations by carefully explaining what kinds of information will be useful and teaching them how to record the information succinctly in appropriate terminology. The observation and record-keeping procedures should be planned in advance with the simplest possible recording forms. Attempting to obtain too much information in each social situation will lead to unnecessary confusion and incomplete data collection.

4. It is best to develop the program of information-recording in advance. In some cases, information can be recorded immediately following the social event, and that is desirable whenever possible since clients are less likely to forget the specifics of the interaction. Should this not prove feasible, the client can be instructed to set aside two or three periods a day for recording information on previous interactions, for example, 12:00 noon, and 6:00 P.M.

Behavioral Assessment through Direct Observation

Theoretically, the most accurate way to assess the client's social skills is by having the assessor observe the client in his or her social environment. Although this is potentially the most objective method, free from the possible biases and distortions inherent in the client's self-report, it is often not feasible from a practical standpoint. The observer usually cannot follow the client around all day making observations in critical interpersonal situations. In addition, the presence of the observer would probably change the nature of the social situations so that they would not be representative samples of the client's "true" behavior anyway. There are some exceptions to the feasibility issue in that it is possible to obtain behavioral observations in the natural environment in some circumstances. The most familiar ones which have been done involve observing children's interaction with teachers and peers in school.

There are, however, several methods of observing social behaviors directly without having to escort clients to a variety of social events. None of these methods is perfect, but they can provide fairly accurate and representative samples of client social behaviors very close to what might be obtained in the natural environment. One obvious method is to observe the social behavior displayed toward the assessor during the interviews. Although the interview may not be representative of all social situations, it is an interpersonal encounter. How the client behaves in the interview is a source of data which should not be neglected.

There are additional methods of creating interpersonal situations which closely approximate the social situations which the client encounters in everyday life. Basically, there are two ways in which we can accomplish this objective. First, we can, in certain circumstances, invite the client's real-life interactional partners to participate in the assessment by having planned interactions with the client and relevant others while the observer is present. This method is most often feasible if we are interested in observing the client interacting with a spouse or with peers. It is more difficult to obtain the necessary cooperation from social partners who have no particular stake in the client's behavior, or those whose involvement in the assessment might jeopardize the relationship with the client. Despite these limitations, whenever it is possible to involve significant social partners of the client in direct observational assessments, it is usually useful to do so.

Probably the most feasible method of obtaining direct observations of the client's social behavior is through simulated interactions involving role-playing. In this method, the client and the assessor role-play, or simulate the interaction that the client has had with natural-environment partners. Role-playing of social interactions is also a useful method of assessment when dealing with clients in groups. Group members can usually portray the behavior of significant natural-environment partners of clients exceedingly well.

The focus of this section will be on how to assess overt social behavior in interview situations, through the arrangement of social situations with the client's natural-environment partners, and by means of simulated interactions through role-playing.

Behavioral Observations through Interviews

In our previous exposition of self-report techniques, we discussed interviews from the perspective of having clients provide reports of their interaction with others. Interviews can also provide relevant data on the client's social interaction with the interviewer. The interview represents a sample, however limited, of the client's social interaction with another person. Pertinent observations of the client's behavior in this encounter should provide some important clues as to how skillfully he or she interacts with others.

General Impressions. The following are some guidelines for making behavioral assessments of social behavior from interviews. During the interview, in addition to noting what the client says, the interviewer should be asking him- or herself some questions about the client's behavior. For example: What kind of impressions is this person likely to make on others meeting him or her for the first time? Does the client appear spontaneous and forceful, or reserved and timid? Does this person have adequate conversational skills to be effective in the sales work he or she does? Does this person come across convincingly enough to perform effectively in his or her occupation as a trial lawyer? How much pressure must I put on the client for him or her to reveal something important about him- or herself? Does this person have a sense of humor? The client has complained that others don't seem to desire his or her company. Is there anything that he or she is doing right now which might cause people to react that way? These and many more global impressions about the client's style and effectiveness can be observed during the interview. These impressions may need to be modified since the interview may not be representative of how the client behaves in other encounters.

Specific Behaviors. Specific behavioral components of social skill can also be observed during the assessment interviews. For example, does the client appear to demonstrate adequate eye contact with the interviewer? Is voice volume sufficient? Are there many speech disfluencies? Are there any strange gestures or mannerisms which might lead to ineffective communication? Do the client's nonverbal communications seem to agree with the content of what he or she is saying? What happens to the nonverbal communications when the interviewer places some stress on the client?

In summary, the interview can be regarded as one of the client's interpersonal encounters. In this interpersonal situation, the client should demonstrate some of his or her behavioral assets and liabilities. The interviewer is in an excellent position to obtain some firsthand impressions of the client's general strengths and weaknesses, as well as an assessment of some of the specific behavioral components of social skill. The observations obtained in assessment interviews may not always be representative of how the client might behave during different interpersonal encounters. Nevertheless, important hypotheses can be made as to how skillfully the client is likely to behave in other situations which will be supported or refuted by other kinds of data.

Behavioral Observation from Natural-Environment Partners

There are circumstances which permit the client to come to the assessment situation with his or her natural-environment partners. This has generally been most feasible when the client's problems in social interaction have been identified as difficulties with a family member, and when the family member has some mutual interest in resolving the interactional problem. However, there is no reason why other natural environment partners who have some interest in resolving mutual problems may not be observed during the assessment, and perhaps become involved later on in the training situation.

At this point, a concrete illustration of the use of natural-environment partners in behavioral observation is warranted. Mrs. Jones is a hypothetical client who has reported having problems in interacting with her husband. Mr. Jones is most willing to join the assessment to resolve problems they both euphemistically refer to as problems in "communication." Typically, couples with problems in communication lack skill in obtaining the behavior they desire from the other. Their expectations of a treatment or training situation are that they will talk about their problems in a general way, and they will receive feedback about who is right and who is wrong, and then there will be some magical solution to the problems so that they can live happily ever after.

Our view of these communication problems are that they often result from a history of social-skill deficits whereby partners attempt to influence the behavior of the other using, at times, unfair but mostly ineffective means of conflict resolution. In this case we would want some background information on Mr. and Mrs. Jones through a conjoint interview where they describe the scope of their problems to us. Next we would want actual demonstration of the problems so that we could directly observe the social behavior of each spouse, and the skill with which they attempt to influence each other.

From our conjoint interview we have learned that the Joneses have conflict-resolution-skill problems in two areas. There is constant unresolved conflict about how they spend their joint income. Additionally, they are both unhappy with the conduct of their sexual interactions. Based on these two problem areas, the interviewer asks the couple to participate in two or three discussions which illustrate how they attempt to revolve problems in these areas. The discussions we ask the Joneses to perform for us should (1) have actually occurred, and (2) be typical of the situations which lead to interpersonal conflict in these areas. These are the sample situations which the Joneses have agreed to display for us.

1. Mr. Jones has just bought a new car without consulting his wife. She feels he should never spend that much money without consulting her, and he feels that since she has a car it was really none of her business.
2. Mrs. Jones is upset because Mr. Jones doesn't agree that their daughter needs a $10.00 per week allowance. He feels that at 15

she is old enough to work for her spending money, whereas Mrs. Jones feels that it is important for her daughter to learn how to handle money whatever its source.

3. Mr. Jones can't understand why his wife isn't interested in sex whenever he feels romantically inclined. She has complained that he doesn't pay her enough attention, and this is, after all, attention. Mrs. Jones doesn't like her husband to initiate sex when she is not interested.

4. Mrs. Jones would like her husband to talk to her about how he felt about the sexual encounters. He feels that this is degrading and ruins the spontaneity of the encounter.

There are several different options whereby the assessor can obtain direct behavioral observations of these encounters without actually going home with them. The couple can be instructed to discuss each one of these problems for 10 to 20 minutes in the presence of the observer. With this method, ground rules would be made that the interviewer would not respond to any aspect of their conversation until they had finished. A second alternative would be that the observer would record their conversation on videotape or observe it through a one-way mirror if such equipment was available. Both these methods guard against the possibility that the couple will attempt to involve the assessor in their communications. The videotape method is very desirable because it has the additional feature of involving the couple more directly in the assessment since they can observe the replay of their interactions on videotape.

The assessor can evaluate observations of the couples' interaction, live or on tape, as if it had occurred in their home. There is, of course, always the possibility that the fact of being observed changed the course of their interaction somewhat compared to what it would have been had they been "truly" alone. However, in our experience, it is clear that couples with a history of interactional problems cannot avoid displaying the primary features of their interactional problems, even if they know that they are being observed. Secondly, the behavioral aspects of interpersonal problems are always more salient through observations of the participants, however unrealistic the observational situation, than through verbal reports of these interactions.

What to Observe. In the case of the Joneses we have defined observations of interest to be their ability to display conflict-resolution skills. Some questions which might be asked of the behavioral assessment are: Does each spouse clearly state his or her position on the issue in question? Does each spouse indicate that she or he understands the other's position? Does each spouse demonstrate a sincere concern or interest in the other's feelings? Can confrontations between the two be handled skillfully without undue acrimony or "hitting below the belt?" Do they show skills in negotiation and compromise? The answers to these questions provide the framework for a comprehensive analysis of what social skills the couple have in marital interaction, and also what deficits prevent their successful resolution. Note that we have changed our focus from the skills of Mrs. Jones to the interactive skills of the couple. It may be that both Mr. and Mrs. Jones display similar interactional problems with others, or just primarily with each other. It may be that we will choose to give training just to Mrs. Jones, or they may both become involved in training.

In summary, the employment of natural-environment social partners is very useful whenever it can be accomplished in a nonthreatening manner. Interpersonal-skill problems of the client and possibly the other can be accomplished by judiciously selecting sample situations that relate to the interpersonal problems. It is often a practical alternative to observations of the participants in their actual locations. Most of the natural-environment features of the interactions are preserved, even though they are "staged" somewhat for the benefit of the assessment.

Behavioral Observations from Role-Played Interactions

The last method of direct behavioral assessment of social skill to be discussed here involves the simulation of natural-environment social interactions through role-playing. Role-played social interactions are used frequently in the behavioral assessment of social skills because it is usually more feasible to obtain direct observations of the client's behavior in this manner than through natural environment observations. Although role-playing is by far the most convenient method of obtaining observational data, the question of how representative role-played interactions are of the client's behavior in natural-environment situations is not entirely clear (Bellack, Hersen, & Lamparski, 1979). For the present time, we probably can rely on the client's report as to how closely his or her role-played responses approximate his or her behavior in the natural environment.

Role-played observations can be employed after obtaining initial impressions of the client's skills from the preliminary assessment. That is, following the assessment of initial self-report data, we should have a general picture of the type of social situations which lead to the client's ineffective social behavior. The role-playing then helps to pin down the specific behavioral components of the client's responses, (e.g., content, nonverbal behaviors, etc.), which should be targeted for remediation. Following the assessment of general areas of client difficulty, we should put some thought and effort into the selection of specific social interactions (scenes) for the client to enact for the role-playing assessment. In addition, some clients need some initial instruction and preparation for how to role-play.

Scene Selection. In most cases, three to six interpersonal-interaction scenes can be prepared which sample each situational dimension of the client's skill deficit. For example, a range of several scenes can be selected which deal with the client's ability to cope with heterosocial situations, or to deal effectively with his or her supervisor, or his or her ability to express anger appropriately. Should we desire to assess the heterosocial ability of a young man, we might present him with a scene in which he enacts a telephone call to a young lady, requesting a date. Another scene might reveal his skills in conversing with a woman at a party, and other scenes might be enacted dealing with how he interacts casually with females at work. In selecting scenes for role-playing, it is best at first to reenact previous social situations in which the client has reported difficulty. Later, hypothetical situations which have not occurred, but with which the client anticipates difficulty, can be enacted.

Client Preparation. In order to obtain maximum benefit from the role-playing assessments, clients need to be introduced to the procedure rather than saying we will now role-play thus and so. A brief rationale for role-playing and how it will improve the assessment process is generally required. Some clients may complain at first that the idea of role-playing seems silly or unnatural. The assessor can counter by expressing his or her opinion that role-playing provides more useful information that just talking about the problem. Should the client's apprehension remain, it is frequently useful to obtain his or her consent to try a few scenes before passing judgment. Most clients will feel very comfortable with the role-playing procedure following the enactment of one or two scenes.

In order to maximize the elicitation of the client's natural-environment responses to role-played scenes, the social situations presented to initiate role-playing should be specified in as much detail as possible. For example, we want to know about the details leading up to the particular social situation, specification of the environmental surroundings of where it took place, who was there, what was the purpose of the interaction, what were the client's thoughts and feelings about the situation, what did he or she want or expect would happen. What did the social partner say or do?

Once the client is prepared for the role-playing and the details of the scenes to be enacted are specified, the assessor in his or her role as the social other can prompt the client to begin the scene with a line which calls for a client response. Following the client's response, the assessor can either continue the interaction with a reply, or stop the interaction and go on to another scene. Typically, three or four reciprocal exchanges between client and role-playing assessor are required to assess the client's skill in dealing with the situation. The following is a transcript of how an assessor might obtain some specific information about how his client obtained some observational data through role-playing. The client in this example is Jimmy, a worker in a plastics plant, and his immediate supervisor is Mr. Phelps.

ASSESSOR: Jimmy you have told me that your boss frequently places demands on you which you feel are unfair. Can you think of a specific situation in the last few weeks where this occurred?

CLIENT: Yes, last Friday Mr. Phelps asked me to stay after work at the plant to complete an inventory of equipment we had at the shop.

ASSESSOR: Can you tell me a little more about Mr. Phelps and what led up to the situation where he asked you to stay?

CLIENT: Mr. Phelps is a pretty nice guy. He feels he can always depend on me to get things done. I think he knows that I have trouble saying no to him so he kind of takes advantage of me. Last Friday he told me that he had to get a report out on our equipment by noon Monday or he might be in trouble with the foreman. He said he knew this had come up at the last minute, but hoped I would help him out.

ASSESSOR: Where were you when Mr. Phelps made this request?

CLIENT: I was standing around at the shop with several of the guys just goofing off.

ASSESSOR: What were your thoughts and feelings at this moment?

CLIENT: I thought that Mr. Phelps had been awful nice to me. In fact he helped me get a raise last month. But I had promised my girlfriend that I would take her bowling Friday night, and I knew she would be mad if I cancelled our date. I also felt that the guys standing around were laughing at me for getting stuck again.

ASSESSOR: Okay, Jimmy, let's role-play this scene with you and Mr. Phelps.

CLIENT: I can tell you what happened, I got stuck again and stayed to finish the inventory.

ASSESSOR: No, that's not what I had in mind. I want to see exactly how you handled this, what you said and how you said it. So let's role-play this. Let's pretend you are back in the shop with Mr. Phelps just like it was last Friday. I will be Mr. Phelps.

CLIENT: Okay.

ASSESSOR: Jimmy, I hate to ask you this, but I know I can depend on you. I have to

send in a report on our inventory by noon next Monday, would you mind
staying late tonight and helping me finish it?
CLIENT: Mr. Phelps I have to go somewhere tonight, couldn't you ask someone
        else to do it?
ASSESSOR: Well, I wish I could, but you are the only one around here who knows
        where everything is, and I'll get in trouble if I can't get it done right away.
CLIENT: Well, I guess I'll have to stay then.

The above illustration demonstrates the interaction between client
and assessor leading up to the role-played interaction, as well as the
role-playing itself. Note that prior to the role-playing, the assessor obtained information on the specifics of the situation, the other person(s) in
the situation, and where and under what circumstances the interaction
occurred. Also, in order to evaluate the client's overt behavior, the assessor wanted to know something about what was going on in the client's
mind as the interaction was taking place. In this case, a little persuasion
by the assessor was necessary in order to have the client role-play the
scene. Once a rationale was offered, the client had no problem in enacting
the scene.

Summary

This chapter reviews practical methods for assessing the client's
social skills and the situations which elicit social behavior. There are
basically two sources of data relevant to social-skills assessment: self-
reported views of the client, and direct observations of the client's social
behavior reported by outside observers. Among the self-report methods,
we have discussed structured inventories and focused interviews, and
we have recommended self-monitoring techniques for obtaining specific
assessment information about relevant social situations and for assessing
the level of client skills before, during, and following the instigation of
training procedures.

Several methods were suggested for obtaining relatively precise
observational data on a client's social skills. These included the use of
simulated social interactions through role-playing techniques, and the
observation of the social interaction of natural-environment partners.
Role-playing is probably the easiest method to employ since it may be
conducted in the training session. However, role-playing may have the
drawback of artificiality, and in some instances, may not be representative of how the client would behave in actual social situations. Observing
the interaction of natural-environment partners was discussed as being

an excellent method for obtaining behavioral data on client skills. However, practical considerations limit the use of this technique to situations in which the natural environment partner, for example, spouse, may be available for assessment purposes.

The last section discussed the importance of appropriate preparation of the client for role-playing and how to select and implement role-playing scenes which are relevant to the client's particular problem. In sum, the effectiveness of training depends on a thorough assessment of all aspects of social skills. This includes the client's knowledge of how to behave in social situations, his or her attitudes and emotional responses, and a precise knowledge of how the client actually behaves in relevant social situations.

Teaching More Effective Social Behaviors

Overview

- Clients require appropriate preparation prior to instigation of training. They should be given a thorough rationale for the procedures to be used and be in agreement with the objectives of training. The role of the trainer as a source of positive social reinforcement is also discussed.
- The advantages and disadvantages of conducting training in group versus individual formats are discussed.
- Training is presented as a four-step process consisting of: (1) providing a description and rationale for learning new behaviors; (2) demonstrating new behaviors through modeling; (3) practicing learned responses through behavioral rehearsal; and (4) improving upon acquired responses through feedback.
- Guidelines for the format of training sessions (e.g., How many? How long?) are presented.

In Chapters 3 and 4 we discussed how strengths and deficits in social skill can be assessed. This chapter will be devoted to the actual acquisition or training of social skills. Our purpose will be to explain how the targeted skills can be taught. This includes preparing for training, choosing appropriate training formats, and actually conducting training sessions.

The techniques covered in this chapter may be considered basic. They are useful for training a wide range of social skills. There will, of course, be differences in emphasis, pacing, and complexity, depending on the population you are working with, the skills you are attempting to train, and the progress of training. Some individuals master skills quickly, and perform well right from the start. For these individuals, training can easily be condensed. For other individuals, especially those demonstrating extreme deficits in social functioning, progress can be very slow, requiring extended practice. Most people are, of course, somewhere between the extremes. In short, though the entire procedure may not be necessary with a particular individual, the combination is generally sufficient.

For example, let us say that you are working in a clinical setting, trying to train an extremely withdrawn patient to acknowledge the presence of others through a simple greeting. In this instance, the skill being trained (greeting others) is elementary. Yet the extreme deficit displayed by the individual makes highly structured training necessary (and usually successful). At the other end of the continuum, you may be working with an experienced executive who wants to sharpen her skills in preparation for sensitive contract negotiation. In this instance, training might be centered around developing negotiation strategies and reacting appropriately to subtle nonverbal cues. In both these examples, a social skill is being taught. Although the specifics of training will differ greatly, given the gross differences in clients and skills to be taught, the basic techniques are the same. In this chapter we will identify these techniques and explore their usage.

Following the initial assessment (described in Chapters 3 and 4), the trainer should have a good appreciation of the client's interpersonal strengths and weaknesses. The understanding required by the trainer needs to be on two levels. First, the trainer requires a global, impressionistic understanding of the client's interpersonal strengths and weaknesses. Let us take the example of a middle-level supervisor named Alan. Following an assessment, the trainer might conceptualize Alan's difficulty as behaving "passively" when demands were placed on him by his immediate superior at work. Further, the assessment might show that Alan was "overly aggressive" when providing feedback to subordinates. The level of understanding illustrated in this example is extremely useful for determining the general objectives of training, as well as its tone. Feedback and coaching can thus be tailored to obtaining these objectives.

However, knowing that Alan is too passive with his supervisor does not specify which particular behaviors need to be modified. "Passivity" can have a wide range of behavioral referents. A person may be labeled passive because of poor eye contact, low speech volume, a high frequency of speech dysfluencies, long delays in responding to questions, frequently complying with unreasonable requests, a failure to express positive emotions, and so on. The list could be varied and extensive.

Thus, the second level of understanding required is a delineation of the *specific* target behaviors to be modified. In the example mentioned above, the trainer may need to instruct Alan to increase his voice volume and eye contact when he is interacting with his supervisor, but decrease both of these nonverbal behaviors when he is interacting with subordinates. A similar degree of specificity would also be required with the verbal content of the client's response. In interactions with his supervisor, Alan might need to make clear, straightforward requests. On the other hand, he might need to make fewer requests, fewer threats, and ask more questions when dealing with the people he supervises.

These two levels of understanding, impressionistic and specific, should both emerge from the assessment data. If they have done so, training can be started. In many cases, the person doing the assessment will also serve as the trainer. If this is the case, many of the preliminaries to training may already be completed. If the trainer is a different person than the assessor, special attention must be paid to the development of a good, cooperative working relationship. In either case, there are a number of factors to take into account when setting the stage for training.

Preparation for Training

If training is to be maximally successful, the client must both develop the targeted skills during training and perform them in appropriate situations outside of training. However, doing these two things may not always be easy or pleasant. Quite often there is a good bit of anxiety associated with trying out new skills. Old, well-learned patterns of social interaction can be difficult to change. Attempts at using new skills can sometimes backfire, resulting in awkward and embarrassing interactions. In short, the process of developing new social skills may be somewhat threatening for some individuals.

Effectively overcoming the inertia inherent in developing new skills requires some advance preparation. There should be clear agreement between client and trainer on the goals and methods of training. Without it, training is not likely to be successful. Further, the trainer should be a source of positive reinforcement to the client. Praise or social reinforcement from the trainer can help overcome the client's reluctance to try new behaviors. It can help motivate the client in the face of early difficulties in applying the skills outside the training situation.

On the other hand, poor preparation for assessment and training can have a detrimental effect on clients' learning. An insensitive or caustic trainer who ridicules the client's performance will undoubtedly increase the client's anxiety, decrease learning, and thereby make it more difficult for the client ever to develop the new skills. Client cooperation is also essential to effective training. If the client does not agree with the goals of training, there is little hope that the new skills will ever be used.

The guidelines for structuring a good working relationship and obtaining client cooperation are not dissimilar from those appropriate to any training situation. Nonetheless, a review of some general considerations is in order.

1. *Informed consent* refers to an understanding on the part of the client of what is to be done with him or her and why. Further, the client should know how any information generated during assessment or training is to be used. This knowledge should be complete, truthful, and *understood* by the client. In addition, the client must freely consent to participate in the described training program. Pressure, applied by the trainer or others associated with the trainer, either overt or subtle, misses the point.

The requirement of informed consent is important not only from an ethical standpoint but also from a practical one. Knowing what is to happen and why can be extremely useful in reducing anxieties associated with an unfamiliar situation and help minimize fears that one's performance will somehow be used in a detrimental manner. In short, the client will have more appropriate expectations along with having voluntarily expressed his or her cooperation.

2. *A training contract.* Closely related to informed consent is the notion of a training contract. As described here, a training contract is simply an agreement between the client and the trainer. This agreement specifies the goals of training as well as the rights and responsibilities of both the trainer and the client. Such an agreement can be a formal, written document, carefully specifying goals, rights, and responsibilities. If this is the case, the training contract can also function as a formalization of informed consent. At the other end of the spectrum, a training contract can simply be a verbal agreement. The trainer and client discuss the client's goals and come to an informal agreement. In either case, the goal is the same—to specify mutual goals and expectations. In most instances, this agreement or training contract is verbal. However, in some cases a written, somewhat formalized agreement may be preferable. Such a written agreement is not subject to forgetting or subtle distortions over the course of training. This permanence can be valuable to client and trainer alike. An example of such a written training contract is shown in

Figure 2. A contract helps make it clear to both the client and the trainer why they are there and what they will be doing.

3. *The trainer as a positive reinforcer.* In most instances the trainer can be a source of positive reinforcement to the client. The client sees the trainer's praise and approval in a positive light and will work to receive it. However, this is not universally true. There are probably a few cases in which the client dislikes the trainer from the very start. For example, the trainer might be a female who reminds the client of his ex-wife whom he intensely dislikes. Or the client may object to the trainer's personal style or manner of speaking. There may be a variety of reasons, most of which should have little to do with training. If these initial differences cannot be overcome, considerations should be given to changing trainers.

Training Contract

1. This contract is between _____(client) and _____ (trainer).

2. The purpose of training is to improve the skill of the client in the following areas:

   _____

   _____

   _____

3. To accomplish this goal, the client agrees to do the following:

   _____

   _____

   _____

4. In return, the trainer agrees to do the following:

   _____

   _____

   _____

5. Both parties freely and without duress agree to the terms of this contract. This contract may not be altered without the consent of both parties.

Signed: _____   Signed: _____
                  (client)   (trainer)

Date: _____   Date: _____

Figure 2. An example of a formalized training contract.

However, in the vast majority of cases the trainer starts out in a good position to become a positive reinforcer. If for no other reason, the trainer is usually looked up to as the expert. Whether the trainer remains a reinforcer depends on his or her behavior. If the trainer's behaviors show the client that he or she is not interested in him or his performance, one cannot expect to remain an effective trainer. The feedback to the client will lose some of its reinforcing value. On the other hand, if the trainer's behavior reflects a respect for the client, and a concern for his or her progress, the trainer will probably become more reinforcing.

There are, of course, no universal rules on how to establish oneself as a reinforcing agent. However, some examples of behaviors that might tend to make a trainer more or less of a reinforcer are shown in Table IV. Although many of the examples may seem obvious, it is unfortunately the case that they are sometimes ignored.

Group versus Individual Training

Social-skills training is clearly a very flexible procedure. This is true not only in terms of the kinds of skills that can be trained and the

Table IV. Some Examples of Trainer's Behavior That Either Help or Hurt Trainer's Efforts to Become a Positive Reinforcer

Less likely to become a reinforcer	More likely to become a reinforcer
Express indifference about the client's difficulties.	Express concern about the client's difficulties.
Ignore positive performance	Praise positive performance.
Allow no opportunities for questions.	Offer opportunities for questions.
Show disdain for client.	Show respect for client.
Use harsh/sarcastic voice tone.	Use friendly/pleasant voice tone.
Be pessimistic/discouraging.	Be optimistic/encouraging.
Be rude/discourteous.	Be polite/courteous.
Criticize poor performance without offering alternatives.	Ignore poor performance and offer positive alternatives.
Ignore client's questions.	Answer client's questions.
Use poor eye contact.	Use good eye contact.
Be interpersonally "cold."	Be interpersonally "warm."
Have no time for the client.	Have time for the client.
Do not explain procedures.	Explain procedures.

populations with which it can be used, but also in terms of the training format itself. In the following sections we will see that the trainer is faced with a variety of options at many points in the basic training procedure. But perhaps one of the most basic decisions is whether to train in a group or an individual format. In an individual format, the trainer works with a single client. If the trainer simultaneously works with more than a single client, training can be considered a group process. The group size can vary from two individuals to a room full of people. Typically, groups are of moderate size (6 to 12 people), and the opportunity to role-play or practice is rotated among group members.

Social-skills training has been successfully used with individual clients (e.g., Eisler *et al.*, 1974; Frederiksen & Eisler, 1977; Frederiksen *et al.*, 1976), pairs of clients (e.g., McKinlay, Pachman, & Frederiksen, 1977; Frederiksen & Peterson, 1975), as well as larger groups (e.g., Argyle, Bryant, & Trower, 1974; Goldsmith & McFall, 1975). Unfortunately, there is a paucity of data on which to base a decision between the two approaches. There is some indication that clients may benefit from being involved in the training of another client with a similar problem. For example, in one recent study (McKinlay *et al.*, 1977), clients with temper-control problems served as role-playing partners for each other when another client with a similar problem received social-skills training. Some improvement in subsequent performance was noted after the clients served as social partners for each other. Thus, it appears that some advantages can occur when the client becomes actively involved in the training of others. Yet, on the whole, there may be few differences in overall effectiveness of the different training approaches.

This latter question was addressed in two recent experiments. In one, psychiatric patients demonstrating deficits in social skills were divided into three groups (Packman, McKinlay, & Frederiksen, unpublished). One group received individual social-skills training, and the second group received similar training conducted in a group format. The third group received no skills training and served as a control group. Results showed that both experimental groups performed better than the control group following training. Importantly, individual and group training did not differ in their overall effectiveness. A similar finding was obtained in a study of nonassertive community women (Linehan, Walker, Bronheim, Haynes, & Yevzeroff, 1979). Here again, the clients were randomly assigned to group or individual training. Results indicated that both training formats were equally effective at the end of training and at follow-up. Thus, the decision on which training format to use may need to be based on considerations other than simple effectiveness.

An individual training format offers maximum flexibility and intensity. The trainee's full attention is focused on the single client. Training can be closely tied to the client's specific deficits and needs. As the client's needs change, training can be appropriately modified. Further, there is more time for practice. Yet, these advantages have their price. Individualized training requires a much greater investment of time for each individual trained.

Group training sacrifices some of the concentrated attention and flexibility inherent in an individual approach. By necessity, training usually involves less practice and attention to specific individual deficits. On the other hand, the potential cost effectiveness is markedly improved. If a single trainer can effectively train ten people at a time, rather than a single client, services can be delivered much more efficiently. Further, the group itself can be an important part of training. As a function of their shared experiences, group members can provide mutual support or reinforcement for improvement in a way that the therapist cannot. They can model alternative ways of responding and evaluate the social effectiveness of certain behaviors or response strategies. Similarly, the group can be a source of background data on problem situations, general information about social norms, and feedback on specific performances. In short, the group can help define what is "socially skillful" and what is not. This is particularly true when the clients are from a subculture that is different from the trainer's. Since effective social functioning is so closely related to social norms, this information can be invaluable to the trainer.

In choosing between an individual or group format, the trainer must be mindful of the nature of the clients and their deficits. If the clients have similar backgrounds and show similar skill deficits, it is probably wise to use a group format. If, on the other hand, the clients have a variety of dissimilar backgrounds and differing skill deficits, an individual format is indicated. Some of the advantages of each training format are summarized in Table V. By taking these factors into account, training can be more closely tailored to the client's needs and desired benefits.

The Training Session

As we have emphasized repeatedly, there is no single best way to train social skills. The training procedures are very versatile and can be modified to suit the particular occasion. To this end, we will place a good bit of emphasis on variations in the training procedure. At almost every stage of training the trainer can tailor the training process to fit the specific situation. As long as the trainer remains in a position to insure that the objectives of training are met, he or she is on safe ground.

Table V. Some Advantages of Individual and Group Training Formats

Individual training	Group training
Maximum versatility to suit specific needs and differing problems.	Can use group as a source of information about social norms and problem situations, motivation, etc.
Maximum intensity of trainer's efforts.	
More time for repeated practice.	Group members may benefit by observing others improve.
Training can be better "paced" to suit client's progress.	
Client has many social deficits which require individual attention.	Access to a variety of models, opinions, and sources of feedback about individual's effectiveness.
	See others with a similar problem if the group is homogeneous.
	Potential for improved cost-effectiveness.

However, this emphasis on variation should not obscure the basic process of training. As indicated in Chapter 1, training consists of four basic phases. The first is a description of the desired social behavior with a rationale for its use. Tell the client *specifically* what he or she is to do and why. Second is demonstration, or modeling. Show the client what to do. Third is practice. Have the client actually practice the desired skills. Typically, this is accomplished in role-playing conducted during training sessions. Finally, the client receives corrective feedback on his or her performance. What is done correctly? What needs to be improved? Here again, a variety of feedback modes can be used. It is this basic four-phase procedure (description of the behavior, demonstration, response practice, and feedback) that forms the basic structure within which variations are employed.

Description and Rationale

Probably the simplest way to get someone to behave in a certain way is to give them instructions on what to do and why. If you want the client to use more eye contact, tell the client this in clear and unambiguous terms. If the client knows what is expected, he is more likely to do it. It is also important that the instructions be placed in context by including a rationale for behaving in the described manner. Why is it important to use eye contact? Why is it important not to apologize when making a request? Providing a convincing rationale can help facilitate a behavior change.

It is in the process of providing instructions on what behaviors to employ and the rationale behind their use, that the trainer starts to apply what he or she has learned from the assessment. The trainer must translate global and nonspecific impressions into the specifics of what the client needs to change. At first blush, coaching the client in what to do may seem like an easy task—but often it is not. The trainer not only needs to understand the client's current behavior in an impressionistic sense but must also be able to tell the client specifically what needs to be done differently and why. It is relatively easy to observe that the client is doing something ineffectively. It is quite another matter to specify clearly what the client should be doing in order to function more effectively. Yet, it is important that the desired behaviors be specified if training is to have maximum impact.

In some cases, the clients may "know what to do" and be able to demonstrate the desired skill on request. Yet they hesitate to actively use the skill because they feel that it may be misinterpreted by others; they don't want to commit themselves to a position; they unrealistically fear "counterattacks" from others, etc. In these instances, the rationale takes on special importance and may take the form of an extended discussion rather than a brief statement by the trainer.

Another area where the trainer may encounter difficulty is in trying to provide specific instructions and rationales for verbal content or for general strategies. It is often not possible to tell the person what words to use or how to react in every possible situation. In these circumstances, it often becomes more a matter of mutually generating some possible alternatives, trying them out, and evaluating the results. Yet even in these circumstances there are some general principles that aid rapid learning.

1. *Be specific.* Tell the client what he or she needs to do in clear and unambiguous terms. Describe the desired target behavior in enough detail so that it is clear to anyone what you expect the client to do. To be unnecessarily vague and noncommital may be easier for the trainer, but it is not conducive to rapid behavior change.

2. *Be positive.* Tell the client what he or she should be doing rather than what he or she should not be doing. It is much more effective to build in an effective behavior than to try to suppress an ineffective behavior. Simply removing a behavior from a person's repertoire leaves a void. What does the individual do now that he or she is in the same situation that previously elicited the ineffective behavior? By training in skillful behaviors that are incompatible with ineffective behaviors, you not only eliminate the problem behavior, but you also provide the needed replacement.

3. *Use small steps.* Work with one or two behaviors at a time. Break the skills the client needs to learn down into component behaviors and

give instructions on only one or two component behaviors at a time. For example, if you are training a person to be a "more effective communicator," you may target the behaviors of asking open-ended questions and using appropriate silences, head nods, eye contact, etc. It is preferable to give instructions and training on relatively few behaviors until the client has mastered them before introducing additional behaviors. This allows the client to concentrate his or her efforts and successfully develop competencies. If a number of behaviors are simultaneously introduced, the client may have a very difficult time in changing his previous pattern of responses. In short, use small steps to insure repeated success and steady progress.

4. *Explain why.* Provide a convincing rationale for why the behavior to be trained is important in meeting the client's goals. Clients should be aware that what they are to learn is in fact relevant to success. Further, they should have some understanding of how changes fit into their overall functioning. The client not only learns what behavior to employ, but also *when* to employ it. If the client feels that behaviors to be learned are irrelevant or superfluous, one cannot expect maximum training effects or generalization of the new skills to the client's day-to-day functioning. This rationale should be in language that the client clearly understands. Further, the rationale should be presented in a way that elicits the client's cooperation.

Let us examine some brief examples of effective and ineffective coaching:

POOR: "I want you to be more authentic and true to your real feelings. Open up and express yourself genuinely."

BETTER: "When you are expressing an opinion, simply state how you feel and stop. Don't apologize or qualify your opinion, it only makes you appear uncertain."

In the poor example, the client is not told specifically what to do or why. Words like "authentic" or "genuine" can mean different things to different people and, consequently, are not appropriate for use in instructions. In the better example, the situation, desired behavior, and rationale are all more clearly specified. The client can get a good idea of what to do and why.

POOR: "Stop being so timid."

BETTER: "Look directly at the person and speak louder. You will appear more confident and assertive."

Here again, the poor example does not specify what is to be done or why. "Timid" is not defined in terms of behavior. In the better example, the desired behaviors are clearly stated as is the likely effect of using those behaviors.

POOR: "When you are dealing with your subordinates, suppress your true feelings so that they may vent their infantile wishes against your authority."

BETTER: "When subordinates approach you with a complaint, listen in silence until they have finished. By listening to their story before you reply, you not only develop an understanding of their side but also convey the impression that their opinions are important."

Once again, the better example tells the person specifically what behavior is expected and the rationale for its use. The desired behaviors and when to use them are presented in clear, unambiguous terms.

In most instances, the descriptions of target behaviors and the rationale for their use will be delivered verbally. Especially in a group setting, the delivery of the instructions and rationale can offer an opportunity for group members to contribute. Quite often group members can add perspective and legitimacy to a rationale or provide additional suggestions for the expression of specific behaviors. The insistence by several other group members that a given behavior, suggested by the trainer, will in fact work can carry a lot of weight with an individual group member. By the same token, several group members insisting that a suggested social behavior is ineffective can markedly reduce the trainer's impact. In any case, it is ultimately the trainer's responsibility to insure that coaching instructions are specific, positive, and appropriate to the particular social context.

A description of the target behavior is clearly important. However, sometimes the behavior to be taught is exceedingly difficult to describe verbally. For example, how does one adequately describe the appropriate use of hand gestures? One might describe the hand movements in great detail, yet the timing and fluidity is lost in a verbal description. One must *see* the gesture in context really to understand it. At other times, the sequence of behaviors desired is lengthy or too complex to describe adequately (e.g., a negotiation strategy). It is in these instances that the importance of modeling or demonstrations in social-skills training becomes clear.

Modeling or Demonstrations

In the first phase of training, the goal was to *tell* the client what to do and why. The purpose of demonstrations or modeling is to *show* the client what to do. The client thus gets a "sample" of the expected behaviors as well as the description. This opportunity to see or hear the desired behavior is especially important when the target behavior is complex, subtle, or not easily described. A good example of such a behavior is hand gestures. It is exceedingly difficult and cumbersome to describe to someone the appropriate use of gestures. On the other hand, it is quite easy and efficient to show them how gestures can be smoothly incorporated into a conversation. This is true for verbal behaviors as well. For example, describing the use of open-ended questions and giving a rationale for their use is important. However, adding examples of open-ended questions and their appropriate use can markedly increase the probability that the client will understand what they are and how to use them.

Modeling can be conducted in several different formats, including the use of live models, audiotape, videotape or film demonstrations, and even mental imagery. In choosing among these formats, there are several considerations to keep in mind.

1. *Accuracy.* The model or demonstration must accurately present the desired target behavior(s) to be learned. If the wrong behavior is modeled, there is a very real danger that the client will perform the inappropriate behaviors rather than the ones actually desired. At the very least, demonstrating an inappropriate behavior can lead to confusion on the client's part.

2. *Reproducibility.* Very often it is desirable repeatedly to demonstrate the target behavior to the client. For example, the first time a social interaction is demonstrated, the client may not be adequately attending to all the relevant component behaviors. In this case, it would be desirable to demonstrate the behavior again. The same is true across training sessions. It is important to have an accurate demonstration of socially effective behaviors available on a repeated basis.

3. *Versatility.* Versatility refers to the ability to change the modeling demonstration to suit changing conditions. For example, the trainer may wish to provide the subject with a number of different models displaying the appropriate behaviors in varying situations. Or the trainer may wish to suit the model to the characteristics of a particular client. In working with an elderly male, the trainer would probably not want to employ a young female model or vice versa. This ability to adapt the modeling demonstration to changing or variable conditions is an important consideration.

4. *Ease of preparation.* This final consideration refers to the cost, in time, effort, and money, required to prepare the modeling display. This cost can vary widely depending on the format chosen. With some modeling formats, there is virtually no advance preparation required, whereas others require a good bit of preparation and production.

Each of the modeling formats has its relative advantages and disadvantages. By keeping these in mind, one can choose a modeling format or formats that are well suited to specific training situations.

Live Demonstrations. In this format, the target behavior is demonstrated "live" in the training session. In most cases the model is the trainer, or one of the group members if group training is used. For example, let us say that the trainer is working with an individual on how to request a behavior change from his or her supervisor. The trainer would first describe the characteristics of an appropriate request (instruction), e.g., it is clear, direct, and unambiguous. The trainer would then explain why it is important to make such a direct request, offering a rationale. At that point the trainer could demonstrate several alternative ways of making appropriate requests. If training was being conducted in a group format, the trainer might also request one or more members of the group to demonstrate direct, appropriate requests that they have seen others use. In this manner, the group would be exposed to a variety of different models.

Live modeling demonstrations are clearly very versatile. Since modeling is done in the training situation, the model's behavior can be organized to emphasize certain things. If certain postures are being demonstrated, they can be clearly accented or exaggerated for a particular cleient who uses poor postures. If the next client uses excessive hand gestures, the trainer can easily minimize or underplay hand gestures to that client's needs. This kind of flexibility is nearly impossible to achieve when some sort of preprepared modeling format (e.g., videotape) is used. Further, live demonstrations are virtually "cost free" in terms of ease of preparation. Although the trainer should probably rehearse these modeling displays before the session, there are no costly tapes or films that need to be prepared.

The disadvantages of live modeling are twofold. First, since the modeling display is not prepared in advance, it is difficult to insure its accuracy. In other words, the model may inadvertently give a poor example of the target behavior. This is particularly a problem when group members are called on to demonstrate a target behavior. The second problem with live demonstrations is reproducibility. There is no way to "replay" the demonstration and insure that it will come out precisely the same way the second time. These problems notwithstanding, live demonstrations have been and will probably continue to be important in the modeling of socially effective behavior because of the economy of effort.

Audiotape Demonstrations. In this modeling format, a prerecorded audiotape serves as the example of the target behavior. After the trainer provides the instructions and rationale for the target behavior, he or she simply plays the audiotape(s) demonstrating the target behavior.

Audiotape models have been frequently used, particularly in some of the early work with social-skills training. Audiotape is an inexpensive, portable, and easy-to-use format. The trainer can prepare audiotapes in advance and review them to insure that the target skills are accurately represented. Further, the modeling displays can be stored, played, and replayed at will. If the client "misses" the target skill the first time, the tape can be replayed on the spot with ease.

On the negative side, since audiotapes are prerecorded, they are not as flexible as live demonstrations. More important, it is impossible to demonstrate nonverbal behaviors in an audiotape format. This is a serious limitation given the importance of nonverbal behaviors in social interaction. It is this consideration, more than any other, that has led to the increased use of the videotape format for modeling displays.

Videotape and Film Demonstrations. These two related formats are used in much the same way as audiotape. Following instructions and rationale, the trainer plays the prerecorded modeling tape or film. As with audiotape, the modeling display can be replayed and stored as desired.

Perhaps the most obvious advantage of videotaped models is that they allow the client to observe nonverbal as well as verbal behavior. In addition, they retain the advantages of insuring the accuracy and reproducibility of the modeling display. Further, perhaps because of novelty, these formats often hold the client's attention exceedingly well.

In terms of advance preparation and cost, these formats are undoubtedly the most expensive. Production of the tapes and films requires advance planning, recruitment of models, rehearsal, sophisticated and sometimes expensive equipment, and often a good bit of time. This is especially true with film. As with audiotape, there is also the problem of lack of adjustability. However, in situations which require high accuracy and reproducibility (skill training in groups), or when the same demonstration is likely to be used repeatedly, it may be well worth the cost.

Mental Imagery. An interesting variant on modeling procedures is to employ the client's own mental imagery to present demonstrations (e.g., Kazdin, 1974). With this procedure, the client first receives instructions and a rationale, as before. However, rather than having the trainer model the target behavior, the client is instructed to *imagine*, or "draw a mental picture" of, a model performing the target behavior. The trainer may assist by providing verbal descriptions or narration (e.g., "Imagine the model approaching her supervisor and looking him directly in the eye").

This procedure has a number of points to recommend it. First, it is extremely versatile. The client can "observe" literally any situation. This is of particular benefit if you are working with social situations that are intimate or otherwise difficult to film or demonstrate live, such as sexually related situations. A client with vivid imagery can also produce a modeling display of great detail and realism. Further, imagery-based procedures require no equipment and minimal advance preparation. And, finally, since the client is the one producing the modeling display, he or she can "review" or imagine the demonstration outside the training session. This can be beneficial in producing transfer of training to the real social situations.

On the negative side, since the client's mental imagery is private and not available to the trainer, there is no way of insuring that the modeling display is accurate. The client may inadvertently be "imagining" the ineffective behavior. There is likewise no assurance that the imagery is clear or reproducible, either immediately or in the future. Further, some clients may have difficulty in developing any images of models. These are all significant drawbacks. Nevertheless, imagery-based techniques do hold promise and may well have a place in the trainer's overall approach.

Modeling or demonstrations can add a great deal of clarity to the desired target behavior. This can be further enhanced by instructing the client to attend carefully to the targeted behaviors when the modeling display is presented. The model should also appear reasonably successful as a result of using the appropriate behaviors. It would quite obviously be contraproductive to have the model demonstrate the desired behavior, only repeatedly to fail to obtain the desired consequences in the social interaction. Also, providing several demonstrations, using different models and even different modeling formats, can aid in developing the client's understanding of what effective social behavior looks like and what it accomplishes. However, as important as this understanding is, the client must also be able to perform the necessary behaviors.

Behavior Rehearsal

The purpose of behavior rehearsal, sometimes called response practice, is to have the client actually practice effective social behaviors in simulated social situations. The techniques of instruction and modeling should provide the client with an understanding of what behaviors will be most effective and why. But understanding alone is not enough. The client must be able to perform the targeted behaviors. Behavior rehearsal gives the client the opportunity to practice and perfect the performance in the training situation, before he or she uses it in the "real" world.

In addition to giving the client an opportunity to practice the targeted behavior, rehearsal also affords the trainer an opportunity to observe the client's performance and provide corrective feedback. Such feedback can be valuable in shaping more appropriate performances. In short, the client can make mistakes in a situation where errors have few negative consequences, and constructive feedback is readily available.

In most instances, behavior rehearsal involves role-playing specific situations in much the same way that they were role-played during assessment. A situation is described, and the client is asked to behave as he or she would if he or she were actually in the situation. The main difference is that the client should be placing special emphasis on using the target behavior that is being taught.

In behavior rehearsal, as in assessment, a variety of role-playing partners can be used to develop approximations to real-life social interactions. A simple procedure, especially when individual training is being used, is to have the trainer serve as the role-playing partner. This procedure has the advantage of actively involving the trainer in the situation, giving him or her a better "feel" for the effectiveness of the client's behavior. On the negative side, by becoming actively involved in the behavior rehearsal the trainer sacrifices some detachment from the situation. The trainer may inadvertently miss an important part of the client's performance.

The alternative is to employ a role-playing partner other than the trainer to reenact different social situations. This person might be someone who is familiar with the kind of situation being role-played and the social norms for effective behavior in that kind of situation. For example, the client might be a personnel manager who wishes to improve her skills in conducting employment interviews. In that situation the role-playing partner should be familiar with how job applicants typically behave in such employment interviews. This familiarity tends to make the situation more realistic for the client, and hence, more relevant to the client's ultimate performance goal. The role-playing partner's familiarity with the situations may come from direct experience, for example he had previously conducted or observed similar employment interviews, or from other sources such as the client's description of how people typically behave. The source of the knowledge is unimportant. What is important is the realism of the situation.

In group social-skills training, one obvious source of role-playing partners is other group members. If the group is relatively homogeneous, it is likely that group members are familiar with the kinds of situation being role-played. They can thus give a realistic role-playing "performance" with minimal effort. Employing group members in role-playing also has the advantage of involving them more actively in the training process. This involvement may actually have some positive training benefits (e.g., McKinlay et al., 1977).

The actual rehearsal or role-playing should be long enough to be realistic, yet short enough to allow for repeated practice and frequent feedback. In the example used above, it would probably be excessive to simulate a full 30-minute employment interview before stopping to give the client performance feedback. A more appropriate tactic would be to start with a role-playing segment one to five minutes in length. The client can then receive some immediate feedback and make the necessary performance adjustments. Behavioral rehearsal can then continue for another brief segment followed by additional feedback. The basic principle is repeated, brief practice trials with frequent feedback, rather than extended trials with infrequent and delayed feedback. In most instances, a practice trial of under 10 minutes is quite sufficient. As training progresses, it may be advantageous to employ some more extended simulations. However, especially in early stages of skill acquisition, the key is *repeated* practice and *frequent* feedback.

Covert Rehearsal. Up to this point, we have concentrated on overt-behavior rehearsal where the client actually engages in the desired behavior. An alternative procedure is covert-behavior rehearsal where the client rehearses the target behavior in his or her imagination. Just as modeling can be either overt or based on imagery, so too can behavioral rehearsal. In covert rehearsal, the client would be instructed to imagine or visualize him- or herself engaging in the target behavior. This covert procedure has two advantages. First, behaviors that would be extremely difficult to rehearse overtly (e.g., intimate/sexual behavior) can be covertly rehearsed with ease. Second, clients can use this procedure on their own in naturally occurring situations. For example, if a client wishes to ask for a promotion, he or she could covertly rehearse what he or she wishes to say just before entering the manager's office. Overt rehearsal would indeed be cumbersome, potentially embarrassing if overheard, and impractical in such a situation. The main disadvantage of covert rehearsal, as with covert modeling, is that the trainer cannot directly observe the client's imagery. Without such observation, the trainer is in no position to provide direct performance feedback. Ultimately, it is the client's overt behavior that must be changed. It would do little good if a client could imagine himself performing well, but could not actually perform the overt behaviors effectively. Thus, although covert rehearsal can be extremely useful, it is doubtful that it can ever completely replace overt-behavior rehearsal in the training process.

Recording Behavioral Performance. Following several behavior rehearsals, the client should receive feedback on his performance. Part of that feedback will be verbal in nature, that is, the trainer's comments. However, it can also be extremely helpful to have an objective record of the client's performance for immediate review. This can be accomplished easily by making audiotape or videotape recordings of the client's rehearsals. Following the rehearsal, the tapes can be replayed and provide an objective basis for feedback. All that is required is that the client understand and agree to such recording. It has been our experience that, in many cases, there is some initial reluctance and anxiety associated with the prospect of being recorded and "critiqued." However, in most cases this reluctance is minimal and is easily overcome as the value of such feedback becomes apparent to the client. Further, as training progresses, most clients quickly acclimate to the presence of the recording devices during behavior rehearsal.

Feedback

Coaching, instructions, and modeling can provide the client with an understanding of what performance is expected. Behavior rehearsal gives the client an opportunity to practice the desired behavior. The evaluation of that practice occurs during the final phase of the training sequence—feedback. Feedback can come either from the trainer, or, in group situations, from other group members.

Feedback has two functions. The first is to provide the client with evaluative information about his or her performance. How does the client come across to others? Did he or she use the target behavior that he or she was practicing? What other appropriate behaviors were displayed? What ineffective behaviors did the client use? What aspects of the performance should be improved? The feedback about the client's performance should be put in a way that makes it easy for the client to correct and improve his or her performance. In short, the information should be nonjudgmental, yet precise in prescribing changes.

The second function of feedback is to provide motivation for more effective performance. The feedback should function to reinforce the positive aspects of the client's behavior rehearsal. As we mentioned earlier, developing social skills can be a difficult task, and it is the trainer's responsibility to insure that the client maintain the necessary motivation. One of the primary ways of insuring adequate motivation is through the reinforcement of appropriate social performances. Usually this reinforcement is of a social nature. The trainer praises the positive aspects of the client's performance. If the trainer has insured that he or she is a positive reinforcer (see the earlier section on setting the stage for training), then the social praise from the trainer will usually have the desired motivational effect.

In some cases, particularly with very unskilled populations, social praise may not function as a reinforcer. In these instances, it may be necessary first to employ more tangible reinforcers (e.g., food, money, cigarettes, trading stamps, prizes, etc.). The systematic delivery of such tangible reinforcers may be conveniently structured through a token economy (Kazdin, 1977a). Through the repeated pairing of these tangible reinforcers with social praise, the praise alone may ultimately come to function as a reinforcer (Stahl, Thomson, Leitenberg, & Hasazi, 1974). However, in most applications it will not be necessary to employ reinforcers other than social priase.

Notice that we have cast the motivational function of feedback in a positive light. Rather than motivating by criticizing poor performance, we are suggesting that the trainer instead reinforce good performance. Poor performance is either ignored or simply pointed out in a neutral fashion with suggestions for how it might be improved. This general approach has the dual advantage of providing the necessary motivation, while simultaneously avoiding the potential aversive side effects of criticism (Azrin & Holz, 1966).

Keeping in mind the dual functions of providing information and motivation, there are several characteristics that feedback should have.

1. *Feedback should be objective and accurate.* The information provided should accurately reflect the client's performance. Inappropriate behavior should not be labeled as appropriate or vice versa. Inaccurate or misleading information is worse than none at all.

2. *Feedback should be specific.* To be useful, the feedback must be specific enough to allow the client to make appropriate adjustments. Simply saying that a rehearsal was "good" or "poor" does not provide sufficient information. What was good about it? Specifically, what behaviors does the client need to concentrate on to improve in the next rehearsal?

3. *Feedback should be corrective.* Feedback should function to correct performance by providing suggestions for alternative ways of behaving. If the client's performance was good, are there other good alternatives available? In this way, feedback can serve both to correct performance and to amplify the client's options.

4. *Feedback should be positive or neutral.* The emphasis should be on reinforcing the appropriate aspects of the client's performance. Praise or reinforce what the client does right. The inappropriate aspects of his or her performance should either be ignored or pointed out in a neutral manner in conjunction with constructive suggestions. It is probably a good idea to have positive-feedback statements outnumber neutral or corrective statements by at least a margin of three to one. In this way, the overall mood of the training session will be positive and constructive rather than critical and aversive. Training should be a positive and reinforcing experience.

Let us examine two examples of verbal feedback and see how these principles of feedback might be implemented.

POOR: "You did an okay job on that one."
BETTER: "That was better. Your eye contact improved, and you did not interrupt the other person this time."

Notice that in the better example the person giving feedback clearly specified what was good about the performance. The irrelevant and inappropriate aspects of the performance were ignored. Notice too that the tone is more positive and constructive.

POOR: "That was a poor request. Try to do better next time."
BETTER: "The request will be more effective if you tell the person *specifically* what you want them to do differently. Also, it is more effective if you don't apologize for making the request."

In the second example, the person giving feedback clearly specifies in a neutral manner how the client's behavior might be improved. The poor example, on the other hand, is both negative and nonspecific.

Within training sessions, there are several sources of feedback on the client's behavioral rehearsal. These include review of audiotape or videotape replays, the trainer's comments, comments from other group members and, finally, the client.

Audiotape Videotape Playbacks. The immediate replay of recordings of the client's behavioral rehearsal can be a powerful form of feedback. Most people seldom get an opportunity to see themselves as others see them. This is particularly true of a person's behavior in social situations. Usually what feedback we receive comes from the way others react to us. The opportunity to see what other people are reacting to can be a powerful learning experience. Further, audiotape and videotape have the capabilities of repeated replay. Segments of behavioral rehearsal can be reviewed periodically to emphasize certain points. Audiotape/videotape have the advantage of being clearly the most objective and accurate forms of feedback we have available. However, sometimes clients may not attend to the relevant aspects of their performance or may have an overwhelming negative reaction to their performance (e.g., "I did just awful! I give up!"). In short, completely objective feedback can sometimes be a painful experience for some clients (Bailey & Sowder, 1970; Griffiths, 1974). For this reason, it is advisable to have the trainer verbally highlight certain specific positive aspects of the client's performance as the tape is being replayed (e.g., "That was a good, direct request"). This is a simple and effective way of insuring that feedback be specific, corrective, and positive, as well as objective. Particularly good or noteworthy segments of the performance can be replayed a second or even third time for special emphasis. In sum, audiotape and videotape replays can be invaluable sources of feedback. It is a good idea to have the trainer comment on the client's behavior as the tape is being replayed, to insure that the client attends to the relevant aspects of his performance, and that the feedback experience is constructive.

Trainer Comments. The trainer's comments on the client's performance are an extremely important form of feedback. The trainer can selectively focus attention, reinforce specific aspects of the client's performance, and provide corrective suggestions. Further, the trainer is in a position to be fairly objective about the client's performance. In many ways, it is the trainer's feedback that integrates the other forms of feedback. If the client seems to be attending excessively to the negative aspects of his or her behavioral rehearsal, it is the trainer's feedback that can correct for this misplaced attention. If a group member provides feedback that is incorrect or overly negative, it is the trainer's responsibility to place it in proper perspective. The trainer's feedback should, of course, be consistent with the principles of feedback outlined above.

Group Members' Comments. If training is conducted in a group format, comments by other group members can become an important source of feedback. As discussed earlier, group members often have a good understanding of what kinds of social behavior will be effective under a given set of circumstances. They can provide valuable feedback about how a particular performance will "come across" in a given situation. Further, the group members can function as powerful reinforcing agents for appropriate performance. Finally, if group members are involved in providing feedback, they are forced to attend to each other's performances. Such involvement will have important learning benefits in and of itself. The possible problems of using other group members as sources of feedback is that their feedback may be too global and nonspecific, inaccurate, or overly negative. It is the trainer's responsibility to insure that this does not happen. In most instances, group members can be taught the "correct" way to provide constructive feedback. One procedure to help insure this is to structure feedback from the group in a way that insures that it is specific and given in a positive manner. For example, one or more of the group members can serve as objective observers. In this role, they will actually count the frequency, or in some other way quantify the target behavior, during a behavioral rehearsal. Feedback then takes the form of reporting the results of that recording. In this way, the group members are encouraged to attend to specific objective behaviors rather than global impressions.

The Client. The client can also be used as a source of feedback. On one level, the client is always evaluating his or her own performance (cf. Eisler, Frederiksen, and Peterson, 1978). However, in most instances that evaluation probably does not adhere to the principles of good feedback. By making the client's feedback overt and deliberate, we can aid the client in developing skills in more accurate, specific, corrective, and positive self-evaluation. If this is successful, the client is in a better position to continue to maintain and improve his or her skill even after training is completed. This self-evaluation can be quite easily structured by asking the client a series of specific questions. For example, the trainer might inquire: How many times did you employ what you have learned? What would you like to change about your performance? What did you feel you did best in that segment?, etc. The client's answers to these questions can then be compared with feedback obtained from other sources. By this kind of questioning and comparison, the trainer can focus the client's attention on relevant aspects of his performance and encourage appropriate self-evaluation.

The Format of Training

Throughout this chapter we have emphasized that social-skills training is a flexible process. Although it involves the basic elements of instruction and rationale, demonstration, behavioral rehearsal, and feedback, these elements are adaptable. There is a good deal of room for tailoring training to the specific needs of the client or the practical constraints under which training must be conducted. The format of training (number and length of sessions, topics covered in each session, etc.) is a prime area for such tailoring. By discussing guidelines for the training format, our purpose is not to limit the options of the trainer. Rather, it is to maximize options by pointing out common practices and alternatives based on previous experience. Unfortunately, there is virtually no research data on which to base format decisions. The trainer must rely on careful consideration of the nature of the clients' resources, skill deficits, and the practical constraints under which training must be conducted.

How Much Training?

The optimal approach to deciding how much training is needed is to link the amount of training to client progress. Start out by assessing the deficit, then provide training and monitor progress. When the client has progressed to the point where he or she is performing the target behaviors consistently and comfortably in their natural environment, enough training has been provided.

Yet, in some instances, it is not possible to link ccompletely the amount of training to the client's progress. A prime example of this would be a group-training workshop. To plan to attend the workshop, particip- ants would need to know ahead of time how many sessions were to be offered, how long each one was going to be, and so on. Likewise, in individualized training, it is important to have some estimate of the amount of training required in order to give the client appropriate expec- tations.

The amount of training to be provided should be based on the nature and severity of the deficit. If the trainer is attempting to make wide- ranging improvements in a client showing marked deficits, much more training is needed than that required for limited changes in circumscribed problem areas. Another factor to take into account is a group or individual format. In an individual format, less training time may be required since there is a much greater opportunity for practice and feedback. A group session, on the other hand, may involve a somewhat greater total training time, since there is relatively less opportunity for each individual to practice and receive feedback on the new behavior.

If the skill to be trained is relatively circumscribed, for example, how to chair a meeting, and the client is well-motivated and learns the skill readily, it may be possible to provide the necessary training in as little as one to three hours. Many training programs focus on somewhat more general skills, such as assertiveness or communication training, and are conducted in a group format. A typical amount of training in this situation might be somewhere between seven and 15 total hours. A situation requiring even greater amounts of training, such as making fairly wide- ranging changes in an individual who has many deficits, would likely require substantially more time, perhaps from 15 to 30 hours of training.

The Distribution of Sessions

How should this training time be distributed? How many sessions? How long should each session be? Here again, there is room for flexibility. The general strategy should be to provide sessions that are long enough to allow for adequate practice, but no so long as to result in excessive fatigue. These sessions should be distributed in a manner that allows for some opportunity to practice the skills between sessions in the environ- ment where they will be used. On the other hand, there should not be so much time between sessions that the client is forced essentially to "start from scratch" at each session. There are at least three basic strategies for distributing or scheduling sessions.

One approach has been to hold training in a "workshop" format. Such a workshop can span one, two, or even several days. Often, sessions are scheduled to cover consecutive days. The main advantage of this strategy is its practicality. It is often easier and more economical to have individuals attend a workshop for several full days than it is to have them attend an extended series of intermittently scheduled sessions. The obvious disadvantage of this "workshop" approach is that it does not allow the client an opportunity to practice the desired behavior in his or her natural environment. An alternative might be to hold a follow-up session a week or more following the intensive training workshop. Such a variation would build on the practical aspects of the intensive workshop format and still allow the client to practice the new skills.

A second basic strategy is to hold briefer sessions on an intermittent basis. An example of this might be a session from one to two hours long held on a weekly basis. The advantage of this "seminar" or "class" approach is that it allows for fairly intensive training while still giving the individual an opportunity to practice the skills as they develop. This strategy is quite often used in group-training formats. It typically involves anywhere from five to 12 sessions, held on a weekly basis. The length of the sessions is typically between one and two hours. Having sessions shorter than one hour is often insufficient for accomplishing much within a group format. On the other hand, longer than two hours raises the possibility of fatigue, boredom, and inattention.

A third common strategy for scheduling sessions is to hold them on a more frequent basis, for example, daily or several times a week. Each session can then be somewhat shorter in length, perhaps thirty minutes to an hour. This strategy also allows for a fairly intensive training experience while still giving the client an opportunity to practice the new skills outside the session. The main disadvantage is that it is sometimes not practical to require a commitment from someone on a daily basis. This strategy is probably best suited to training conducted in a restricted environment, such as a hospital, residential care facility, or a specific organization. It is also possibly better suited to individual rather than group training since the logistics of having an individual attend daily sessions are often less complicated than assembling an entire group.

The three strategies outlined above provide the trainer with a range of options. Depending on the condition under which training occurs, ease of scheduling, and related considerations, the format of training can be adapted as needed.

The Content of Sessions

How much can be covered in a single session? Quite obviously, the amount to be covered varies with the length of the session. However, as a strategic point, it is probably best to limit the number of topics covered during each session. The purpose of limiting content is to provide for the gradual and systematic development of skills and avoid overwhelming the client with "too many things at once." In a typical session (e.g., 45 minutes for an individual or one and one-half hours for a group), it is probably advisable to concentrate on a single skill (e.g., making an appropriate request). Instructions about the rationale and use of the skill can then be introduced and discussed. Appropriate behaviors can then be modeled, practiced, and feedback received. As the session progresses, this same sequence can be repeated, using different role-played situations. In this way, each session is focused on mastering a particular component of the skill. That component can then be practiced outside the session. If each session were to involve a focus on several targeted aspects of a skill (e.g., nonverbal behavior, and several verbal content behaviors) in several situations, it might tend to overwhelm, confuse, and preclude sufficient practice.

A slightly different strategy is to have each session focus on skill training for one type of situation, for example, refusing unreasonable requests from friends. Using this approach, the entire session would involve practicing different ways of responding to such a request. The trainer would focus on training different behaviors that would be useful in such a situation. Subsequent sessions would focus on different problem areas (e.g., negotiating a disagreement or speaking in front of a group). This strategy aims at mastery of a problem area without overwhelming the client by introducing new training situations before skills are developed on earlier ones.

In summary, we may say that any particular session should have limited objectives. It should focus either on one aspect of a skill, or on one type of problem situation. Attempting to cover many skill components and many types of situations does not allow for sufficient practice to master any particular aspect of the skill.

Summary

This chapter focuses on the basic training procedures that are used to train clients in the components of social skills. Not all of these procedures are equally applicable to every client; however, the combination is generally sufficient to train a range of social skills. In preparing for training, the client and therapist should agree on the purposes of training and how training will proceed. This agreement can be formalized or verbalized; in any case, its existence is important for structuring mutual expectations and providing for maximum benefit of training. Further, it is very important that the trainer establish him- or herself as a positive reinforcer. This can facilitate training and avoid many potential problems.

The benefits of group versus individual training were also discussed. In general, individual training offers maximum versatility and allows for maximum intensity of training for a specific individual. On the other hand, group training may be more cost-effective, as well as providing a range of role-playing partners, opinions, and sources of feedback.

The training session itself generally follows a standard format consisting of four steps. First a description of the behavior to be trained, as well as the rationale for its use, is presented. Next, the behavior is demonstrated or modeled. This model can either be done "live" or by means of videotape, audiotape, film, or it can even be imagery-based. The third step involves actual practice of the behavior. Here again, role-playing is most often used. The provision of feedback is the final step. Some of the desirable characteristics of feedback are that it be accurate, specific, corrective, and positive. Finally, alternative formats for conducting training were discussed. Major considerations include the total amount of training to be offered, the distribution and length of sessions, and the amount of material covered in each.

6

Promoting Transfer to the Natural Environment

Overview

- Transfer of the newly acquired skills to the client's natural environment is a critical concern. Eight strategies for promoting transfer are identified.
- Four of the strategies center around the training sessions. They are: (1) train effective behaviors; (2) make training realistic; (3) train strategy; and (4) extend practice.
- The other four strategies are centered in the client's natural environment or following the initial training sessions. They are: (1) use graded homework assignments; (2) involve others; (3) develop self-management skills; and (4) provide follow-up or booster sessions.

In Chapter 5, we focused on basic training procedures for learning new social skills. In this chapter, we will cover some principles of training that can be used to help ensure that the client will be able to employ effectively the new skills in his or her natural environment. With the techniques already described, we can be quite confident that the client will learn the new skills during training. But learning the skills is not enough. They must actually be performed in appropriate social circumstances. Knowing how to ask your supervisor for a raise, or how to refuse an unreasonable request, does little good unless you actually do it at the appropriate time.

In this chapter, we shall cover eight different principles or strategies than can be used to help ensure that the social behaviors learned during training will transfer to the client's actual life situation. Four of these strategies focus primarily on the training sessions themselves, either on what is trained or on the way the sessions are conducted. These principles are:

1. *Train effective behaviors* that will maximize the client's success and minimize failure.
2. *Make training realistic* so that it is easier to transfer the skills to extra-training situations.
3. *Train strategy* so that the client learns flexible overall approaches to interpersonal situations rather than simply rigid patterns of behavior.
4. *Extend practice* so that new patterns of behavior become more habitual.

The second four strategies are primarily focused outside the initial training sessions, in the client's natural environment and/or following the completion of the initial training. They are:

1. *Use graded homework assignments* to allow the client regularly to practice the developing skills outside training sessions.
2. *Involve others* in the client's environment to help provide support for the client's progress.
3. *Develop self-management skills* that allow the client to maintain his or her new skills.
4. *Provide follow-up or booster sessions* that allow for monitoring the client's progress and providing any needed additional training.

On the Training Sessions

Train Effective Behaviors

In Chapter 1, we introduced the concept of the effectiveness of given behaviors. Are a particular set of behaviors effective in obtaining the desired results? The more effective a client is in obtaining the desired outcome in a social interaction, the more social skill he or she has displayed. For example, let us say that a supervisor has difficulty with his boss making unreasonable requests. He decides to approach her with the problem. If he is successful in getting her to reduce the demands on his time, he has displayed effective interpersonal behavior. In short, he was socially skilled in that situation. If his behavior was ineffective in reducing the unreasonable demands, he was not socially skilled in that situation. The key is, the degree to which the behavior has been effective.

This functional or effectiveness-based definition of social skill has some important implications for ensuring generalization to the client's natural environment. If you want to train skills that the client will actually use, train skills that produce the desired consequences. If the skills get the client what he or she wants, he or she will be reinforced. If the client is reinforced for using the new skills, the skills will be more likely to be used again. If the behaviors employed are not reinforced, or are actually punished, they will not be used (cf. Baer, Wolf, & Risley, 1968). At first blush, this principle may seem self-evident. No one would purposefully train ineffective behaviors. The point is that, without deliberate and careful attention to the functional effectiveness of the behaviors, it is easy to slip into a habit of training a particular set of behaviors simply because they "seem like they should work" or "that's the way I've always done it in the past."

What makes a skill effective? First, the skill must produce the desired consequences. Second, it must work in the client's natural environment. A behavior that is effective in rural North Carolina may not work in New York City. The behavior must be effective in the client's situation. Third, the behavior should have a minimum of negative side effects. In the example we mentioned earlier, the supervisor might approach his boss and launch into any angry outburst about the unreasonable demands she was placing on him. Now, this approach might well function initially to reduce the demands. However, it might also get our supervisor fired in the long run. If such were the case, the behavior would clearly not be effective. *In summary then, we can say that an effective behavior is one that accomplishes the client's goals (i.e., is reinforced) in his or her natural environment with a minimum of negative side effects (i.e., is not punished).* If the trainer wants to train behaviors that the client will actually use, he or she should train behaviors that are maximally effective.

How can the trainer be sure that a behavior will be effective? There are no certain ways. However, the greater the trainer's understanding of the client's situation or natural environment, the more likely he or she will be to select behaviors that actually work. This understanding can be gained from firsthand experience or observation, interviews with the client, or information provided by group members or other people from the client's natural environment. The important thing is that the behaviors to be trained are effective. If there is reasonable doubt as to whether the behaviors will be effective, there is little point in training them, since in the long run they will not be used anyway.

Make Training Realistic

The second important principle in promoting transfer of training involves making the training situation as realistic as possible. By this we mean making the conditions under which the client practices closely resemble the situation he will encounter outside training. *This is accomplished by maximizing the number of identical elements between the natural environment and the training situation.*

Let us take the example of the supervisor who was having difficulty with his female boss. To increase the chances that our young supervisor will continue to use the new social skills he has learned, we would want to have the training situation closely resemble the situation in which the problem occurs. If the boss was a female somewhat older than the client, we would want the role-playing partner during training also to be an older female, or at least act like one. Similarly, if the problem typically occurs in the supervisor's office, we would want practice to occur in a situation which at least looks like an office. Finally, the situation and interpersonal partner's behavior should also closely resemble the problematical situation. If the boss makes unyielding, repeated demands, the role-playing partner should also make such demands. By maintaining this close correspondence between the "real" situation and the training sessions, the client's practice will help prepare him for the actual problem situation. To the extent that the training does not resemble the actual situation, a greater burden is placed on the client. Experience in an unrealistic situation may not only be of limited value, but may also be counterproductive.

There are three general areas in which to concentrate when trying to make a training situation realistic. First is the physical environment. Does the problem situation occur in an office? At a bar? In a crowded restaurant? Although obviously it would be extremely cumbersome to duplicate these environments exactly, it is quite simple to "set the stage" using some minimal furniture arrangement and instructions to the client. For example, the trainer could arrange two chairs facing each other across a table and instruct the client to "imagine you are in your office." This simple procedure provides at least a measure of relevance to the natural environment.

There should be some similarity between the training environment and the actual social environment. Role-playing partners should share at least some characteristics with the people in the client's actual situation. If the client was having difficulty with young females, it would be preferable if the role-playing partners were young females. As with the physical environment, it may not always be practical to have the ideal role-playing partner available. In these cases, instructions to the client can also be used, for example, "imagine that this person is your boss." However, in most cases, it is possible to have a role-playing partner of the appropriate sex available.

The final area of similarity is in the situation and behavior of the role-playing partner. The partner's behavior should reflect what actually would happen in real-life circumstances. If the client's behavior would be likely to precipate a verbal attack in the natural environment, it should also do so in the practice situation. It is not appropriate to leave the client with the impression that is or her behavior would be effective, when in all probability it actually would not be. In this area, making the situation realistic requires a good understanding of the client's environment. As mentioned earlier, such an understanding is usually obtained through interviewing the client and/or the direct observation of his or her environment. If training is conducted in a group setting, other group members can often be important sources of such information.

Training in Social Strategy

In our model of social skill (Chapter 1) we placed a good bit of emphasis on the cognitive component of interpersonal effectiveness. To be maximally effective, a person must be able to accurately assess social situations, select behaviors to perform from among alternatives, and adjust subsequent performance based on feedback from the social environment. Effective social functioning is a dynamic process requiring ongoing adjustments in one's behavior. *It is not possible to train the client in a rigid group of behaviors that will work in all situations. Clients must learn to adjust their behavior to varying situations and reactions.* In short, they must learn to pursue an interpersonal strategy.

Let's return to the example of the supervisor who is having difficulty with his boss making unreasonable demands. There are a wide variety of strategies he could take to achieve this goal. Our young supervisor might display a temper outburst the next time his boss makes a demand. Yelling and pounding on her desk, he could threaten to quit if she doesn't stop making these demands. Alternately, he could attempt to catch her "in a good mood" and make a joking reference to the excessive demands. Each of the potential approaches or strategies would likely have somewhat different outcomes. For example, both of the above strategies might get the boss to reduce her unreasonable demands. However, with the "angry" approach, the boss may label the supervisor as "hostile and immature" and pass him over for promotion. Thus, in the development of any strategy, all the probable effects need to be taken into account.

An effective interpersonal strategy is not limited to choosing an initial approach to a situation. It also involves being able to adjust one's behavior to the changing requirements of the situation. Let us say, for example, that the supervisor chooses to approach his boss when she is in a "good mood" and makes subtle references to her unreasonable demands. However, as the conversation proceeds, it becomes clear that the boss is not "picking up on" these subtle hints. Recognizing this, the supervisor must adjust his strategy. Should he become more direct? Drop the issue until a later time? In short, he needs to adjust his strategy, based on the effects of his behavior.

From the above examples, it should be clear that strategy is an integral part of social skill. The client needs to develop effective interpersonal strategies if he or she is to be expected to improve interpersonal functioning outside the training session. But how can effective strategy be taught? Many of the procedures for improving strategies have already been covered in the previous chapters. However, let us review and consolidate them here:

1. Emphasize the importance of strategy when providing a rationale for various behaviors being taught. Explain how particular behaviors fit into an overall strategy.
2. Suggest and discuss different strategies with the client. This is particularly useful in group training where group members can contribute their ideas and evaluations.
3. Train the client to generate and evaluate multiple strategies before choosing one. Often a *problem solving approach* (e.g., D'Zurilla & Goldfried, 1971) is quite useful for the client who has difficulty in evaluating multiple strategies.
4. Practice using different strategies in the same situation. When this is done during training, the client can get the benefit of objective feedback on the differing outcomes of the different strategies.
5. Have the role-playing partners vary their reactions during behavioral rehearsal. This will force the client to change his or her strategy to suit changing conditions. Again, the availability of feedback makes this an excellent opportunity for learning.

Our social environment is complex and ever changing. We typically approach interpersonal situations with a sense of objectives. What do we want from the situation? Friendship? A sexual partner? A promotion? A pleasant conversation? To be successful in most any interaction we must be able to adjust our strategy or approach to the changing social environment. Teaching a client that there is a single "right" way to handle a situation is an oversimplicication. The effects of training cannot persist in the client's natural environment. To be maximally effective outside training, the client must learn how to use strategy and how to adjust to changing conditions.

Extended Practice

All other things being equal, when faced with a novel situation, a person will tend to behave in the same way that he or she has previously behaved in similar situations. We may say that the person is in the habit of behaving a certain way in that kind of situation or that a particular response is "easier" or more comfortable. This presents something of a problem in social-skills training. We are attempting to train the person to behave in a new or different way in a given situation. Yet, because the new behavior is still untested, there is a tendency for the client to continue to use the old behaviors. We might say that the new behavior hasn't yet become established as a habit and is consequently less comfortable.

However, this inertia can be at least partially overcome during training by extending practice of the new behavior. By having the client repeatedly practice the new behavior, he or she tends to "overlearn." The new skill then becomes more firmly established as a habit and is more available when the client encounters the given situation outside training. There are two dimensions on which practice can be extended. First, the client can practice the same situation on repeated occasions. For example, the situation might be asking a casual acquaintance for a date. The client could practice this situation with minor variations at each training session. The goal here is "more of the same." The second alternative is repeatedly to practice situations that differ in a number of respects. In the example mentioned above, the client might ask different people for a date, request different things of the same person, receive markedly different responses to the request, etc., over repeated practice trials. The goal here is "more variety." In most cases it is appropriate to extend practice on both dimensions; more variety and more of the same. *The general principle is that the client should receive extended practice on a variety of situations that are most relevant to those he or she will actually encounter outside training.* In this way, the new behaviors will be more likely to be employed when the situation is actually encountered. How much is enough practice? That is a difficult question to answer. In general, the more the better. At minimum, each situation should be practiced until (1) the client has performed satisfactorily on *repeated* occasions, even when the role-playing partner varies aspects of his or her response and attempts to make it difficult for the client; and (2) the client reports feeling comfortable using the new skills. An even better criterion for terminating practice is when the client is regularly and successfully employing the new skill outside the training sessions. This, after all, is the goal of training. The only real danger in extending practice is that the trainer will become "bored" and discontinue adequate reinforcement for the client's performance. If this happens, the new skill will tend to again become less available and, consequently, less likely to be used (Goldstein & Sorcher, 1974). If the client fails to show continued improvement and enthusiasm, this possibility should be considered.

Outside of Training

Use Graded Homework Assignments

The final goal of training is to have the client regularly and comfortably performing the targeted interpersonal skills in his or her natural environment after training is completed. The starting point for achieving this goal is getting the client to approximate the desired behavior in the training setting. One particularly useful procedure for helping to bridge the gap between the starting point and the final goal is graded interpersonal homework assignments. This procedure involves having the client systematically practice more and more of the new skills in social situations that occur outside training. This outside practice (homework) is presented in a graded fashion. The client starts out by practicing the skills that are easiest. As training progresses, the homework assignments get more difficult as they approximate the final target behaviors. The principle is to make the assignments gradually more difficult while simultaneously ensuring the client's continuing success. The homework assignments thus parallel the training sessions and extend them to the client's actual social situation.

During the training session, the client can report back on the assignment and how it went. Difficulties that were encountered can be discussed or even role-played. The trainer and group members can offer ssuggestions or demonstrate different approaches to the situation. The client can then practice these new behaviors and subsequently try them outside training. The review of the homework assignments also offers the opportunity to reinforce or praise the client's appropriate performance. As in other situations, feedback on homework assignments should be heavily slanted toward reinforcing positive performance. Poor performance should be played down and met with suggestions for improvement.

There are two important points to keep in mind when giving homework assignments. First, the assignment should be relevant to the achievement of the training goals. Assignments should not be given just for the sake of giving them. They should parallel the course of training. Second, the assignments must be at a level of difficulty that the client can master. By the same token, the assignments should not be so lengthy or burdensome that they cannot be easily and successfully accomplished.

The principle is to give the client successful practice in using the targeted skills outside training.

Let us take the example of a recently divorced female who complains of an inability to talk to men. Our assessment reveals that she does not initiate or maintain conversations with men when it would clearly be appropriate to do so. She also describes great discomfort associated with the prospect of dating and has repeatedly refused invitations despite her avowed desire to the contrary. Her goal is to be able to interact comfortably with men in all social situations.

In using homework assignments with this client, the trainer would not want to start with the assignment of having her ask a man out for a date. Given the results of the assessment, this would clearly be asking too much and would be putting the client in unnecessary discomfort. A more appropriate assignment would be to have her initiate two brief interactions, such as asking for directions or the time of day. In this case, the assignments are close to where she is now performing. The situations could be role-played in the training session where they were assigned and again when they are completed. The client could then move on to a somewhat more difficult assignment.

Table VI shows an example of a series of graded homework assignments that might be used with the client mentioned above. In practice, these assignments would be determined on a session-to-session basis (rather than in advance), depending on the client's progress. Notice that the steps are gradual and that the critical behaviors required of the client are specified. It is important that there is little room for ambiguity on what the assignment actually involves. In many instances, it is appropriate to write out the homework assignment in detail and have the client self-monitor its completion by taking notes on his or her performance, the outcome of the situation, etc.

Graded homework assignments offer an excellent opportunity to

Table VI. An Example of a Series of Graded Homework Assignments

Week 1	Initiate a brief (30 sec) impersonal interaction with two different men whom you don't know very well.
Week 2	Initiate two brief (1–3 min) conversations of a social nature with men that you know but would not date.
Week 3	Initiate two brief (1–3 min) social conversations with men that you know and would be interested in dating.
Week 4	Engage in at least one extended (over 10 min) social conversation with a man you would be interested in dating.
Week 5	Accept an invitation for a date.
Week 6	Ask a man out for a date

bridge the gap between the training session and the client's natural environment. The assignments should be clear, relevant, and within the client's growing ability. Their completion should be closely monitored, and feedback should be provided.

Involve Others

We have placed a good deal of emphasis on the notion of developing social skills that are functional or effective. Clients should learn behaviors and strategies that allow them to achieve their goals and obtain maximum reinforcement with a minimum of negative side effects. These skills should be well learned in training and practiced in the client's natural environment. Yet, even if all these suggestions are followed, there can still be problems in the transition from training to the day-in-and-day-out usage of the skills.

The people that the client interacts with on a day-to-day basis have grown used to certain patterns of behavior on the client's part. They have come to expect certain predictable behavior patterns in given situations. When a change occurs in the client's behavior, it quite often requires that those around the client must also change their behavior. The client may no longer be "inflexible" in negotiations, or passively accept unpleasant tasks. Things have changed. This behavior change may or may not be welcome by everyone. If it is welcomed by those around the client, it will readily be strengthened and maintained. If it is unwelcome, a greater strain is placed on the client. In either case, there may be a period of adjustment where those in the client's environment must adapt to the client's changing behavior and develop new expectations of the client.

Let us return to our example of the young client who was having difficulty with his boss making unreasonable demands on him. What will happen when he starts refusing these demands? The boss may initially be a little startled. She may wonder "what's wrong" with the client. If the client continues to use the new skills, she will be forced to change her own behavior pattern. She will likely stop making so many unreasonable requests. Even if she views this change in the client's behavior as positive, she will have to go through a period of adjustment. This adjustment may be difficult or unpleasant to make. In short, the period during which the client is starting to use the new skills outside training is a stressful one from two perspectives. Both the client and those around him or her must make changes—changes that may be somewhat difficult or uncomfortable.

One way of smoothing out this transition period is to involve others in the client's natural environment. This involvement can be of two basic types. Preparing others for changes in the client's behavior is the first type. Enlisting their active help in generating or monitoring changes in the client's behavior is the second.

Preparation for change can take many forms. Significant others can be brought in for a session to discuss the kinds of changes that the client is trying to make, and how those changes may affect them. Questions can be answered and concerns discussed at length. Such a session can go a long way toward reducing fears and making adjustments easier and less stressful. Having others come in for a session, though effective, can be an obtrusive and time-consuming procedure. In addition, it may not always be necessary or desirable. A trainer working in a clinical setting may not find it appropriate to have the client's supervisor in. Alternatively, the trainer may find it quite acceptable to talk to significant people in the client's environment by telephone. Written material, such as a description of what social-skills training involves and how the client may change might also be sufficient to prepare people for changes in the client's behavior. The form of the communication is probably not so important as the fact that significant others have an opportunity to prepare for changes in the client.

People in the client's environment may also be used to help the client make changes. This help often takes three forms. First, they may help to evaluate the client's behavior. Is the client using the new skill in the appropriate situations? Are graded homework assignments being completed? This evaluation can range from global and impressionistic to very detailed and specific. For example, a co-worker of the client could report whether he is in fact refusing the boss's unreasonable requests. The co-worker could also provide information on how the client came across and what particular behavior deficits and excesses were still evident. Clearly, this kind of information could be of tremendous value in training. Between the client's reports on his own progress and the observer's reports, the trainer would be in an excellent position to make training more relevant, appropriately paced, and effective.

A second way in which others can be actively involved in training is to prompt the client. By prompting we mean giving the client instructions, suggestions, or reminders to use new skill in appropriate situations. In this way, the situations in which a specific skill could be useful and appropriate become more salient for the client.

Finally, people in the client's environment can be used to reinforce the client for the use of the appropriate skill. Some of the client's early attempts at using a new skill may not lead to "naturally occurring" reinforcement. Reinforcement from a significant other, in the form of praise or encouragement, can help bridge the gap until such time when the client's skill develops to the point where the naturally occurring reinforcers start to occur regularly.

Let us take the example mentioned above, of the client working on her dating skills. The first few times she tries to perform the homework assignment of asking a man out, she is unsuccessful. This lack of reinforcement for her attempts could easily lead to discouragement and slow progress in her attempts to develop the targeted skills. However, let's say that the client's close friend was involved in training. The friend could then provide praise to the client for trying and point out the things the client was doing appropriately and how she was improving. Employing the other two strategies, the friend might also point out situations that would be conducive to using the new skill, for example, "You said you'd like to ask Bill out and I see you talking to him after lunch just about every day. Why don't you ask him out, then?" and then observe the client's progress. Adding this kind of natural-environment support to training can greatly enhance the probability of successful skill development and maintenance.

In involving others in social-skills training, there are a number of important considerations to keep in mind:

1. The closer the relationship a person has with the client and the more affected they are likely to be by the changes, the more important it becomes to involve them. For example, if the trainer was working on marriage-related social skills with a client, it would be important to involve the spouse. At minimum, they should be prepared for the changes in the client. If, on the other hand, the trainer was working on helping the client become more assertive with strangers, it is not critical to involve the strangers!

2. If significant others are to be involved, make sure that they are in a position to observe the skill. If they don't have the opportunity to see the client use the skill, they are in no position to add much beyond what the trainer can.

3. Make sure that the people you involve are capable and willing to do what you are requesting of them. If you are asking someone to observe the use of a client's skill, they must be both able to identify the skill accurately and willing to monitor it. Similarly, if the person is to reinforce the use of specific skills, they need to be able accurately to identify the occurrence of the target behavior, know how to "deliver reinforcement" and be willing to actually do it.

4. Perhaps most important of all, you must have the client's permission before involving others in his or her natural environment. This requirement is part of the principle of informed consent (see Chapter 5). Contacting people in the client's environment (e.g., a supervisor) could

potentially be harmful to the client's best interest. For this reason, it is important to ensure that the client understands and agrees to your request to involve others in the training process.

Develop Self-Management Skills

The past decade has seen a growing trend in the behavior-modification literature. There has been a sharp increase in the development and use of self-management (or self-control) approaches to behavior change. Obesity, smoking, study skills, alcoholism, psychiatric problems, and classroom misbehavior are just a sample of the problems to which this approach has been applied. In a self-management approach, the client is taught skills that can be used to control his or her own behavior (e.g., Mahoney & Thoresen, 1974; Stuart, 1977). For example, let us say that a person is in the habit of overeating. In a self-management approach, that person might be taught to monitor food intake, make food less available, reward himself for not overeating, etc. By using these self-management skills the individual him- or herself can control the troublesome behavior, in this case overeating.

A behavioral self-management approach specifies the situation in which the person needs to exercise self-control and goes about training practical self-management skills. In this respect, behavioral self-management is analogous to social-skills training. With this conceptual procedural correspondence, it would seem that training in self-management would be an excellent way to help the client develop the habit of using new social skills in his or her natural environment. The client could use self-management skills such as prompting, cognitive rehearsal, self-monitoring, or self-reinforcement to strengthen the use of new skills in troublesome situations. Yet, the use of self-management in concert with social-skills training is currently not widespread. Presumably, this situation will be changing in the future.

There is probably a variety of self-management techniques that are applicable to social-skills training. We shall review a few of the techniques that seem promising and illustrate how they might apply to effective interpersonal behavior. It is not our purpose to provide detailed instructions on self-management. Rather, we wish to suggest how the techniques of self-management might apply to the problem of promoting transfer of social skills to the client's natural environment. For more detailed discussions of self-management, the reader is referred to other sources (e.g., Mahoney & Thoresen, 1974; Stuart, 1977).

Covert Rehearsal/Modeling. In Chapter 5 we discussed how covert (imagined) modeling or rehearsal could be employed within the social-skills training session. An even better use of these imagery-based procedures is in promoting transfer of training. The client can use the covert modeling or rehearsal in his or her natural environment with minimal embarrassment or interruption of ongoing activities. This allows the client to "observe" or "practice" the desired target behavior prior to its use. Let us say, for example, that our client wants to ask his boss for a raise. He has already practiced the necessary behaviors during the training sessions. Now it is time for the real test—he is about to approach his boss. This would be a very appropriate time for him to employ covert modeling/rehearsal. He could take a couple of minutes to sit down and imagine someone like himself approaching the boss and making an appropriate request. The image could be quite detailed and include both what the model said (verbal) and the way in which he said it (nonverbal). This would be an example of covert modeling. The client could then imagine himself approaching the boss and successfully making the desired request. This covert rehearsal would give the client an opportunity to practice the target skill again just prior to using it. Such practice can be very useful in bridging the gap between the training situation and the actual performance of the skill. The reader will probably recognize these techniques, especially covert rehearsal, as being in common use. Many people often "mentally rehearse" a task before they attempt it. However, the "commonsense" nature of these procedures doesn't make them any less valuable.

Prompting. Prompting is a technique of presenting a cue or "reminder" to increase the probability that a person will perform a desired behavior. When it is used as a self-management technique, the client will present his or her own cues. By associating the cue with a desired social skill, the client can increase the likelihood of employing the new skill following the presentation of the cue. For example, let us say that our client is a busy corporate executive who has difficulty asking for help. Following a course of social-skills training, she has learned the new skill of how effectively to ask for help. However, at times she still "forgets" and fails to employ the skills. We might suggest that she associate use of the new skill with an event (cue) that occurs frequently in her day-to-day routine—let us say the ringing of the telephone. If she does this successfully, she will be prompted or reminded to use the new skill each time the phone rings. If this is done regularly, it won't be long before the new skill of effectively making appropriate requests becomes a habit. What cues can be used for prompting? The choice is limited only by the ingenuity of the client and trainer. Generally, cues that are (1) encountered fairly regularly, and (2) occur at times when the skill might be appropriately employed are best. Examples of cues include a ringing telephone, a note on a desk calendar, a distinct mark on the client's wristwatch, a signal reminder from a friend or co-worker, etc. The nature of the cue is not so important as is ensuring that it is both associated with the desired skill and presented at appropriate times.

Self-Monitoring. This procedure was first introduced in the context of assessment (Chapter 4). In self-monitoring, the client attends to his or her own behavior, determines when a particular target behavior has occurred, and systematically records that behavior. This recording may be as simple as a frequency count or a tally of the target behavior. At the other extreme, it may be a detailed description of the situation in which the behavior, its consequences, and the concomitant thoughts or feelings that the client might have experienced are given. Although we are probably all enthusiastic, if not objective, observers of our own behavior, self-monitoring makes the process *systematic.* Let us take the example of the divorced woman who wishes to improve her dating skills. The trainer may suggest that this client self-monitor "asking men out on dates." When the client asked a man out, she might be instructed to write down the date and time, where she was (e.g., in her office), what she and what the man were doing (e.g., leaving work), the phrase she used in the request, his reply, and, perhaps, how comfortable she felt (e.g., 1–10 rating). Clearly, this kind of information could be helpful to the trainer. It could serve both as a way to monitor the client's progress (i.e., assessment) and as the foundation for a self-reinforcement program (see below).

Self-Reinforcement. In self-reinforcement, the client presents a reward (reinforcement) to him- or herself contingent upon the use of a desired behavior. This reward may be something tangible (e.g., a new record album, or a pair of jogging shoes), a special privilege (e.g., a trip to a sporting event or to the movies), or covert (e.g., a pleasant thought or a mental "pat on the back"). If the reward that is delivered is in fact reinforcing, then the targeted behavior will be strengthened. Let us return to our example of the busy corporate executive who has difficulty requesting assistance. She has already participated in social-skills training sessions and is using prompting techniques (see above). To further enhance skill generalization, the trainer might arrange for the client to reward herself each time she appropriately obtained assistance. The reward should, of course, be something that is pleasurable or enjoyable to the client. In this case, let us say that for each request the client sets aside $2.00 toward the purchase of tickets to a hockey game. If she does not make the appropriate request, she does not accumulate the money to attend the hockey game—an event which she enjoys very much. Thus, by using the new skill, she will not only receive the rewards intrinsic in effective social functioning, but she will also get the "bonus" of attending the game. Although the use of self-reinforcement may seem trivial or ineffective, the technique can be very useful in promoting desired behavioral performance. Self-reinforcement is a way of making the performance of the desired skill immediately reinforcing. For self-reinforcement to occur, three things must happen. First, the client must discriminate the occurrence of the target behavior. Put another way, the client must realize that the behavior has occurred. Second, the behavior must be compared to a standard. Is the behavior correct? Is a reward "earned"? If the answer is yes, then the client must actually deliver the reward to him- or herself. If the client doesn't deliver the earned reward (i.e., too strict) or rewards himself when he has not performed appropriately (i.e., too lenient), the *desired* behavior will not be strengthened. There are several basic principles to keep in mind when designing and implementing a self-reinforcement program

1. *The rewards should in fact be reinforcing.* What is reinforcing for one person may not be for another. Make sure that the client finds the reward enjoyable.

2. *Make rewards reasonable.* If the reward is too small, it will not be effective. If it is very large, the client may not "stick to the rules" and may be too liberal in dispensing it.

3. *Reward small steps.* Just as with the graded assignments, it is better to build effective performance with small, easy-to-achieve steps.

4. *Consequences should be fairly immediate to have maximum impact.* It is better to self-reward right after the target behavior occurs, rather than at the end of the week.

5. *Be consistent.* The contingencies of self-reinforcement must be followed consistently. The standards for reward should not change from day to day.

To help structure these self-reinforcement programs, it is sometimes useful to negotiate a self-control (self-reinforcement) contract with the client. Such a contract would specify what behavior is to be rewarded, under what conditions, and what the reward is to be. Further, the contract should include an agreement by the client to follow its terms. An example of such a contract is shown in Figure 3. This contract is very similar to the treatment contract illustrated earlier.

Provide Follow-up or Booster Sessions

This final procedure for promoting transfer and maintenance of new skills is perhaps the most obvious of all. Yet very often social-skills

---

Self-Control Contract

I _____ agree to do the following: _____

_____

_____

_____

in the situation described _____

_____

_____

I understand that for each time I do this I will reward myself with _____

_____.

If I fail to do as agreed I will not reward myself.

This contract may not be suspended or renegotiated until _____

_____, 19_____.

I agree to the above freely and without duress and pledge to follow the terms of the contract.

Signed: _____   _____
                    (client)   (date)

Witness: _____   _____
                    (witness)   (date)

Figure 3. Example of a self-control contract.

training is conducted on a time-limited, no-follow-up basis. It is common to see a social-skills group meet for a predetermined number of sessions only to disband. This is sometimes quite unfortunate. The clients may learn some very useful new skills in the training sessions. They may even begin to employ these skills regularly in their natural environment by the end of training. But things can go wrong. A boss is replaced with someone who is more difficult to deal with. New stresses are encountered, and the client begins to have difficulty. The effects of the intensive training experience begin to fade.

It is at this point that a booster session could prove to be very effective. The client has an opportunity again to practice in a training situation. The trainer and/or group can once again provide reinforcement, suggestions, modeling, and feedback. Strategies for overcoming new problems can be developed and practiced. Even a brief session can reinforce new skills.

There are, of course, the problems associated with reconvening a group (or individual session). For example, clients or trainers can move or be otherwise unavailable. Yet, it may prove to be quite useful for those who do attend. Unfortunately, we have little concrete data to guide us on this point. How much follow-up is enough? Here again there are no good guidelines. A conservative suggestion might be two or three sessions over a several-month period. If it is much less than this, there is probably not much point in doing it. If much more is needed, training probably should have been extended.

Follow-up or booster sessions can be a low-cost and convenient way to help promote generalization. Minor problems that might otherwise inhibit transfer of training can be identified and overcome before they become major. It also provides an excellent opportunity for additional practice, discussion, and reinforcement.

Summary

This chapter focuses on strategies that can be used in promoting the transfer of training. It is important that the client not only learn the new skills, but actually use them in his or her natural environment and maintain them over time. Eight principles have been identified that can be used either within the training sessions themselves, or outside training.

Focusing within the session, the therapist should: (1) Train effective behaviors. The skills taught should be those that are actually effective. The therapist should exercise care and judgment to insure that the client does not erroneously learn ineffective skills. (2) Make training realistic. It should parallel the client's actual situation where the skills will be needed. Attention should be paid to making the setting realistic, and the role-playing partners as authentic as possible, both in terms of their appearance and of their behavior. (3) Train strategy. The client should be taught to be flexible in his or her approach to situations and adjust his or her behavior, depending on the changing social environment. (4) Extend practice. Training over a longer period of time and over a wider variety of situations allows the client to be more comfortable in the use of his or her new skills and increases the chance that he or she will, in fact, employ them when the situation arises.

Techniques that focus outside the session include: (1) Use graded homework assignments. Clients should be given assignments that allow them to practice successfully their new skills as they are being developed. Care should be taken so that the assignments are not too difficult, thus resulting in failure experiences. (2) Involve others. Change in a client's social skills usually necessitates change in the behavior of those around the client. Involving others allows them to prepare for the change and/or help reward the client for progress. (3) Develop self-management skills. These self-management skills can include monitoring one's own behaviors, rehearsing a situation before you are going to use it, self-reward, and the like. These techniques can help increase the probability that the clients will actually use the skills they have learned. (4) Provide follow-up or booster sessions. If possible, the client should be followed to ensure that the newly developed skills are being used. Too often training ends abruptly and, with the passage of time, skills are no longer used. The provision of booster sessions helps head off problems before they become serious and helps to ensure the maintenance of the skills.

III

Applications

The purpose of this section is to illustrate a range of applications of social-skills training. Although these applications are certainly not exhaustive, they do cover a variety of different populations and problems. The illustrations should allow the reader to gain a better understanding of how social-skills training can be used, based on how it has been used. Second, we have sought to make the training procedures described in Part II "come alive" through the excerpting of interactions between the trainer and the client in the training sessions themselves. Put another way, we have tried to illustrate the implementation of the training principles described earlier.

In each chapter we have included a discussion of the problem area in general, along with some of the special considerations that may be relevant to planning for training. In addition, we have presented a social-learning prospective of the problem in question to illustrate the reasoning behind the use of social-skills training for this particular problem. Finally, we have included some specific results that have been obtained through the use of the procedures and illustrated the conduct of sessions at crucial points in the training process.

Chapter 7 deals with marital problems and places special emphasis on some of the unique characteristics of the marital relationship that make social-skills training not only particularly difficult, but also particularly applicable. Social-skills training with children is the topic of Chapter 8. Although this relatively new application area offers some unique challenges, it also holds much promise for the remediation of skills deficits before they evolve into more serious problems. Chapter 9 focuses on applying this approach to the difficult problem of inappropriate aggression. Although the chapter points out many of the problems inherent in working with overly aggressive individuals, it also presents an approach that is widely applicable, and shows much promise. Finally, a range of job-related skills is the topic of Chapter 10. Within this broad area, three specific types of application (job-interview skills, supervisory skills, and communication skills) are illustrated and discussed.

The applications of social-skills training discussed in this section should give the reader a feel for how training can proceed and be adapted to a variety of different situations and populations. In this sense, the reader should be better able to anticipate new areas of application and be better prepared for the decisions and practical difficulties that are part of any intervention.

7

Marital-Skills Training

Overview

- Social-learning perspectives on the development of positive and negative marital-interactive styles are presented. The implications of social-learning principles to the evolution of training objectives are discussed.
- Couples require appropriate preparation prior to the employment of assessment and training procedures. How the trainer explains the rationale for training and develops a collaborative relationship with both spouses are presented.
- Assessment for marital-skills training consists of obtaining information on how the spouses evaluate each other, as well as trainer observations of their marital-interactive behavior. The uses of marital inventories, spouse-observational procedures, and behavioral observations by the trainer are discussed.
- Training consists of helping spouses resolve marital problems through the use of corrective feedback from the trainer, and coaching in more effective interactive behaviors. Illustrations of the processes are made, using a case example.
- In order to maintain the effects of training, additional marital skills are often required. The couples are instructed in the use of spouse monitoring, and in positive reinforcement strategies which can be applied at home.

Probably no interpersonal task faced by couples in contemporary society requires as much social skill as the marital relationship. Part of the reason for this is that the social and legal bonds of marriage require long-term commitments on the part of spouses to each other. In addition, marital partners have been conditioned from early childhood to expect a great deal from their eventual mates. The difficulties faced by couples attempting to have mutually satisfying marital relationships is attested to by the rather formidable statistics on couples seeking divorce, not to mention the numbers of dysfunctional marriages not terminating in divorce.

The reasons for the increasing divorce rates have been attributed to many sociocultural factors, including shrinking extended family networks, greater geographic mobility of couples, relaxation of social and legal barriers to divorce, and, more recently, the increased economic viability of women. The causes of marital disharmony and divorce stemming from frictions within the marital unit have only been studied extensively during the past few decades. For purposes of the present chapter, it will be worthwhile to become briefly acquainted with the broad scientific perspectives on marital interaction based on social-learning theory. This will serve as the basis for the application of social-skills training to the marital relationship.

At the outset, we should make it clear that our presentation on social-skills training for couples is not meant to be a panacea to remediate all the social- and sexual-adjustment problems of individuals experiencing marital difficulties. Instead, we propose to formulate a broadly based training program for couples which can be used educationally to enhance existing marital adjustment or be used as part of a comprehensive marital-intervention strategy for more seriously disordered marriages.

Social Learning Perspectives on Marital Interaction

In order to explain the acquisition and maintenance of socially adaptive and socially maladaptive patterns of marital interaction, theorists have elaborated concepts of two-person (dyadic) interaction developed by social psychologists. Prominent among these has been Thibaut and Kelly's (1959) view of dyadic interactions. According to Thibaut and Kelly, in any relationship involving two people, both individuals are striving to maximize "rewarding" consequences, such as pleasures and satisfactions, while at the same time attempting to minimize "costs," that is, unpleasant or negative consequences (Thibaut & Kelly, 1959). The relationship is thereby maintained by each individual's perception of high rewards relative to costs. Over a period of time, according to this view, the interaction between the pair becomes governed by a set of norms based on each partner's expectations of positive versus negative consequences for remaining in the relationship. Thus, when a husband chooses to spend more of his spare time with his friends than with his wife, it may be concluded that his friends offer greater satisfactions relative to costs than his wife.

Another important social-psychological concept relevant to marital interaction and the issue of marital satisfaction is based on the theory of *reciprocity* governing the relationship. According to Stuart (1969), reciprocity develops as a history of one spouse's pleasing or rewarding the other, confident that he or she will be rewarded or pleased by the other in the future. Conversely, when one spouse displeases or punishes the other, the marital partner will reciprocate these negative interactions. In recent studies of marital behavior, Birchler, Weiss, and Vincent (1975) and Wills, Weiss, and Patterson (1974) found very high reciprocity of "pleasing" behaviors in marital interactions. Birchler, Weiss, and Vincent (1975) compared the reciprocity of pleasing and displeasing behaviors of couples in distressed and nondistressed marriages. The results indicated that distressed couples evidenced very low rates of spouse-pleasing behaviors and higher rates of punishing behaviors relative to the nondistressed pairs.

It further appears that in marriages characterized by low reciprocity of desired behaviors, each spouse attempts to obtain his or her due rewards through coercive threats and punishment. Spouses who seek marital gratifications through hostile actions only serve to produce further deterioration in the relationship which becomes characterized by negative expectations. For example, if a wife "nags" her husband into compliance with her wishes to have her mother stay with them for two weeks, he will probably not be very pleasant during the mother-in-law's visit. Therefore, she can expect him to be "grouchy." By complying with her wishes under coercion, the husband can expect his wife to become "a pain" whenever she wants to have her way.

From studies of successful and unsuccessful marriages, it appears that marital harmony is based on doing a variety of things which please your spouse and are then reciprocated by the marital partner. Why then do so many spouses adopt interpersonal strategies based on coercive force, withdrawal of affection, and other punishing acts? One answer is that the punishing strategies, although mutually defeating in the long run, often produce the immediate effects which a spouse desires. Intimidating the wife into a sexual encounter works, although perhaps only for that night. Another is that spouses are not skilled in the use of positive methods of communication and problem-solving (Jacobson, 1977; Peterson, Frederiksen, & Rosenbaum, in press). Training in a number of social skills relevant to marital communication and problem solving is a practical approach to implementing positive behavioral exchanges. The social skills taught can be explicitly defined with sequential steps well within the capacity of each spouse to acquire.

Marital-Skills Training

Let us now turn our attention to the practical issue of how to teach couples interactive skills aimed at increasing marital satisfaction. For purposes of organization, the presentation will be divided into four main sections.

Establishing the relationship. The first section will be on how to introduce couples to the assessment and training procedures. This includes explaining the purpose and rationale for our approach and establishing a collaborative working relationship with the couple.

Assessment. This second section deals with methods and issues of assessment. Here we will be interested in the spouse's observations of each other and their perception of satisfaction within the relationship. We will also be interested in assessing the couple's interactive skills from direct observation of their interaction.

Skill development. In the third section we will discuss how to conduct conversational-skills training. Some of the more important areas covered here will be how to teach spouses communication and negotiating skills.

Maintenance. In the fourth and final section we will discuss how to teach couples to maintain marital behaviors which they mutually desire. This will include such topics as spouse reinforcement and spouse monitoring.

In order to clarify our exposition, we will refer to a hypothetical couple who have sought marital-skills training. A brief summary of the background information on the couple relevant to training is as follows:

> Mr. Bill Roan and Mrs. Jan Roan have been married for ten years. They have two children, a six-year-old daughter and a nine-year-old son. Mr. Roan is an electronics technician who works for a large manufacturing firm.
>
> The Roans have indicated that they had been happily married during the early years of their married lives, but now sense that there has been increasing unresolved conflict between them. Jan wants Bill to take an increasing interest in the day-to-day care of the children, and give her more support to go back to her career in teaching. She also views Bill as a person who spends money beyond what they can afford. Bill

feels that he has always been an adequate provider for the family. Although he sympathizes with Jan's desire to go back to work to resume her career, he feels that his wife has started to neglect her responsibilities with their children. Jan has gained some weight since they were first married, and feels that Bill doesn't love her as much as he did then. Bill feels that Jan's worries about his love for her are unfounded, but does complain that his wife has become a "nag."

The couple feels that these conflicts have been growing steadily over the past two years. Both feel that they have an important stake in continuing the marriage, although each feels that changes in the other are the reasons for their current problems. When they try to discuss the areas of conflict, they claim that they can't "communicate." Frequently Bill has given up talking about problems and leaves the house feeling angry. When Jan feels angry, she either cries or has temper outbursts. Finally, the frequency and enjoyment of their sexual encounters has decreased in the previous year.

Establishing the Collaborative Relationship

Successful training depends on establishing a collaborative relationship with the couple in which objectives of training are agreed on by each spouse and the trainer. In this relationship, each spouse must perceive the trainer as fair and impartial in his or her dealings with the couple. Training is not to the advantage of either spouse, but to improve the behavioral exchanges which is to the mutual advantage of both spouses.

The foregoing summary of background information about the Roans was obtained during a conjoint marital interview. Neither spouse had any specific ideas about what to expect from marital-skills training, although they were both highly motivated to try a new approach to their marital difficulties. At this point, the trainer should, in a preliminary way, explain the rationale for training so that the couple has some idea of what to expect from training. The following rationale was given to Jan and Bill Roan by the trainer toward the conclusion of their first meeting.

TRAINER: I would like to try to summarize your situation as I understand it, and tell you how I think marital-skills training might be helpful. From what you have told me, I gather that your marriage had been more satisfying in the earlier years, but you now find yourself engaging in frequent conflicts which have not been resolved. These conflicts have led to a loss of confidence and trust which you previously had in each other. There is nothing particularly unusual about these developments. Many couples experience changes in their lives, and in what they expect from each other after they have been married awhile. How well couples adjust to each spouse's changing wishes and expectations while maintaining marital satisfactions depends to a large extent on their skills in negotiating differences, and solving mutual problems.

In earlier years of your marriage, you were undoubtedly doing things to please each other more often than you are now. As time went on, you both wanted different things from each other, but the methods you used didn't work very well. In fact, your tactics for change which you have described to me resulted in mutual anger and disappointment. Although you both obviously have the social skills to deal with others outside of your marriage, you have had difficulty in producing necessary changes within your relationship which, after all, is a special relationship with greater obligations and expectations.

I have found that couples can regain and even improve their satisfaction with each other when they can resume their former ability to please one another more, and disregard the unpleasant emotions which were generated in the past. You can learn to make more pleasant accommodations to each other by thoughtful negotiation rather than by criticizing or withholding important satisfactions from each other.

Learning how to deal with each other without one partner's feeling resentful or "taken" by the other requires personal skill much like that of diplomats who must resolve disagreements between countries. The purpose of our training program is to help you acquire and practice these skills. This is to be done without blaming either of you, or by my deciding who is right about a particular issue and who is wrong. You will be expected to learn skills in describing your relationship more accurately, skills in communicating what each of you desires more specifically, skills in how to express emotions in a more constructive way, skills in how to negotiate conflicts more successfully, and how to maintain changes in your relationship. What are your reactions to this plan as I have outlined it?

The trainer has attempted to summarize his or her views of the Roan's marital situation in an objective, nonjudgmental manner. At the same time, the trainer has provided the couple with a general rationale for marital skills-training based on social-learning principles. The trainer has also indicated that the Roan's marital situation is not unusual and that improvements can be made when they learn more skillful ways of influencing their mates. In his or her closing remarks, the trainer paused for questions from the couple demonstrating that he or she too is open to negotiations about how they will conduct training.

During the course of explaining the rationale for training, and in making preliminary assessments available to the couple, the trainer has an opportunity to emphasize the collaborative nature of their venture. In all such situations, the trainer must indicate by his or her behavior that the interactive aspects of the marital difficulties are of paramount importance and must balance his or her comments to reflect equally on the behavior of both the husband and the wife. For purposes of illustration, we have chosen two such opportunities from the hypothetical case of the Roans. With each illustration we have developed two alternative trainer responses which are either "more" or "less" likely to facilitate a collaborative relationship. In the first situation, Bill Roan directs a question to the trainer which indicates that he wants the trainer to take his side in an issue relating to the expression of affection in the marriage. Depending on how the trainer responds to this question, he or she is more or less likely to establish a collaborative relationship.

BILL: How can Jan expect me to be more affectionate with her when she spends so much time putting me down?

LESS LIKELY TRAINER: Bill, you have buried your feelings for Jan because your ego is easily hurt which causes you to constrict emotionally. During the course of training you will learn to express your feelings better despite what she does. Your wife will learn that the nasty comments you speak of are really not useful.

MORE LIKELY TRAINER: You have both done things to hurt each other when you have been angry or felt that you have been treated unfairly. Unfortunately, none of us here can do anything about what has happened in the past. During the course of training, I will ask you to do some things to please Jan even though you may not feel like doing them, and she will be asked to do some things for you to help reestablish more positive feelings for one another.

In the *less* likely reply, the trainer seems to indicate that the problem of affection is inherent in Bill, rather than a problem with their interaction. The trainer also seemed to indicate that each spouse would be treated individually for his or her problem. The alternative trainer comments were more likely to establish a collaborative relationship because they focused on the interactive nature of the problem. The trainer also revealed his or her expectations that previous interactive failures could not be used as an excuse for currently not attempting changes. Finally, the trainer presents a preview of training during which time they will both be asked to change their behavior in a reciprocal fashion.

Another juncture at which the trainer can facilitate the collaborative nature of the training relationship is when he or she is presenting the couple with feedback on his or her observations of the couple's interactions. Feedback statements to the couple should always emphasize the interactive behavior of the spouses, and not be a comment on one spouse's behavior. Further, feedback from the trainer should be expressed in a neutral and nonjudgmental manner. Here are some examples of trainer feedback statements which are either "more" or "less" likely to facilitate a collaborative relationship.

LESS LIKELY TRAINER: Bill, I've noticed that you have tended to become hostile and bitter toward Jan whenever she has brought up the issue of your sexual relationship. As you must realize, this problem cannot be resolved in an atmosphere of anger and recrimination.

MORE LIKELY TRAINER : I've noticed that you both become a little irritated at each other whenever the topic of your sexual relationship has come up. Perhaps we can find out more about what each of you expects from the other in terms of your sexual relationship.

Notice that in the *less* likely option, although the trainer has accurately labeled the emotional tone of anger in relation to sexual topics, Bill was blamed for having angry feelings. Moreover, the trainer's expectation that the problem could be solved if the spouses would just quit being angry was not realistic or conducive to a collaborative solution. In the *more* likely response option, the trainer's labeling of the observed emotions as irritation was applied to both spouses. In addition, the trainer's suggestion that further exploration of the topic is warranted underscored the importance of the sexual issue which was more conducive to a collaborative solution.

In summary, establishing a collaborative relationship with the couple is a prerequisite for ensuring the effectiveness of training. Both husband and wife must perceive the trainer as impartial with respect to either spouse's grievances. The trainer sets the tone for collaboration through his or her preliminary explanations of the rationale for training, the way in which he or she handles each spouse's attempts to gain special favor, and the manner in which he or she emphasizes the interactive nature of marital problems in giving feedback to the couple.

Assessment Procedures

As we have pointed out in Chapter 3, assessment of interactive behavior is an integral part of social-skills training. Assessment is a continuous process which begins during the first interview with the couple and continues throughout the training. Since general issues in assessment have already been covered in earlier chapters, our intention now will be to focus on special assessment issues and procedures which have a particular bearing on marital-skills training.

In marital-skills training, we are primarily interested in making three kinds of interrelated assessment: (1) to evaluate each spouse's degree of satisfaction with the marriage before and after skills training; (2) to evaluate each spouse's observations of the other partner's behavior so that we are in a position to know precisely what each spouse desires from the other; and (3) to formulate our own views of the couple's marital skills direct from observations of their interaction.

Assessing Marital Satisfaction. Evaluation of each spouse's marital satisfaction is important because it helps us understand the skill deficits leading to unresolved marital conflict. It also helps us to determine how effective skills training is for each couple following training. In some instances, marital dissatisfaction may be related to the failure of each spouse to express their wishes adequately. In other instances, low levels of marital satisfaction may stem from a failure to negotiate and compromise effectively. Consequently, assessment of spouse's general level of satisfaction with the marital relationship is a barometer as to how skillfully each spouse behaves in balancing his or her own satisfactions with those of his or her partner.

Assessments of marital satisfaction are typically obtained at least once prior to the initiation of skills training, either before or after the first interview with the couple, and at least once following the conclusion of training. Assessment can, of course, also be conducted at each meeting. Global indicators of marital satisfaction in various areas of the couple's marriage, such as satisfaction with the partner's expression of affection, are easily obtained with one of several standardized self-report questionnaires.

Stuart and Stuart (1972) have developed a comprehensive self-report survey called the *Marital Pre-Counseling Inventory*. This questionnaire, which takes about an hour to complete, elicits a fairly detailed picture of how each spouse views himself or herself, and his or her spouse in terms of marital goals and expectations. It also surveys numerous areas of marital satisfaction, including sexual interaction, management of children, family finances, family obligations, division of spouse-related responsibilities, etc.

Also available are briefer measures of marital satisfaction which can be completed by each spouse in twenty minutes or less. These are the *Marital Happiness Scale* developed by Azrin, Naster, and Jones (1973) for use with their reciprocity-counseling procedures, and the *Marital Adjustment Test* developed by Locke and Wallace (1959). Both these questionnaires can be scored for a global impression of how satisfied each spouse is with the marital relationship. The *Marital Pre-Counseling Inventory* by Stuart and Stuart (1972) is more useful for evaluating specific areas of spouse discontent prior to training. Either the *Marital Happiness Scale* (Azrin, Naster, & Jones, 1973) or the *Marital Adjustment Test* (Locke &

Wallace, 1959) would be a good choice to obtain impressionistic information on areas of marital discontent which could be pursued in subsequent
interviews.

In completing self-report questionnaires, couples provide general
information about their marital behavior which is further developed
during conjoint marital interviews. Interviews with the couple serve
several purposes, some of which have been discussed earlier in reference
to establishing a working relationship. In addition, conjoint marital interviews are important in the assessment of each spouse's observations of
the marital partner.

Assessment and Training Observational Skills. One of the most
important functions of conjoint marital interviews is to clarify how each
spouse views the behavior of the marital partner. During the interview
each spouse provides detailed information about their perceptions of
their partners which often suggest ways in which skill training may be
useful. In addition, the couple can begin to learn how to describe accurately their own and their spouse's behaviors in ways which are conducive to improving the relationship.

During the initial interview, the assessor/trainer should begin to help
each spouse pinpoint specific behaviors the marital partner would like to
see changed in the other. Most couples, no matter how well they are
suited to one another, have probably gotten into the habit of assessing
their spouse's behavior using global trait labels which communicate little
useful information. For example, Jan Roan has described her husband as
being "irresponsible." Bill Roan has described Jan as acting "empty-
headed." In addition to the provocative nature of most such assessments,
these global trait labels do not communicate what each spouse finds
distressing about the other, or what behaviors should replace the negative ones. In assisting the couple assess the positive and negative aspects
of their interaction, the trainer should teach them more precise ways of
observing the behavior of the other. Let us take an example from a
conjoint interview with the Roans. Jan is in the process of describing what
distresses her about Bill, and the trainer is helping Jan clarify her assessment in *behavioral* language.

JAN: The problem with Bill is that he acts like an irresponsible child. I wish he
would grow up and be a husband.
TRAINER: I'm not sure what you mean Jan when you say that Bill is "irresponsible"
and "doesn't act like a husband." Could you explain what you mean by those
terms?
JAN: Well, Bill tends to forget important responsibilities which means that I have
to handle the problem.

TRAINER: Can you think of some specific examples of this behavior, and when it occurs?

JAN: Yes, when bills come in, Bill says that he will take care of them, but weeks go by and he does nothing about them. I'm the one who gets calls from the bill collectors when he isn't around.

TRAINER: Does Bill do other things like this which you consider to indicate his irresponsibility?

JAN: Well, he does take the children to school on time every morning, and he does (laugh) put his underwear in the laundry. I guess I'd have to say it has to do with his handling of money that bothers me the most. He doesn't attend to the bills, and also, he has a bad habit of charging things on credit cards which we have trouble paying for.

TRAINER: So that when you say that Bill is irresponsible, you don't mean that he is that way in all areas of your marriage, you mean specifically that he tends to spend more money than your income allows, and that he seems to ignore the consequences of excessive spending by not attending to unpaid bills. When you say that you want him to grow up and act like a husband, you are specifically referring to his spending money without seeming to worry about whether the family can afford it.

JAN: Yes, that's exactly what I mean.

Note how the trainer helped Jan reformulate her generalized observations about Bill in specific behavioral language. The trait label of Bill as being "irresponsible" turned out upon closer examination not to be entirely accurate, for example, it did not apply to his getting the children to school on time. Moreover, it is much more likely that the couple is in a better position to learn how to negotiate changes skillfully in how they handle money than in trying to change Bill's "irresponsibility."

The ability of each spouse to pinpoint behaviors observed in their marital partner is an important skill which must be assessed early, and if found to be lacking should receive a high priority for training. In addition to the corrective feedback given to the couple during assessment of their observational and reporting skills, the trainer can present spouses with additional "homework" exercises which will sharpen their marital-observation skills. Since accurate spouse-observational skills are so important to effective marital-skill training, it is recommended that these exercises be given following the initial interviews. The general elements of these exercises can be reported orally to the trainer or written in a diary.

1. *Each spouse should formulate two or three behaviors which they would like to see increased in their partner.* These formulations should be in precise descriptive terms. For example, Jan wanted Bill to act more affectionately. This was restated in behavioral terms as meaning that she wanted Bill to kiss her and tell her that he had appreciated something she had done.

2. *Specify where and when these behaviors are to be observed.* For example, if Jan wants affection from Bill, when should it occur? When he arrives home from work? In the evening when the kids are in bed? At either or both of these times?

3. *Instruct each spouse to give feedback to their partner whenever the spouse feels that he or she has observed the specified behavior.* For example, Bill was to acknowledge positive feedback from Jan by saying something like, "I appreciate the compliment."

Assessing Marital Skills through Behavioral Observations. The most relevant of all assessments for marital-skills training results from the trainer's first hand observations of the spouses interacting with each other. It is here that the couple's skills in marital interaction are assessed, and plans for remedial action made.

The most practical and convenient way to carry out behavioral assessment is to request that the couple actually discuss three or four of the most cogent issues which they have raised during the initial interview with the assessor/trainer. It is important that the trainer does not take part in these discussions or attempt to influence them in any way until the assessment is completed. If possible, it is desirable to record the couple's discussions on audiotape or videotape so that the assessment data can be shared with them, and suggestions for change can be shown more graphically. We have found that a 10- to 20-minute discussion by the couple on each of several topics is usually sufficient to provide a useful sample of the couple's typical interactive behavior. Not infrequently, we have found that observations of the couple made in this manner are far more revealing than information obtained through self-report questionnaires or conjoint interviews.

In the case of Jan and Bill Roan, we might ask the couple to discuss several of the following issues in their marriage: (1) How will Jan's return to work affect the family's ability to provide care for the children, and what changes need to occur in this eventuality? (2) How will the couple rearrange their handling of finances so that neither one of them bears the full responsibility alone? (3) What should the spouses do when either of them feels hurt and angry by the other's critical comments? (4) How do they both desire to handle their sexual relationship in the future?

While observing the couple grapple with these issues in their marriage, the trainer should be formulating and finding answers to pertinent assessment questions such as the following:

1. Does Bill or Jan take most of the initiative in these discussions?
2. How does Jan present information to Bill about her point of view, and vice versa?

3. Do the spouses seem to use positive constructive tactics to influence each other, or do they attempt to coerce their partner into a solution which is likely to breed resentment?

4. Are both Bill and Jan able to express genuine concern for one another during the discussions, or do they seem oblivious to their partner's feelings?

5. Do Jan and Bill indicate by their responses that they have really listened to their partner's point of view, or are they so busy trying to win points that they fail to comprehend the other's position?

6. What kind of skills do they have in negotiation and compromise?

7. Does either Jan or Bill indicate to the other that certain topics are "off limits" to the other and cannot be negotiated?

8. What are the spouse's abilities in the way of offering constructive alternative suggestions on how their differences may be solved?

9. Do Jan and Bill stay on the topic which they have agreed to discuss, or do they bring in irrelevant problems from the past which obscure the issue before them?

10. Finally, do the discussions lead to definite agreements about what to do to try to solve the problem, or are they as far from a solution at the termination of a conversation as they were at the beginning?

Let us briefly summarize our views on marital assessment. Assessment of the couple's satisfaction with their spouse's behavior is important because it helps focus training on real issues relevant to the marriage. Brief self-report questionnaires are useful in providing global information on each spouse's satisfaction within broad areas of the couple's interaction. Conjoint marital interviews help pinpoint specific behaviors which produce marital conflict and dissatisfaction. Also, interviews help establish the necessary collaborative relationships between spouses and between the couple and the trainer. Finally, direct observations of the couple interacting around crucial issues in their marriage provide the trainer with a firsthand assessment of the couple's strengths and weaknesses in marital-interaction skills.

Marital-Skills Training

The procedures which are used to train spouses to interact more effectively with one another are based on the principles described in Chapter 4. Based on the trainer's observations of the couple's interactive behavior, corrective feedback is given to both partners regarding various aspects of their performance which appear counterproductive. Then the couple is presented with a rationale and description of the new behaviors. Coaching the couple in new modes of interaction may be supplemented by demonstrations of more effective behavior by the trainer or a spouse from a different couple in a couple's group. In the latter circumstance, the trainer must be confident that the spouse chosen can effectively display the desirable responses. Problem areas are then discussed further, with the trainer continually providing additional corrective feedback and making suggestions for further improvements in interactive skill. Examples of some of the skills that might be learned by the spouses in this manner include being able to state one's position clearly and effectively, learning to provide the marital partner with alternative solutions, obtaining feedback on one's position, learning how to express feelings appropriately, learning how to listen effectively, and learning how to compromise and reciprocate.

Using our example of Jan and Bill Roan, let us illustrate how this training process might influence stagnant and unproductive marital interactions.

BILL: Jan, that's my final word. As long as I'm head of the household, I will be the one putting bread on the table. You are needed by the children at home. There is no reason for you to go back to work just to prove a point.

JAN: You really don't give a damn about how I feel about working. All you care about is seeing that I put a hot meal in front of your face every night and keep the kids off your back so that you can bury your head in the T.V. screen every night.

TRAINER: Let's stop right there! Its clear that you both have strong conflicting opinions about Jan's going back to work, but your interaction is overheated and completely unproductive. Your personal attacks on each other are preventing the issues from being presented at all.

Bill, you can't begin a discussion by presenting Jan with "your final word." Jan, you really don't know that Bill objects to your returning to work just so you can continue to serve his dinner. Jan, I'd like you to state your position on the issue of resuming your teaching career to Bill directly, and without second-guessing his reasons for opposing it. Bill, I'd like you to respond directly to her presentation by first acknowledging that you've heard her position and then by voicing your opinion. Jan, why don't you start first?

JAN: Bill, before we were married, I enjoyed teaching very much. It made me feel worthwhile, like I was getting somewhere in my life. I feel that I can carry out all the responsibilities of being a wife and mother and still pursue my career in teaching. I'd like you to support me in this decision.

BILL: Jan, I understand that teaching makes you feel good about yourself. But I am concerned that if you and I both work five days a week, the children will be neglected. Besides, I just don't know how to run things around the house like you do.

TRAINER: That was much better. Jan, it was very good that you stated your reasons for wanting to go back to work without bringing in extraneous issues. This time you came out directly and asked for Bill's support. Bill, your response was also much better this time. You acknowledged Jan's feelings about teaching for the first time. Also, you began to state your concerns about Jan's being away from the home without attacking her. However, you haven't been very specific about how the children will be neglected if Jan goes back to teaching. When you are not specific, Jan can imagine all sorts of reasons why you might not want her to resume teaching. Tell her precisely what you think might happen. Okay, let's go on. Bill you start.

BILL: Jan, you usually spend some time getting the children ready before I take them to school each morning, you know how they dawdle. Also, the children come home from school at three-thirty, and if you went back to work, you wouldn't be home until after five. What will they do until you come home?

JAN: The children are not babies anymore. I think the children will cooperate by getting ready on time in the morning if they know I have to leave by eight. About the matter of their getting home before I do, I think that our ten-year-old son is entirely capable of looking after his sister for an hour or so.

TRAINER: That was very good, I'm very pleased with both of you. Bill, you stated your concerns directly so that Jan had an opportunity to propose a solution to your concerns. Jan, you stated your feelings about the children's being old enough to cooperate with changes in your schedule. But I don't think the issue is resolved yet.

I think we've all learned something, based on the differences in your approach to each other so far. We learned that it's best to state your position clearly, so that your partner has a chance to respond. Also, it is better to ask questions about the other's opinion rather than try to bully him or her into your position. However, when discussing differences of opinion, it is often wise for you each to offer a variety of alternative solutions to the problem which you both can evaluate. Let's continue this discussion, but I'd also like each of you to propose alternative solutions to the problem. At the same time, try to get some feedback from your partner on the proposed solutions. When you ask for feedback, the other person feels that you are really interested in his or her opinion. Bill, why don't you start this time?

BILL: Jan, I think that you are probably right about the children's being able to look after each other for an hour or so after school, but I'd feel a lot more comfortable if an adult were in the house with them in case one of them should get sick or something. How about asking your mother to come over, she lives only about four blocks away?

JAN: I have no doubt that my mother would be only too happy to come over for a few hours a day to look after the children, but I don't think it would be fair to ask her to do it every day. Besides, I think she might become too involved in our affairs. I really don't think I would want her to be that close to us. I do

agree with you that we should have an adult in the house in case something
came up that the kids couldn't handle while I was away. I know some
retired teachers through the PTA who would probably be willing to do some
light housekeeping while watching the children.

BILL: I can see what you mean about your mother. She's a very nice woman, but
she does have a tendency to interfere in our personal business. I guess I
would feel better if the housekeeper, or whoever, was someone we know
personally. I wonder if I could talk to the person we got from the PTA?

JAN: I do think you should be involved in the selection of the person we would
hire. In fact, I can probably arrange for us both to interview several possibilities before making a final decision.

BILL: Well, I feel much better about the whole thing now that I understand how we
plan to handle the situation with the kids.

TRAINER: That was very good. You both came up with alternative solutions and
made some decisions which you both appear to be comfortable with.

Through the use of corrective feedback and coaching in more effective interactive behavior, the trainer has helped Bill and Jan develop skills
in resolving one of their major problems. On this particular problem, the
couple has learned that stating one's position without anger, suggesting
alternative solutions to the controversy, and requesting and receiving
evaluative feedback from one's spouse were useful in resolving the disagreement. Training continues by having the couple practice these skills
on additional problems which have not yet been resolved. In addition,
discussions of other problems will demonstrate the need for learning
additional skills which may not have been required for solving earlier
problems.

TRAINER: I have had the impression from talking with you both earlier that your
sexual relationship was not entirely satisfactory to either of you. I wonder if
this is an issue worth talking about now. It may also provide us with an
opportunity for you to practice your problem-solving skills. Would you like
to start the discussion, Jan?

JAN: Sex has been a rather difficult topic to discuss. Bill kids me a lot about being
overweight, and that makes me feel that I'm unattractive to him.

BILL: Well, the fact that you're a little plump doesn't have anything to do with our
sexual relationship from my point of view. I suppose I haven't felt like
making love to you as much as I used to because you always seem to be
putting me down whether its sex or anything else.

TRAINER: Your sexual relationship does seem to be an important issue to resolve.
Bill, why don't you tell Jan how she puts you down and how that affects your
sexual interest in her?

BILL: Jan, I have felt uncomfortable about approaching you sexually lately because you seem so unenthusiastic; you make excuses that you're too tired, or something else is on your mind.

JAN: Usually when you approach me it comes as a complete surprise. Like you come to bed after watching T.V. all night and expect me to turn on like a light switch.

TRAINER: Why don't you both state your feelings on how you would like to be approached for a sexual encounter, and how you would like the other to respond to the offer.

JAN: Bill, I would like to spend some time talking in the evening before you approach me in the bedroom. It doesn't have to be all that romantic, but I would like you to say how you feel about me, something complimentary, I would hope.

BILL: You know that I have trouble finding the right words. If I come out and say that I want you and/or need you, I feel terribly vulnerable to your rejecting me. Even if you're not interested in making love, I would appreciate your doing it in a way which wouldn't make me feel ridiculous—like I was some kind of depraved sex monster.

TRAINER: That was very good. You both are starting to open up and state how you feel about your sexual relationship. Sexual feelings usually cannot be negotiated, but sexual behavior can. Each of you have some expectations about the conditions under which you will be interested in engaging in sex. Let's see if you can come to some agreement about how you will signal each other that you are, or are not, interested in sexual relations.

JAN: I can become interested in sex almost any time that I feel you are really interested in me as a person and treat me like I'm the most voluptuous woman in the world. Sometimes I may really be tired from a tough day, but that usually doesn't mean I don't love you anymore.

BILL: I guess I never knew that. I can agree to spend more time with you prior to our lovemaking. But if you're not in the mood, I would expect you to tell me in a nice way rather than trying to change the subject or by pretending that you are sleeping. Sometimes I would like you to be the one to initiate making advances so it doesn't seem that sex is just my thing.

JAN: I guess there have been many times when I have wanted you sexually but felt too embarrassed, or was afraid of what you might think if I suggested it. You really mean that you would like me to make the first move sometimes? You won't think that I'm a dirty old woman?

BILL: Yes, I'd really like that. It would make me feel terrific! All you'd have to do would be to put on that sexy nightgown, and I'd get the message. Do you think you could do that?

JAN: Well, I might be a little embarrassed at first, but now that I know you approve of the idea, I'm sure I could do it. Remember, you have to tell me how sexy I look when I put it on.

BILL: If that's all it takes, its a deal!

TRAINER: It is very gratifying to find out that you both can express your feelings so well. You should do it more often. When feelings are stated openly, the other person can react to them rather than having to draw conclusions based on their imagination. Also, congratulations on your negotiating a new sexual contract in your marriage.

The failure to express feelings appropriately is often a drawback to the successful resolution of sensitive marital problems. Through coaching and corrective feedback, the trainer helped the Roans learn how to express their feelings about the difficulties in their sexual relationship which paved the way for constructive solutions. Additionally, the trainer showed the couple how to negotiatve behavioral exchanges necessary to meet each other's needs for sexual encounters, for example, Jan desired conversational closeness, and Bill desired that his overtures be reciprocated with a kindly expression of feeling, irrespective of Jan's decision to engage in sexual behavior.

In the course of training, it will become apparent that the skills the couple learns in solving one problem become utilized or transferred to solving the next problem. As additional skills are required to solve different and possibly more complex problems, the couple tend to build their repertoires of more effective interactive skills. Toward the end of the series of skill-training sessions, the trainer will want the couple to develop skills which will help them to maintain effective interactional behavior on their own initiatives.

Maintenance of Marital Skills

Thus far, we have discussed training procedures which are employed by the trainer to develop more effective spouse interactions during training sessions. How well these trained skills work and how long their effects last ultimately depends on the extent to which the couple can develop additional skills to maintain positive and effective interaction at home. In order to maintain the effects of more skilled verbal interactions, the trainer must help the couple see to it that negotiated agreements are carried out with some consistency. To accomplish these objectives, spouses can be taught systematically to observe each other's behavior and give appropriate feedback to each other. In addition, spouses should be taught positively to reinforce each other when the marital partner exhibits behavior the other desires, thereby strengthening it.

Spouse Monitoring

In spouse monitoring, the trainer teaches spouses to observe how frequently and under what circumstances their partners engage in specified behaviors which they have agreed to perform for one another, for example, how often a spouse makes statements of affection, or how much time a spouse actually spends with his children. For example, Bill Roan has agreed to spend more time in pleasant conversatioon with Jan as a precondition to her willingness to engage in sex.

In order to be certain that these behaviors will occur and persist, the trainer might ask Jan to record the amount of time Bill converses with her, and ask Bill to record the frequency with which Jan agrees to sexual encounters over a period of several weeks. While this might seem a little artificial at first, most couples find that spouse-monitoring procedures can be employed with very little effort and, in fact, be somewhat entertaining.

More specifically, Jan is instructed to keep a daily record, with Bill's awareness, of when and for how long he converses with her. To make spouse monitoring more interesting and useful, she can rate his conversational ability on a 10-point scale with 10 being most pleasant. Following each conversation, Jan can present Bill with feedback as to how he performed and explain why she gave him the rating she did, for example, he expressed a lot of interest in what she was saying. For his part, Bill can monitor how often pleasant conversations with Jan lead to her willingness to engage in sex. To make it absolutely fair, he can even rate how enjoyable he found the encounter with her and why he gave her the rating he did. Both the monitoring and the feedback each spouse gives to the other tend to prompt and maintain the behaviors that each spouse has verbally agreed to perform by making them more aware of when, where, and how often they deliver on their promises.

Spouse Reinforcement

Another skill which can help prompt and maintain the behavior which an individual desires in his or her marital partner is spouse reinforcement. Basically, spouse reinforcement involves one spouse's delivering a positive consequence to the other, contingent on the second spouse's performing a behavior that the first desires. This skill is taught by offering spouses a rationale for the use of positive reinforcement and giving couples guidelines for its use. Let us illustrate the teaching of spouse-reinforcement skills by showing how the trainer would teach Jan to increase and maintain her husband's attention to paying the bills on time.

JAN: I've tried everything to get Bill to handle our debts on time, but he delays paying them. I've tried pleading, crying, screaming, and even putting them under his pillow at night.

TRAINER: The problem is that all the methods you've used to coerce your husband into paying the bills have been aversive and not likely to be effective in the long run. You need to replace the "nagging" with a positive reinforcement approach so that he'll associate positive consequences with bill payment.

JAN: I'm not sure I understand how that would work.

TRAINER: A positive reinforcement strategy simply means that when your husband does something you want him to do, you should go out of your way to notice it and reward his behavior by expressing approval or by doing something special that he will find appealing.

JAN: Well, how do I get him to do it in the first place? He typically agrees to take care of the bills, but only follows through once in a while.

TRAINER: In this case, you can prompt him by saying in a very neutral way that a payment is due and offering him a positive incentive for carrying it out right then.

JAN: Like offering to prepare his favorite dessert, a lemon pie, if he does it?

TRAINER: Yes, exactly. Its important that the reward follows very soon after he takes care of the bill.

JAN: That's terrible; I treat my nine year old son that way with cookies and milk for doing his chores.

TRAINER: I'm sure it works very well with him, too.

JAN: What if he doesn't pay the bill like he agreed to?

TRAINER: I would suggest that you do not say anything further about the bill, but don't carry out your part of the bargain by making the lemon pie either. Eventually he will want to know where your lemon pie is, and at that point you can gently remind him of his promise.

Summary

An important aspect of marital-skills training consists of the trainer's teaching verbal interactive skills which are employed by spouses to resolve disagreements effectively. Skills which appear to be the most useful consist of (1) the ability to express feelings appropriate to the problem; (2) the ability to state one's position clearly and effectively; (3) the ability to develop and evaluate alternative solutions, and (4) the ability to negotiate and compromise. When these skills are employed effectively, each spouse should be able to obtain a good deal of what they want from the other without rancor or bitterness.

Training in these skills involves the elements of coaching, modeling, practice, and feedback described in earlier chapters. In order to maintain positive marital interactive exchanges, verbal agreements between spouses must be carried out behaviorally at home. This is accomplished by teaching spouses additional interactive skills, the purpose of which is to accelerate and maintain positive behavioral exchanges. Spouse-monitoring exercises carried out at home will help spouses to evaluate the progress they have been making and to increase the effectiveness of their verbal agreements. Additionally, prompting and positive reinforcement skills employed by both spouses will help maintain the behaviors which they desire in their marital partners.

8

Skills Training with Children

Overview

- Childhood behavior problems of social withdrawal and antisocial aggression can lead to profound interpersonal problems in adult life.
- Children learn much of their social behavior by observing peer and adult models, and through reinforcement of their social-behavior patterns during their earliest interactions with others.
- Evaluations of social skills in children can be obtained by observations of their behavior in the natural environment, through role-playing, and from reports of parents and teachers.
- In planning social-skills training for children, one should consider utilizing the potent influence of peers, parents, and teachers.
- Social-skills training with children utilizes many of the same principles of learning as are employed with adults, although some of the training techniques may differ.
- Social-skills training techniques are illustrated, using several different social problems presented by three children.

Social skills necessary for confident and mutually satisfying relationships with peers, parents, and teachers are among the most important skills that children must learn if they are to maximize their potential in adult life. At the present time, research and the availability of social-skills training methods has lagged behind developments in remedial programs for adults. Therefore, the assessment and training programs which we will propose for children in this chapter may be viewed as somewhat more experimental than those presented in other sections of this book.

The reader is invited to use these proposals as a starting point upon which to make further innovations to suit his or her specific circumstances.

In order to obtain the necessary perspectives on social-skills training with children, we shall first explore the kinds of problems children have which manifest themselves as the absence of adequate social skills. Based on this overview, we shall develop some preliminary ideas about the nature of social skills in children which will provide our basic framework for assessment and training.

Over the past thirty years or so, there appears to be a growing body of evidence which relates the role of poor social functioning in children with the personal adjustment problems faced by adolescents and adults in later life. What are the characteristics of these early social problems in children which give rise to more serious problems as they mature? At one end of the spectrum, a high proportion of school-age children appear to experience excessive shyness, passivity, and fear in social situations which culminates in withdrawal from interactions with peers. This problem has been documented by Gronlund (1959), who reported that 18% of the children surveyed in the third through sixth grade at one school either had no friends or only one friend in their classes. At the other end of the spectrum of childhood social dysfunction, there is a range of aggressive behavior problems. These children may be characterized by throwing temper tantrums when frustrated, ignoring the rights and feelings of others, teasing or embarrassing peers excessively, making demands for immediate compliance with their wishes, and the use of physical assault to settle conflicts with others. Although these undesirable social patterns are all too familiar to the teachers, parents, and siblings of aggressive children, more serious problems arise when these patterns are carried on into later life (Robbins, 1966). Aggressive children are more likely to do poorly academically (Kornrich, 1965), and be involved in a variety of delinquent and antisocial acts (Cowen, 1973).

Further documentation of the relationship between dysfunctional patterns of social behavior, that is, withdrawal or aggression as a precursor to serious adjustment problems in later life, was presented by Kagan and Moss (1962). These investigators concluded that

> passive withdrawal from stressful situations, dependency on family, ease of anger arousal, involvement in intellectual mastery, social interaction anxiety, sex-role identification, and patterns of sexual behavior in adulthood were each related to reasonably analogous behavior dispositions during the school years. (p. 266)

Clearly, patterns of social behavior established during the early years have profound implications for the development of effective interpersonal behavior which carry into adulthood. Both patterns of social with-drawal and aggression appear to be significant handicaps which have detrimental influences on further social development.

Perspectives on Social-Skills Development

How do such different patterns of social interaction in children develop? Why do some children learn healthy adaptive social patterns, whereas others fail to acquire basic social skills necessary to an effective adjustment in life? Although we cannot answer these questions at present with a high degree of certainty, we can speculate about social-learning influences which are likely to provide some preliminary explanations.

Influence of Models

Children learn much of their social behavior by observing and emu-lating others who serve as models. Parents, teachers, peers, and even fictional characters portrayed in the media serve as models which young children are likely to imitate (Bandura & Walters, 1963). An important aspect of model influences depends on the social consequences of the model's behavior. A young boy is likely to imitate the tough but honest social behavior of the Lone Ranger because he elicits admiration and respect from everyone.

If a child observes her brother "bully" mother into giving in to his demands to stay up late every night, she may be tempted to employ similar tactics. On the other hand, a child who observes an older sibling doing chores around the house which results in parental praise and attention, may be more likely to adopt similar behavior patterns.

In addition to modeling their behavior after parents and other family members, children learn much of their social behavior from peers. A child who observes his or her age mates interact with the teacher with much trepidation may learn to be fearful when the teacher calls on him or her. Similarly, observing another child speak fearlessly in front of the class will serve to encourage the observer to attempt a similar feat.

Influence of Social Reinforcement

Although it is true that observations of a model may prompt a child to imitate certain kinds of social behavior, relatively consistent conse-quences in the form of social reinforcement may be necessary to establish the behavior pattern. The consistency of social reinforcement is necessary to establish either maladaptive or relatively functional social behavior patterns. For example, if parents frequently attempt to silence the threats of a bellicose and defiant child with toys and ice-cream cones, the youngster will quickly learn that aggressive acts are the best ways to obtain the good things in life on a regular basis. On the other hand, if parental praise and attention are generously supplied when the child expresses consideration and affection for others, a different behavior pattern is likely to emerge.

Influence of Peers

A number of studies have pointed toward important reciprocal relationships between a child's social behavior and his or her popularity with peers (e.g., Hartrup, Glazer, & Charlesworth, 1967). Gottman, Gonzo, and Rasmussen (1975) found that children who were popular with their age mates both received and distributed more social reinforcement toward other children in the form of positive attention and affection than did the less popular children Conversely, aggressive children who engaged in teasing, threatening, or fighting behavior were found to be relatively unpopular with their peers (Winder & Rau, 1962). Further, it appears that once maladaptive patterns of social interaction are initiated, negative respones from peers tends to increase the social isolation of both aggressive and withdrawn children. Thus, a vicious cycle is begun whereby socially unskilled children are removed from exposure to potentially useful social experiences which would teach them more functional behavior patterns.

Definitions of Social Skills in Children

As we have pointed out in Chapter 1, no single definition of social skills is likely to be adequate for purposes of assessment and training in all social contexts. This is as true of social-skills training with children as it is with adults. However, it is probably equally true that there are some distinctions between "effective" social behaviors engaged in by adults, and those which would be judged effective if engaged in by children. At this juncture, it should be instructive to see how some writers have conceptualized social skills in children, with the expectation that these views will be useful in formulating strategies of social-skills training programs for children.

Combs and Slaby (1977) define social skills in children as the ability to interact with others in a given social context in specific ways which are societally acceptable or valued and at the same time personally beneficial, mutually beneficial, or beneficial primarily to others. (p. 162)

Combs and Slaby also point out that the skills in question would have no adverse effects on others. This would rule out the possibility of including exploitation, deceit, and aggressive "abilities" in any definition of social skills. Finally, these authors indicate that social skills in children should be assessed from the perspectives of the child, peers, teachers, and parents.

Rinn and Markle (1979) define social skills for children as

a repertoire of verbal and nonverbal behaviors by which children affect the responses of other individuals (e.g., peers, parents, siblings, and teachers) in the interpersonal context. This repertoire acts as a mechanism through which children influence their environment by obtaining, removing, or avoiding desirable and undesirable outcomes in the social sphere. Further, the extent to which they are successful in obtaining desirable outcomes and avoiding or escaping undesirable ones without inflicting pain on others is the extent to which they are considered socially skilled. (p. 108)

The definitions of social skills as outlined above suggest several generalizations which can be made about identifying the characteristics of social skills in children. First, social skills are learned behaviors children engage in which are designed to influence others in their environment to respond favorably toward them. Children desire others to express interest in their behavior and are motivated to obtain affection and approval from others. Social skills in children therefore, should help maintain the flow of these reinforcing consequences from the social environment necessary to sustain the growth and development of their abilities. Lack of skill in eliciting these rewarding consequences from others can lead to frustration, loss of self-confidence, and eventual isolation from others.

Second, social skills must be evaluated in relation to specific interpersonal situations. As with adults, few behaviors are appropriate or effective in all social situations. For example, social skills which elicit enthusiastic approval from peers may not be effective in positively influencing parents or teachers. Finally, both the above definitions stress that the interpersonal behaviors which are deemed effective must not result in harm to others. This generality emphasizes the maladaptive nature of aggressive behavior patterns which might help a child obtain what he or she wants in the short run, such as another child's toy, but which produce long-term negative consequences such as loss of peer acceptance, retaliatory behaviors, etc.

Evaluation of Social Skills in Children

Consequently with our general notions about the characteristics of social skills in children, we now turn to take a closer look at some of the concrete skills which appear to be important in the daily living of most children. Table VII illustrates some examples of positive social skills displayed by children. These examples are listed in categories reflecting either impressionistic descriptions of behavior or more specific descriptions of behavior.

The classification of social skills in Table VII as either impressionistic or specific does not imply that one level of description is necessarily better than another. Depending on the purpose of our evaluation, we may rely on either impressionistic analysis of skills, or a more specific assessment of the child's social behaviors. For purposes of illustration, we shall refer to the following hypothetical situation to help concretize assessment procedures with children.

An Example

Let us assume that we have been invited by the principal of a public school to plan and implement a social-skills training program for a "special" class of children who have exhibited a variety of social-behavior problems at school. The children in this class range in age from five to seven years. They have been previously assessed as being within the average range of intelligence, but have not been performing well academically in their regular classes. A special education teacher, Ms. Goodwin, has the responsibility for teaching and managing this class.

Table VII. Examples of Prosocial Skills in Children

General impressionistic level

Is able to communicate needs effectively.
Is able to appear friendly and outgoing.
Is able to respond appropriately to others.
Is able to engage in cooperative play.
Is able to express emphathetic understanding of others.

More specific level

Is able to offer an apology for hurting someone's feelings.
Is able to share toys and other possessions with another child.
Is able to ask an adult for an explanation of what a word means.
Is able to ask another child for help on a task.
Is able to express affection toward a teacher.

At our first meeting with Ms. Goodwin, she appears to be over-whelmed in attempting to manage this class of children. She describes the problems in impressionistic terms. Some of the children are described as withdrawn, and seem incapable of interacting with the others at all. Other children in this class are described as hyperactive, and cannot seem to attend to any task or social activity for more than a minute or so. A few of the children are described as being very belligerent and more specifi-cally reported as having threatened or attacked others with little provoca-tion.

As a rule, most teachers have had a good deal of experience in developing lesson plans and dealing with routine misbehavior in the classroom. However, children who present extreme problems in social behavior, as do those described above, tend to make teachers feel anxi-ous, inept, and angry. When this happens, teachers want to turn the responsibility of dealing with difficult children over to "the experts" for a complete overhaul. Our objective, in this case, however, is to support Ms. Goodwin so that she can be employed as an effective agent in the process of social-skills evaluation, and later on in training.

Evaluation from Teacher Observation

Our first step here is to reassure Ms. Goodwin that she does in fact have problem-children who would be very difficult for anyone to handle. Second, we indicate that we hope to devise some training programs which will help her manage the social behavior of the children, as well as be of benefit to the children's development. Third, we would have to admit that we have no instantaneous solutions which we can apply successfully without her help. In order to obtain more specific informa-tion about the children, we first ask about seeing any records that she may have on the chilren which might be helpful. Second, we ask Ms. Good-win to describe the social behaviors she has observed in each child and indicate how she has responded to it. The evaluative information we obtain from the teachers on three of the children might look something like this:

SCOTT: Scott is a withdrawn child who cries when his mother leaves him at school almost every morning. He appears to watch the other children at play with keen interest, but he never joins them. Instead, he constantly tries to involve the teacher in what he is doing, frequently asking for help. Ms. Goodwin admits that she feels sorry for Scott, and often spends time playing with him as a gesture of reassurance. Whenever she tries to involve him in games with other children, Scott has refused.

LAURA: Laura is a child who constantly wants to be the center of everyone's attention. She talks constantly, and has a habit of interrupting the interactions between the teachers and another child, or groups of children playing together. She tends to be verbally aggressive and domineering which results in compliance from the quiet children and frequent arguments with the less docile children. Ms. Goodwin has asked Laura to sit in the corner when she becomes disruptive, but Laura gets around this by singing loudly or by removing her clothes.

JOE: Joe is the tough guy in the class. He tends to be physically aggressive and is frequently found on the floor pummeling a classmate who has not knuckled under his demands. His parents have been invited to take him home from school regularly because of his fighting behavior. Joe tends to act put upon and defiant whenever he is confronted with his misbehavior. Ms. Goodwin has tried everything short of corporal punishment to bring him under control. The teacher feels that Joe is more difficult to manage than any five of the other children.

Based on the teacher's observations of the three children, we can identify a number of descriptive labels applied to the children's social behavior which range in degree of specificity. At the impressionistic level, one or more of the children has been described as (1) socially withdrawn; (2) aggressive; (3) defiant; (4) disruptive; and (5) domineering. At the second, "more specific" level, the children's behavior has been described as: (1) inappropriate crying; (2) inappropriate interruptions; (3) physical pummeling or fighting; (4) verbal arguments; (5) inappropriate singing; and (6) removing clothes. It is important to note that all the social-behavior descriptions reported by the teachers could be characterized as reflecting negative or antisocial behaviors. We have virtually no information on whether, or to what extent, the children have demonstrated behaviors which could be characterized as prosocial or socially skilled. As we prepare to obtain more specific behavioral observations in the children's natural environment, we want to select several observational categories which would reflect the possible presence of prosocial behaviors as well as the antisocial ones.

Evaluation from Natural Environment Observations

Following Ms. Goodwin's descriptions of the social behaviors of all the children, we decide to obtain additional observational data on Scott, Laura, and Joe. Although a number of relatively complex rating schemes have been developed to assess the complete range of social behaviors of children in a classroom for research purposes (Wahler, 1975), we recommend that assessments for purposes of remedial training involve a sampling of no more than four or six of the most relevant behavior categories. Then the remaining assessment task is to focus on observing the children over a specific period of time. In most instances, 30 to 45 minutes of observation will be sufficient to determine *how frequently* children engage in the specified behaviors, or to note *how long* they engage in them.

For purposes of this illustration, we have decided to rate our three problem-children on three behavior categories which reflect antisocial behaviors demonstrating lack of skill, and three categories which reflect prosocial behaviors. These behavior categories are shown in Table VIII.

Obviously, we could have chosen additional behavior categories on which to rate the children. However, consistent with other notions about not rating too many behaviors at one time, we have tried to choose those behaviors most related to the impressions described by the teachers. To facilitate the observations in the classroom, we have decided to use an available one-way mirror which permits our observations without the possibility of the children noting our presence. Should a one-way mirror not be available in the particular natural-environment setting, it may be possible to observe from within the social situation. Observations which are made within the situation may involve some degree of participation in the interaction with the children. Although this is not desirable from the standpoint of influencing the children's interactions with each other, it may provide some useful information on how the children interact with the assessors.

Let us now look at the information which we have obtained by

Table VIII. Categories Reflecting Prosocial and Antisocial Behaviors for Scott, Laura, and Joe[a]

Behaviors	Scott	Laura	Joe
Prosocial			
1. Initiates conversation with another child	1	5	4
2. Offers to share materials or toys with another child.	0	0	0
3. Praises or compliments another child.	0	0	0
Antisocial			
1. Physically hits another child during social interaction.	0	0	1
2. Verbally threatens or intimidates another child.	0	5	6
3. Inappropriately interrupts social activities between two or more children.	0	4	2

[a] Observations made during 45-minute recess.

observing Scott, Laura, and Joe interacting with other children in the class during the 45-minute recess. Scott's social withdrawal was more precisely defined by the observations which showed that he engaged in almost no interactions with the other children. Both Laura and Joe exhibited some skills in initiating social interactions, but it did appear that these exchanges often became negative as evidenced by their relatively high frequency of making threats or verbally intimidating another child. Joe was observed pushing another child once during this period of observation. Both Laura and Joe were observed to interrupt inappropriately the social activities of other children. None of the three children was observed sharing materials with the others, or offering praise to the other children.

The behavioral observations of the three children's prosocial and antisocial activities have given us some important leads regarding social behaviors in need of training. Scott appeared to lack the ability to interact with the other children at all. He probably will require some very basic training in how to initiate social activities, how to greet others, how to ask appropriate questions, etc. Both Laura and Joe's social behavior, though apparently more developed than Scott's, seemed to reflect a preponderance of antisocial compared with prosocial behaviors. These children will probably require training in how to resolve differences effectively, or to obtain what they want in a more socially skilled fashion. Other possibilities for Laura and Joe might be training in how to share possessions, and how to deliver praise and other verbal reinforcements to others which would make them more acceptable to the other children.

Evaluation from Observations of Role-Playing

Recently, role-playing has been used for assessing specific social deficits in children (Bornstein et al., 1977). Although there is not much evidence at the present time to conclude that social behaviors observed during role-playing perfectly reflect behavior in the natural environment, role-playing does seem to provide important clues about the nature of social abilities in children. In role-playing, children are invited to use their imaginations and "pretend" that they are interacting with a child or another adult. These simulated interactions are fun for children to engage in, and they represent a convenient method for assessing how children might react to actual social encounters. The following are some examples of role-playing tasks from Bornstein et al. (1977) to which we have asked the children in our class to respond. The following role-playing information is given to the child to set the stage, followed by a prompt which invites the child to respond.

SCENE 1: You're playing a game of kickball in school and its your turn to get up next. But Bobbie says that he wants to get up first.

PROMPT: I want to get up next.
SCOTT: O.K.
LAURA: That's not the way you play, I'm going to tell Ms. Goodwin on you.
JOE: I'll knock your brains out if you do.

SCENE 2. Pretend that you lent your pencil to Joanie. She comes over to give it back to you and says that she broke the point.

PROMPT: I broke the point.
SCOTT: (starts crying)
LAURA: You shouldn't have done that. I'm never going to let you have any of my things again.
JOE: That does it, I'm going to kill you for that.

The advantage of the evaluations by role-playing is that role-playing scenes pinpoint the specific nature of the deficit which is likely to be displayed in particular circumstances, for example, unwarranted aggressive threats, unpopular tattling, crying when frustrated, etc. Second, role-playing lends itself nicely to training, in that alternative behaviors can be taught, rehearsed, and evaluated prior to implementation in the child's natural environment. We shall have more to say about role-playing as a tool in providing specific assessment information in the following sections on training.

Preparing for Training

At the outset, we should make some decisions regarding where training is to take place, and who will be involved in the process. We believe as do Combs and Slaby (1977) that, in most instances, training can be most effectively accomplished in the child's peer-group setting, whether it be a day-treatment center for "disturbed" children or in the average classroom. In some instances, it may be more desirable and feasible to conduct training for children in the context of a family-treatment program. The use of natural environments to promote learning and transfer of training does not rule out opportunities to individualize training. Therefore, the trainer will want to spend some time with each child individually to explain the program and obtain his or her cooperation to ensure appropriate motivation.

Training which is structured in the child's natural environment has certain advantages not to be found by working with the child exclusively on an individual basis. Training accomplished in the context of the child's social system either at home or in the schoolroom tends to facilitate the acquisition, maintenance, and transfer of learned skills to additional social situations. The natural social network affords the child opportunities for practice and exposure to reinforcing consequences for demonstrating skillful responses.

Peer Influences

The most obvious reason for including other children in the training process is that children can learn a great deal from observing and responding to one another. Children usually comply with peer-group norms once they understand what is expected of them. They imitate the behavior of other children and are influenced to change their behavior as a result of positive and negative consequences provided by peers. Also, children can be coached to ignore the socially maladaptive behavior of their socially unskilled colleagues, and to give them increased attention for prosocial behavior. For example, children in our special class could be coached to walk away from Joe when he becomes belligerent, and to provide him with increased acceptance when he plays in a cooperative fashion. Likewise, children in Scott's class could be taught how to approach him gently, and to reward him for his initial attempts at social interaction. Finally, the other children in the class could be prompted to ignore Laura's inappropriate singing and other interruptions, or remind her that they will play with her only when she learns how to ask for their attention in a more socially appropriate manner.

Teacher Influence

Teachers can facilitate skill training in two ways. As a valued model and source of approval, teachers can encourage and support the socially unskilled child while he or she is attempting new ways of communicating and behaving with others. Perhaps, even more importantly, teachers can structure social activities in the classroom which will facilitate the social activities of both relatively skilled and unskilled children. For example, let us suppose that Joe and Laura are playing that they are operating a grocery store while Scott is off in a corner by himself playing with a truck. The teacher can suggest to all three children that Scott should use his truck to deliver goods to the grocery store, thereby including him in the interaction. Further, the teacher can praise Laura and Joe for including Scott in the game. Another example of how the teacher can structure prosocial activities with unskilled children is to appoint them to various positions where they can become important sources of reinforcement for the others. For example, Scott could be appointed to deliver snacks to the children during recess. While Scott is practicing what to say to the others during his "deliveries," he will receive positive recognition for performing an important service.

Family Influences

Parents and siblings can affect the outcome of a child's social-skill training whether they are directly participating in family-training sessions or have merely consented for training to take place at school. Family members have this impact on whatever training program is decided upon because they are important sources of material and social reinforcement to the child on an everyday basis. For example, Scott's family can greatly facilitate his acquisition of specific conversational skills by gently prompting him to employ his training to greet people, or by praising him for speaking a few words to a stranger. Joe's parents can assist the training processes if they are encouraged consistently to withhold attention from him when he is belligerent, and offering to comply with his requests when his expressions are socially appropriate.

Meetings with Parents

It is a good idea to meet with the child's parents to prepare them for training and to secure their help in facilitating mutually agreed on goals and objectives. In the context of our present example with Scott, Laura, and Joe, we might decide to see all the children's parents in the context of an evening meeting arranged by the teachers. At this meeting, we should try to accomplish the following objectives:

1. Provide the parents with feedback based on our observations and conclusions regarding the social behavior of their children.
2. Solicit additional information from the parents about their child's social behavior at home.
3. Thoroughly explain our rationale for social-skills training, how it is done, and how it might be helpful for their children.
4. Obtain parental consent (preferably written) to include their child in the training program at school.
5. Provide specific suggestions about how *they* might alter their responses to the appropriate and inappropriate social behavior of the children at home.

6. Provide time to answer any questions which they might have.
7. Agree upon some system either by phone or through additional meetings to discuss any problems which might arise during training. With this system of communication we might be able to assist them with any problem which arises during the training which is not obvious to us at school. Also, we will have the opportunity to receive feedback from them as to how well the training is working at home.

Training

During our evaluation of the social behaviors of Scott, Laura, and Joe, we utilized a variety of sources in obtaining information relevant to training. We have received impressionistic descriptions from parents and teachers. This information has reflected behavioral observations of the children interacting in their classroom to look at their relative frequency of engaging in prosocial and antisocial behaviors. In a sense, training has already begun because we have involved teachers and parents in our plans for training. Now it is time actively to involve the children.

At both the impressionistic and the specific levels of analysis, these three children require somewhat different strategies for training, although it is clear that all three are very deficient in social skills. Scott exhibited very little interactive behavior of either a prosocial or an antisocial nature. He is not getting any of his needs met through social interactions with other children. He is too dependent on the teachers. Laura can initiate some activities in a prosocial manner, but does not get very far with her coercive, disruptive, and verbally aggressive tactics. Joe is at the other extreme from Scott. His output of social behavior is almost entirely aggressive, using threats and physical aggression to accomplish his ends. Although antisocial tactics used by Laura and Joe might be temporarily successful in achieving their goals, the discomfort and retaliation these behaviors generate in other children prevents either of them from forming relationships necessary for consistent social development.

Training for Scott

At the general impressionistic level, Scott needs basic training in initiating social activities, and in learning how to engage in cooperative play. For purposes of effective training, we must break these general skills into more specific components. Thus, for Scott to initiate social activities, he must learn how to look and smile at other children in a friendly manner. He must also learn how verbally and nonverbally to indicate to the other children that he desires to engage in a particular social activity. Later, he will receive training in the basic components of skill in cooperative play, such as the ability to touch others affectionately, the ability to share materials, and the ability to offer constructive suggestions for games. Since the more complex social skills in children require at least minimal abilities in initiating social activities, we will begin working with Scott on an individual basis before introducing training in conjunction with the other children.

Scott's initial training will sequentially consist of learning how to look and smile at another child, how to offer to share a toy with another child, and how to offer constructive suggestions. After spending some time playing and talking with Scott to establish rapport with him, the trainer begins in this manner:

TRAINER: Scott I've watched you playing by yourself a lot, and I just know by the way you've looked at the other children that you would like some friends to play with.
SCOTT: (Nods head affirmatively).
TRAINER: Well, one of the best ways I know to make friends is to smile at people like this (trainer smiles). Do you think you could smile like this when you look at me?
SCOTT: Like this? (smiles)
TRAINER: Yes that's very good Scott. Let's see you do it again (trainer smiles).

After smiling has been practiced with the trainer for a while, Scott is asked to practice smiling first at Ms. Goodwin and then at another child. Once Scott has mastered this with a number of other children, training is begun on the next skill, offering to share toys.

TRAINER: One of the best ways to make friends is to share one of your favorite toys with them in a game. Do you have any toys that you think the other children would like to play with?
SCOTT: I have a big red fire truck.
TRAINER: Let's call Andy over here to see if he wants to play with your fire truck. Watch how I do this, Scott. "Hey Andy, want to come over here and play with my truck?"
ANDY: How does it work?
TRAINER: Scott, why don't you show Andy how it works?
SCOTT: Well, you wind it up here in the back and then push this button here to make it go.
TRAINER: Scott that was very good. Let's see if Andy can make it go.
SCOTT: O.K. Andy, would you like to try it?

Comment. The reader should note that many of the principles of training that we have previously discussed in relation to the training of adults is equally applicable in training children. We begin by training the skill which is the least complex to master, that is, smiling. Note also, that the training techniques employed are similar to those used with adults. The rationale for training was offered to Scott as a way to make friends. Given Scott's apparent inability to initiate interactions, the trainer first modeled the desired responses and then used a liberal amount of prompting to get Scott started performing them on his own. Once Scott started smiling, and demonstrating his toy, the trainer immediately reinforced him with praise and approval. Later, the other children's reinforcing responses to Scott's initiatives should maintain them. With the hopes of sensitizing others in the environment to the training process, and promoting transfer of training, the trainer employed the teacher and some of the other children for practice. It is important to bear in mind that the trainer must initially be very much involved in structuring the practice with others and then gradually withdraw his involvement when it becomes apparent that the child can perform under these circumstances and the natural responses of others will maintain the new behavior.

TRAINER: Scott, why don't you see if you can get Linda to help you put together that doll house over here.
SCOTT: I don't think she wants to play with me.
TRAINER: Sure she does. Remember how we've said that smiling at people will help to make friends. Go over to Linda—Remember to smile at her, and then take her hand to bring her over here.
SCOTT: O.K. (*Goes over to Linda, smiles, takes her hand.*)
TRAINER: That was very good Scott. I see that you have a new friend. Linda, Scott and I are going to put together this house, and we need someone to help us pick out the furniture.
LINDA: I will help you pick out the furniture. It's in that box over there, if Scott will help me bring over the box.
SCOTT: O.K. Let's go get the box.

In this series of training interactions, the trainer is prompting Scott to perform the initiations on his own. Scott is somewhat reluctant at first, possibly because he feels awkward or doesn't know how Linda will respond to his overtures. The trainer then goes back one step and prompts Scott in what he has learned earlier, simple nonverbal smiling and handholding initiatives. To make sure that the purpose of the initiative does not fail on the first attempt, the trainer picks up the interaction and models some of the behaviors for cooperative play. Linda responds to this by directing her social responses toward Scott by asking for his help.

At this point, the trainer was able to withdraw from the interaction until needed again. Had Linda not interacted with Scott at this point, the trainer would have remained involved and continued modeling until Scott and Linda were interacting.

Training for Laura

Our evaluation of Laura showed that she had developed some basic prosocial skills in initiating social activities with others. She did look and smile appropriately at others. She could, at times, engage other children in play. She did, however, seem to become frustrated rather easily, especially if the other child objected to her having her way. When this happened, she attempted to coerce the other child, and, failing that, used threats which escalated in intensity. In her relationships with her teachers, Laura has used inappropriate methods of gaining attention. She frequently interrupted what was going on in class by yelling or by engaging in outlandish acts which were difficult to ignore. The initial stages of Laura's training will be to teach her, via role playing, how to request what she wants in a more socially acceptable manner. Second, by coaching the other children and the teachers in different ways of responding to her disruptive behaviors, she will learn that there are better ways of getting attention.

We begin the first stage of training with Laura by initiating a series of role-playing tasks to increase her repertoire of prosocial responses. Laura is already familiar with the role-playing tasks from the initial assessment so we need not repeat the rationale for role-playing given to her previously.

TRAINER: Let's play the pretend game again. I will pretend that I am someone in your class. First, I will describe what we're doing, and then you will imagine that we're really doing what I describe to you. Remember to answer just like you would if we weren't pretending, O.K.?

LAURA: O.K.

TRAINER: Pretend that you are watching Mike work on a puzzle. I'll pretend that I'm Mike. You notice that Mike is trying to put together two pieces of the puzzle that don't fit. He says, "Laura, can you help me with this puzzle?"

LAURA: That's stupid what you're doing. Let me do it (*belligerent tone*).

TRAINER: Laura, if you really called Mike stupid in that nasty tone of voice, he would probably get angry and not want to play with you any more. Mike would like you better if you had said, "Mike, I think I know how it should go." Then you could show him which piece fits. Let's try it again to see if you could say something like that.

TRAINER: Laura, can you help me with this puzzle?

LAURA: That's not the way it goes, Mike. Let me show you which one goes there.

TRAINER: That's much better, Laura. When you are helping a friend, you should try not to make them feel bad by calling them names or sound angry. Instead, you should show them how to do things in a nice way.

LAURA: I want to be friends with Mike.

TRAINER: O.K. Let's try another one. Pretend that you are watching Sarah and Dennis playing the drums. You want to play too, but Sarah doesn't want to give you the drum sticks. She says, "You can't play, we're playing with the drums now."

LAURA: I'm going to tell Ms. Goodwin that you're not being fair.

TRAINER: Laura, it's not a good idea to tattle to the teacher on other people. Nobody likes a tattler, even when the other person has said or done something which is not very nice. You should have asked Sarah if you could play with the drums next, or you could have told her that she wasn't being very nice for not letting you play with the drums.

LAURA: But what if Sarah still didn't let me play with the drums?

TRAINER: Well, sometimes we can't have what we want right away. Sooner or later I think that Sarah would have gotten tired of playing the drums, and then you would have been able to play the drums with Denny.

The above role-playing scenes are illustrations of how training was structured to deal with two of Laura's social deficits: (1) how appropriately to offer to help another child, and (2) how to respond skillfully to a conflict with another child. In actual practice, the trainer would have role-played additional scenes in each of the two problem areas, in order to increase the strength of her prosocial responding through practice. Additional scenes would also increase the likelihood that the learned responses would transfer to similar situations. It should also be noted that, in these illustrations, the trainer was careful to point out to Laura the negative consequences of her belligerent responses, for example, loss of friendship. Coaching in alternative responses was offered as a way of obtaining more favorable consequences, for example, getting to play the drums. Following successful training in role-playing, the next step would be to encourage Laura to use similar responses in the classroom.

In order to deal with Laura's more extreme disruptive behavior in the classroom, it was decided to coach Ms. Goodwin in how to decrease the attention Laura received when she was misbehaving and increase their positive responses to her when she was behaving appropriately. From our evaluation, it was clear that Laura was receiving a good deal of teacher attention for behavior similar to temper tantrums. Even though the attention from the teachers was negative, for example, scolding, it did serve to keep all eyes riveted on Laura.

In order to reduce the amount of attention Laura received for tantrums, we coached the teachers in a procedure called "time-out." Simply put, time-out is a method for isolating a child from all social consequences following his or her misbehavior. Typically, an empty room is selected, such as a large closet or coatroom. Since there are no toys or amusements in the empty room, most children find time-out terribly boring and unrewarding. The teachers were instructed to take Laura to the time-out room and leave her there for 15 minutes whenever she engaged in a tantrum. This procedure was followed for two weeks when we observed the following interaction between Laura and Ms. Goodwin.

LAURA: (*loudly*) I don't want to draw with these crummy old pencils. I want new pencils like Brenda has.

MS. GOODWIN: Laura, you know very well that's not the way to ask for something.

LAURA: (*screaming*) I don't care what you say, I'm not going to use these pencils.

MS. GOODWIN: Laura, you're starting to have a temper tantrum. I'll have to take you to time-out again unless you can talk properly.

LAURA: (*more calmly*) Well, could I *please* have some new pencils?

MS. GOODWIN: That was much better, Laura. We don't have any more new pencils, but I'll be happy to sharpen yours for you if you'd like.

LAURA: Well, O.K. but I still don't like them.

The reader may note that the training program for Laura was composed of both individualized coaching in more socially skilled ways of interacting with the other children, and in instructing the teachers as to how to respond to her disruptive behavior. Once Laura has learned more appropriate ways of responding to conflicts of interest with the other children, the teachers will be encouraged to prompt and reward Laura for using her new skills in her everyday interactions. As Laura begins to engage in more socially appropriate behavior as a means of gaining positive attention from others, it is expected that her use of disruptive behaviors will decrease. Therefore, the need for the "time-out" procedures should diminish, and corrective feedback will be employed whenever she slips back into using antisocial behaviors.

Training for Joe

Our evaluation of Joe indicated that he was a socially active child who had few problems in initiating interactions with his peers. However, he typically employed belligerent and sometimes physically aggressive modes of response to settle disputes and get his way. Although the aggression usually accomplished what he wanted in the immediate situation, he soon became exceedingly unpopular with the other children, and elicited continual reprimands from the teachers. This rejection only served to intensify his aggression in a vicious spiral which led to further rejection.

The training program we planned for Joe had similar objectives to the one proposed for Laura in that the goals were to increase prosocial behaviors and eliminate antisocial ones. However, because Joe's antisocial aggression was even more disruptive than Laura's antisocial behavior, we wanted to concentrate more intensively on reducing his aggressive behavior as quickly as possible. This goal required more active participation on the part of the teachers than we employed with Laura. To accomplish this, we began training by using a *token-economy program* which we felt would produce rapid results in bringing Joe's aggression under control.

The first step was to explain to Ms. Goodwin the rationale underlying the use of token-economy procedures (see Kazdin, 1977). In a token economy, a child is rewarded with tokens for engaging in prosocial behaviors. These tokens can be exchanged later for games, toys, or access to activities in which the child desires to engage. In Joe's case, we knew that he liked toy soldiers and loved to play kickball during recess. Access to these toys and activities would be contingent upon his earning tokens in a manner which will be described in a moment. In addition, we designed the token economy for Joe so that he would be fined or lose accumulated tokens for engaging in undesirable or antisocial acts. The idea here was to increase Joe's frequency of engaging in prosocial behaviors by making them "pay off," and decrease his antisocial behaviors by making them "costly."

Following our explanation to Ms. Goodwin, we brought Joe into the discussion and asked him the things he would like to do to earn tokens. We also informed him what would happen should he engage in various antisocial acts. We then gave Joe a money belt in which he would receive tokens for (1) cleaning up the classroom, (2) assisting the teachers pass out materials to the other children, (3) helping another child put together a puzzle, and (4) eating his lunch quietly without getting into a fight with the others. We should point out here that both the child and the adults involved in setting up the token economy should discuss mutually acceptable activities which would result in the token rewards. They also should discuss what toys and activities accumulated tokens can be exchanged for. It was further pointed out to Joe that he would be fined or have to give up tokens for threatening other children, or for fighting with them, no matter "who started the fight." In addition, should he be observed shoving or hitting another child, he would loose all his accumulated tokens for that day and be placed in "time-out" for twenty minutes.

Following implementation of the token program for three weeks, Ms. Goodwin reported a dramatic decrease in Joe's physical aggression toward peers which was reduced from several instances per day to once or twice a week. Joe initially continued his bellicose attitude toward the teacher when she fined him or placed him in time-out. However, it appeared that over time he did begin to accept the consequences of his antisocial acts in a stoic fashion. On the other hand, the earning of tokens for helpful and cooperative activities did seem to intrigue Joe, and he was proud to show the others how much "money" he had earned. With the threat of Joe's overt aggression under control, some of the children found Joe a far more acceptable playmate. In these activities, Joe did seem to exhibit a quality of leadership which heretofore had been masked by his hostility. Although he was not yet a "model" child, Joe exhibited an ability to initiate activities and converse in a far more socially acceptable fashion. In turn, he delivered more reinforcing consequences for his prosocial behaviors.

Token economies, such as the one described for Joe above, typically impose controls on a child's behavior by making explicit rules which determine what consequences follow which behaviors. Token economies by their very nature are not designed to *teach* a child new social behaviors in the same way that coaching, modeling, and role-playing do. However, in many cases, such as with Joe, children who display inappropriate aggression are also capable of behaving in socially skilled ways which they rarely display. This is in part because their aggression is somewhat successful in producing the results that they desire, and in part because of the retaliatory behavior they elicit on the part of those whom they intimidate. What the token economy accomplishes is merely to increase the payoff for exhibiting prosocial skills and increase the penalty for antisocial activities. When reductions in a child's antisocial aggression are not accompanied by increase in prosocial behavior, we must assume that he or she lacks the necessary skills. In these instances, the prosocial skills must be taught through individualized instruction much the same as that we employed with Laura and Scott.

Summary

It is well documented that the social problems of withdrawal and antisocial aggression in children may lead to serious interpersonal problems in later life. Children correctly or incorrectly learn much of their social behavior by imitating the behavior of peer and adult models. Early patterns of interaction are then established by the natural-environment consequences of their interactive behavior. Similarly to adults, children employ social behaviors with varying degress of skill, in their attempts to elicit responses from parents and peers consistent with their needs and desires.

Evaluation of social skills in children can be obtained from multiple sources. Teachers and parents are considered to be excellent sources of information as to how a child responds to others at school and at home. More specific information about a child's prosocial and antisocial behavior can be obtained through direct observation of his or her interactions in the classroom or with his or her family. Finally, most children enjoy role-playing which can be used in the continuous assessment and training of target social responses.

Prosocial skills in children frequently requiring training involve abilities such as initiating activities with peers, communicating needs appropriately, engaging in cooperative play, and settling conflicts without resorting to antisocial aggression. These skills and many others can be trained and reinforced in the child's natural environment. Individualized training approaches utilizing coaching, modeling, and feedback can be employed during the role-playing of socially skilled responses. Teachers can develop social situations in the classroom designed to elicit and shape more skillful responses. Finally, specialized procedures, such as time-out and token economy, can be employed to decrease the reinforcing properties of antisocial behavior and increase the opportunities for developing prosocial skills.

Training Alternatives to Aggression

Overview

- Aggressive behavior is a pervasive problem facing society. Different meanings ascribed to the term "aggression" make the problem difficult to conceptualize.
- Although a variety of different theories have been used to explain the problem of inappropriate aggression, a social-learning perspective seems most useful in terms of its implications for understanding and amelioration.
- Within this perspective, one of the major goals of intervention is to provide the client with more appropriate skills for handling interpersonal-conflict situations.
- This process is illustrated through the presentation of a case study which is followed through the four stages of intervention. These stages are: (1) establishing a working relationship; (2) assessment; (3) skill development; and (4) maintenance.

Aggression is clearly one of the most difficult problems we face. One only need pick up the daily newspaper to see the magnitude of this problem. On an international level, one nation is pitted against the other. On a national level, there seems to be a steady stream of civil wars, guerrilla uprisings, and unrest. The problems also reach into the daily lives of many of us. Crime statistics seem to report ever increasing trends of assault, murder, rape, and every other conceivable violent crime. The problem, of course, does not end at our doorsteps. The home is clearly one of the most dangerous places to be. Family violence, either abuse to one's spouse or one's children, is one of the most pervasive forms of interpersonal aggression. The problem of aggression is, of course, as complex as it is pervasive.

It is probably a mistake to think of aggression as a single kind of behavior. In the first place, the term "aggression" can refer to many different kinds of verbal behaviors and physical acts. We may speak of a very achievement-oriented and capable executive as being "aggressive." In this instance, we may value this person's behavior, award him or her raises, and point to him or her as an example to be emulated. We may also use the very same term "aggressive" to refer to an individual who assaults or even kills another. A related problem is that the very same behavior may be viewed as aggressive in one situation but not in another. Let's take the example of one person aiming a handgun at another, pulling the trigger, and shooting at the other individual. If the person holding the gun were a robber shooting an innocent bystander at the scene of a crime, we would undoubtedly all agree that the behavior could appropriately be labeled aggressive. If, on the other hand, the person doing the shooting was a policeman "defending himself" when another individual was shooting at him, we would label this individual a hero and certainly not think of his behavior as being aggressive. Our point is not to belabor the problems in defining aggression. The study of factors affecting the labeling of an act as "aggressive" is in itself a fascinating area of inquiry. Rather, it is important that the person attempting to work with aggression be mindful that it is very situationally based. Just as we cannot point to a single set of behaviors and say that these are socially skilled, we can likewise not point to a single set of behaviors and say that these are aggressive. The appropriateness or inappropriateness of any behavior must be judged in the context where it occurs.

Just as there are many meanings of aggression, so also there is a variety of causes. A detailed accounting of these many factors that may play a role in the occurrence of attack is well beyond the scope of this chapter. Specifically, there are a number of situations that we will not direct our attention to. These include the use of socially sanctioned aggression, as in the case of the police officer or soldier using force in the legitimate course of duty. A second area we will not cover is the calculated use of force by professional criminals in the attainments of their antisocial ends. An example of this might be a professional strong-arm or killer who makes his living by inflicting injury on others. A third form of aggression, also beyond the scope of our discussion, is that displayed by individuals with severe mental disorders. An example of this might be the psychotic individual who attacks another upon the command of an hallucination. In this case we are talking about someone who is basically out of contact with the reality of the situation and is responding in accordance with a delusion. Finally, we will not be considering those individuals for whom a clearly identified physiological cause of aggression can be isolated. An example of this might be someone with a severe brain tumor, extreme irritability, certain rare forms of seizures, and the like.

Even with the exclusion of the above individuals, we are left with a large group of people for whom aggression and violence is a significant problem. The individuals we are talking about may display very mild forms of aggression, such as "a bad temper" where they lash out verbally at people with minimal provocation, or much more severe forms of violence, even ending in injury and death. These individuals may be upstanding "normal" model citizens of the community, or they may be very disturbed individuals, evidencing patterns of aggression that markedly interfere with their life functioning. It is out of this broad category of people that most of the family and interpersonal aggression occurs.

There have, of course, been numerous attempts to explain the diversity of behaviors called aggression. Some of the theories have focused on aggression as an instinct which impels one person to attack another (Lorenz, 1966). Other theories view aggression as an inevitable response to frustration (Dollard, Doob, Miller, Mowrer, & Sears, 1939). Unfortunately, none of these theories has received unequivocal support. More important, neither the instinct nor the frustration theories of aggression have been particularly useful in helping us deal constructively with the problem of inappropriate aggression. We turn next to the social-learning perspective on aggression which appears to have received some empirical support and is of practical significance in the modification of human aggressive behavior.

A Social-Learning Perspective on Aggression

A social-learning perspective recognizes that we are constantly faced with a wide variety of situations that have the potential for leading to aggression. We are faced daily with frustrations and a range of emotionally arousing situations. The individual has a variety of options as to how he or she may label these situations and choose to respond to them. For example, if the person becomes emotionally aroused and labels that arousal as anger, he or she may then respond aggressively. If the individual were in the same situation but labeled that arousal as anxiety, there would be less of a chance that he or she might resort to aggression in that situation. This labeling may be related to the individual's past experience in similar situations, the effect of modeling of other people in the situation, etc. The point is that it is how the person labels the situation, and not the objective nature of the situation, that is the first determinant of the person's response.

A second major consideration is the kind of skills the individual has for handling the conflict situation. If the individual does not possess appropriate skills in conflict negotiation, assertiveness, or the like, he or she will be forced to use some other mode of responding. This may be a passive acceptance of the situation, or it may be an explosive attack directed at the presumed antagonist.

A third major determinant of aggressive behavior is the consequence that follows the episodes. If a person is consistently rewarded for aggressive behavior, that is, "he gets what he wants," it is more likely that he or she will again use aggressive behavior in a similar situation. If, on the other hand, the individual is unsuccessful or is severely punished, it is less likely that he or she will use an aggressive response in a similar situation.

Although the above presentation is something of a simplification of a detailed and comprehensive theory (see Bandura, 1973, for a more comprehensive presentation), it highlights the essential features. There is a wide variety of situations which have the potential for eliciting aggressive behavior. Whether that potential is realized depends on how the situation is labeled, the skills the individual has at his or her disposal, and the anticipated consequences of various actions (including past history in similar situations).

It is important to note that this theory does not preclude considerations such as the individual's biological makeup and the effects of drugs on behavior, or the like. Rather, it recognizes that any display of aggressive behavior is determined by a variety of different factors. This position is probably best presented by Bandura (1973):

> The social-learning theory of human aggression adopts the position that man is endowed with neurophysiological mechanisms that enable him to behave aggressively, but the activation of these mechanisms depends upon the appropriate stimulation and is subject to cortical control. Therefore, the specific forms that aggressive behavior takes, the frequency with which it is expressed, the situation in which it is displayed, and the specific targets selected for attack are largely determined by social experience. (pp. 29–30)

Thus, although our biology plays a part in our aggression, it is not the sole determinant. The situations which lead to aggression and how it is expressed are largely determined by our social experience, the models we see, and the consequences of our own actions.

It should be noted that this view of aggression has important implications for the use of social-skills training. *Skills training teaches individuals to label situations appropriately, and gives them appropriate alternative ways to respond.* When faced with an interpersonal conflict, the individual thus has an alternative to aggression, or another way to handle the situation. This approach very much relies on accelerating or increasing appropriate alternatives to aggression, rather than simply attempting to punish the individual when he or she behaves aggressively. Rather than teaching the individual what not to do in the situation, this approach teaches the individual what he or she should do (Frederiksen & Eisler, 1977).

The rationale for this approach is nicely outlined by Bandura (1973):

> Socially and verbally unskilled persons, having limited means for handling discord, are likely to become physically aggressive on slight provocation, especially in contacts where violent conduct is viewed favorably. Assaultive people can therefore profit greatly from a treatment program that teaches them nonviolent techniques for handling interpersonal conflicts. By enlarging their repertoire of skills, aggressors achieve greater freedom in meeting present and future problems. (pp. 255–256)

Does it work? Does training people in more appropriate conflict-resolution skills actually reduce the incidence of inappropriate aggression? As with many similar areas of research, it is difficult to give a definite answer to the question. Yet, the data that are available are very encouraging. This general approach has been reported successful in studies with children (Gittleman, 1965), adolescents (Elder, Edelstein, & Narick, 1979; Kaufman & Wagner, 1972), as well as adults (Matson & Stephans, 1978; McKinlay, Pachman, & Frederiksen, 1977; Foy, Eisler, & Pinkston, 1975; Frederiksen & Eisler, 1977; Frederiksen, Jenkins, Foy, & Eisler, 1976; Rainwater & Frederiksen, 1978; Rimm, Hill, Brown, & Stuart, 1974; Simon & Frederiksen, 1977; Wallance, Teigen, Liberman, & Baker, 1973). These positive results have been obtained with a wide variety of individuals, who were both in and out of an institution, covering treatment in both individual and group contexts. Although much research remains to be done, these preliminary results are indeed encouraging.

This is not to say that social-skills training should be applied uncritically, nor is it meant to imply that social-skills training constitutes a complete therapeutic approach to any particular individual. Individuals with problems of aggression need comprehensive assessment and may be appropriate for a variety of other interventions. However, social-skills training is an effective way to equip the individual with more appropriate means of solving interpersonal conflict.

Applying Social-Skills Training

Let us now turn our attention to how social-skills training can be used with the inappropriately aggressive individual. There are four topics to be considered: (1) *Establishing a working relationship.* In this phase, the rationale for the approach to be taken is presented and discussed with the client. The goal is to get the client's active support and agreement on a course of action. (2) *Assessment.* In this stage, a comprehensive assessment of the client's interpersonal functioning in areas to be changed is conducted. (3) *Skill development.* Here, the training techniques are applied to develop the needed skills that were identified during assessment. (4) *Maintenance.* In this phase, increasing attention is directed toward getting the client actually to use these skills in his or her natural environment and maintain their use over time. To help illustrate this entire process, we will follow an individual case through all four stages. The case we will use is based on an actual individual; however, it has been altered to protect the individual's identity.

Joey Wallace is a 29-year-old male. He was recently separated from Barbara, his wife of six years. Joey and Barbara have two children, a boy, Joey, Jr., six years of age, and a girl, Nadine, three years of age. Joey came in seeking help shortly after he was separated from Barbara. He complained of feelings of depression and remorse following the recent separation which he blamed on his "bad temper."

Joey's temper has been getting him in more and more difficulty lately. About a year and a half ago he lost his job and a chance for rapid advancement after he "blew up" at his boss when he asked him to stay late and work one Friday. He has also gotten into other heated arguments and threatened his co-workers. Another area of concern has been his relationship with his family. Joey has been resorting to more and more physical force around the home. This has taken the form of slapping Barbara during arguments and using excessive force when disciplining the children. Joey dates his difficulties back to his time in the service. When he was an adolescent he describes himself as shy and having few friends. In the service he entered into a circle of drinking buddies who would frequently top off the evening with at least one brawl.

During the interview, Joey sits with his eyes downcast, speaks in a low tone of voice, and sounds remorseful and depressed. He protests that he's "at the end of his rope" and doesn't know what to do. "I try and take as much as I can but sometimes its just more than I can handle. When a person says too much I blow up; I just lose it and end up yelling or hitting. It's almost like I'm another person."

Establishing the Relationship

The relationship between the trainer and the client is particularly important in the case of excessive aggression. These individuals very often feel alone with their problem and rejected by society. It is important that the trainer be accepting of the individual and help him or her feel comfortable in discussing and working on the problem.

The rationale for the social-skills approach to inappropriate aggression also presents something of a challenge to the trainer. For many potential helpers, the ideas that something like assertive training would be helpful with an aggressive individual is very alien. They tend to feel that such individuals are "too assertive." This, of course, is an inappropriate view. Assertiveness, or expressing one's opinions and wishes directly, is not to be confused with inappropriate aggression. Excessive aggression or excessive passivity can both cause problems since they are both ineffective ways of achieving one's aims.

TRAINER: Now that I understand something about the problem that brought you here, I would like to discuss how we might proceed from here. I would like to try an approach called social-skills training.

CLIENT: What's that?

TRAINER: Social-skills training is an approach where we first do a thorough assessment of how you interact with other people. We pay close attention to those problem situations that have led to your temper outbursts in the past; then we go about training you in more effective ways to handle those situations.

CLIENT: But my problem is temper. It doesn't have anything to do with other people.

TRAINER: Yes, your temper is a problem, but in discussing this difficulty it became clear that your temper problem is always tied to other people. In each occasion when you have lost your temper, it has always been following some kind of a conflict or problem with another person. That's why we focus on what it is about those situations that brings on the temper problem.

CLIENT: But I get along with most people. It's only some people that bother me and that's only once in a while. That's normal, isn't it?

TRAINER: Yes, having difficulty with some people is normal. But sometimes that normal conflict leads to trouble. We'll look at what you actually do in a variety of situations. Sometimes what we do or the way we handle the situation can lead to problems. Rather than working the situation out, we become frustrated and angry and get to the end of our rope. When that happens, it is easy to lose your temper and do something that you are sorry for later.

CLIENT: That sounds a lot like me. I try to take as much as I can, but sometimes its just too much and I blow my cool.

TRAINER: That's where the social-skills training might be very helpful. It might give you better ways of handling those situations before you get to the end of your rope. Our goal would be to give you a new tool or a skill at handling these difficult situations before you feel backed into a corner or at the end of your rope.

Notice that even in this brief passage, the trainer has attempted to give the client an outline of what is to come and why his approach might be useful with the client's problem. He also responded to the client's doubts about whether social-skills training would be useful for him. When the client is comfortable with this approach and has agreed that this is the way to proceed, it is time to begin a more detailed assessment. However, it is important to remember that the client's cooperation must be ongoing. It is not enough to get grudging acceptance of the approach at the beginning of training and then forget about the client's cooperation. Lack of cooperation can hamper the trainer's effectiveness, slow the client's progress, and even result in the client's dropping out of training altogether.

Assessment

When the client's full, informed cooperation is obtained, a more detailed assessment can begin. During the initial phases of working with a client, the trainer has probably developed a good overall feel for some of the client's social-skills deficits. For example, based on the client's history, the trainer may develop the hypothesis that the client has difficulty in refusing unreasonable requests, giving praise or feedback, or negotiating conflicts with other people. These general impressions are useful and help guide the course of more detailed assessment.

To conduct this more detailed assessment, the trainer must first pinpoint the problem situations. In what specific situations does the client have difficulty? What is the client not doing that he or she should be? Who is the client typically with when aggressive episodes occur? These and similar questions help the trainer to understand the nature of the specific deficits the client has and set the stage for subsequent training.

A good way to begin this detailed assessment is to start with some of the most recent aggressive episodes. The trainer can then question the client in some detail to understand the nature of the situation. When the trainer has enough information about the situation, it can then be role-played.

TRAINER: When we talked earlier, you mentioned that one of the most difficult situations for you is when your boss makes an unreasonable request.
CLIENT: That's right—it just drives me through the ceiling.
TRAINER: Describe the last time that a situation like that happened.
CLIENT: Boy, do I remember that one! It's the time I blew up at the boss and he fired me.
TRAINER: When was this?
CLIENT: Well, it was the day I lost my job. It was a Friday, and I was planning to go bowling that evening with some of the guys.
TRAINER: What did the boss do?
CLIENT: He asked me to work late.
TRAINER: How did he ask you?
CLIENT: Well, he came up to me about five minutes before quitting time; some of the other guys had already left early, and he looked around for someone and then saw me. He came over and said that I needed to stay late.
TRAINER: What did you say?
CLIENT: I told him I couldn't do it.
TRAINER: What happened then?
CLIENT: Well, he just got real mad, and said I was fired.
TRAINER: Let's see if I have this right. The last time the situation occurred, it was on a Friday evening, five minutes before quitting time. The boss approached you, looked around for someone else and then said, "Can you stay late and work?" Is that about the way the situation started?
CLIENT: That's pretty close. Actually he was kind of smart-alecky about it and said, "Hey, you, I need you to stay late."

With this kind of pinpointed information about problem areas and specific problem situations, the trainer can begin to structure role-playing situations. With the role-playing situations, the trainer has a chance actually to observe how the client acts in the situation rather than rely on the client's report of how he or she acts in the situation. This is an important advantage because the behavior of the client may be distorted by the client's selective memory, a desire to look better in the trainer's eyes, or simply an inability to observe one's own behavior accurately.

The identification and pinpointing of problem areas can also come from information supplied by people other than the client. For example, a client's spouse, or someone else who is in a position to know something about the client, may be able to identify problematic situations that the client has forgotten or chooses not to reveal. The use of other informants is particularly important when working with the problem of aggression, since the client may be prone to minimize the severity of the problem.

TRAINER: Now that we've identified a number of situations that are a problem for you, let's role-play some of these and see how you actually handle the situation. You will remember from our earlier discussions that role-playing is a way for me to see what you do in a situation rather than having to rely on memory, or other people's descriptions of the situation. To start with, I will first describe the situation, and then you react to me as if I were actually the other person in the situation. Remember to do what you would do if you were really in the situation. Don't describe what you would do, actually say the words you would say in the way you would say them.

CLIENT: But I'm not really in the situation. Isn't this kind of artificial?

TRAINER: Yes, it may seem a bit artificial at first, but it still gives me a better idea of the way you act in the situation than just having you describe it. I think you will also find that after we do some of this role-playing it will become quite natural and seem much more realistic.

CLIENT: Okay, let's give it a try.

TRAINER: Okay, let's start with the situation you described about your boss asking you to stay late. Imagine that we are actually in that situation, and I am your boss. It is Friday evening, five minutes before quitting time. You have plans to go bowling with some of your friends. Your boss walks up, looks around for someone else, and then spots you. He comes over and says, "Hey, you, I need you to stay late today."

CLIENT: Well, I would tell him "no way."

TRAINER: Don't describe what you would do, actually say it. Let's start again. "Hey, you, I need you to stay late."

CLIENT: (*eyes downcast, hesitating*) Uh, well, I don't think I'm really going to be able to.

TRAINER: (*gruffly*) Look, fellow, it's important. I'll only need you for about two hours.

CLIENT: (*long pause*) Well, I don't know, it's, uh, just that, uh, I've, uh, got something else, uh, that I would kind of like to do.

TRAINER: (*gruffly*) Look fellow, I said it's important!

CLIENT: (*angrily, yelling*) Well, goddammit, I've had enough of this shit, it's too much. I'm not going to take any more of it. You can just take that job of yours and shove it!

TRAINER: Look, fellow, if that's the way you feel about it, you can just pick up your paycheck. I don't have to listen to this kind of stuff from you, you're fired.

After the role-playing is completed is an excellent time to question the client about his thoughts and feelings in that situation. This kind of information can add important assessment data to guide the trainer in developing more appropriate strategies and evaluations of the situation.

TRAINER: Was that close to the way it happend?

CLIENT: That is the way it happened! You're just as bad as he was.

TRAINER: What were you thinking when the boss approached you and asked you to stay late?

CLIENT: I was thinking I was caught in the trap. There wasn't much I could do, and I knew it was going to be trouble.

TRAINER: Why was that?

CLIENT: Well, this kind of thing had happened before, and I knew there was nothing I could do. I had taken as much of it as I could.

TRAINER: What other alternatives did you consider in this situation? What other way could you have handled it?

CLIENT: Well, there wasn't really any other way that I could see except to stay late, and I had about all I could take.

The trainer now has a good idea of how the client would handle this problem situation. He not only has had a chance to observe a sample of the client's behavior, but he also has an idea of what some of the client's thoughts and feelings were. In this case, the client behaved very passively. He hesitated, did not explain his position, had poor eye contact, poor voice volume, and generally behaved in a passive manner. When the boss persisted, the client countered by becoming angry. This is a clear example of where training the client in behaving more assertively gives him an option he did not previously have. In other words, it gives him an alternative to the aggression; something which the client felt was not possible.

Assessment would proceed in the above manner until the full range of problem situations was sampled. When this sampling is complete, the trainer should have a relatively complete listing of the specific behaviors to be changed. For example, with the illustration used above, some of the specific behaviors might be eye contact, appropriate gestures, more appropriate requests for behavior change, etc. When this assessment is complete, the task of actually training the client in the new skills can begin.

Skill Development

The purpose of the skill-development phase is to give the client more effective ways to handle the situations that previously led to difficulty. For each situation, the basic four-step training procedure is used: (1) rationale and instructions; (2) modeling; (3) behavioral rehearsal; and (4) feedback.

The sequence starts out with the therapist describing the behavior to be trained and giving a rationale for its use. Why is this particular behavior important, and how will it help meet the client's goals?

TRAINER: I would like you to try something different the next time we role-play this situation. This time I want you to tell the boss directly that you are not able to stay after work, even though you understand his need to have someone there. Also, offer another suggestion about how you might help solve his problem some other way. For example, staying late on another night, or something of that nature. By doing this, you not only make it clear that you are not able to help him on this particular occasion, but you also show him that you understand his problem and are willing to help him in some other way. That way the boss can feel that you are responsible and care about getting the job done even though you are not available to help at this particular time.

CLIENT: But that won't work.

TRAINER: Well, its possible that it might not work, but at least it has a greater chance of success, because you show the boss that you are interested in helping him even though you can't help him on this particular occasion. It makes you seem like a more responsible person.

CLIENT: I don't know if I can do it.

TRAINER: Well, we'll give it a try and practice it until you feel comfortable doing it. Let me give you an example of what I mean.

At this point the trainer is now ready to model the desired behavior. As we mentioned in earlier chapters, this modeling could be done with audiotape models, videotape, or film models, live by the trainer, or even by other members of a group if training is done in a group context. In this particular instance, the client is working one-to-one with the trainer so the therapist has chosen to model the behavior live.

TRAINER: To demonstrate it, why don't you play the part of the boss in the situation, and I'll be you. Let's start with the same situation. It's Friday late, and the boss comes up to you and starts talking.

CLIENT: (*in gruff voice*) Hey, you, I need you to stay late.

TRAINER: (*assertively*) I'm sorry, I'm not going to be able to stay late this evening, but if you need some help, I might be able to come in tomorrow or work late Monday.

CLIENT: Well, okay. Why don't you come in tomorrow morning.

TRAINER: (*laughing*) You didn't put up much of a fight as the boss that time.

CLIENT: Well, there really wasn't much I could say.

TRAINER: That's the point. It's pretty effective when you show the person that you are interested in the problem and offer them alternatives even though you can't help at that time.

CLIENT: I guess so. I guess I'd never really thought of it that way.

When modeling is complete, the client should then have an opportunity to try the behavior. It is usually more effective to give the client the opportunity to role-play immediately following the modeling demonstration. In this way the client has the opportunity to apply the new behavior right away.

TRAINER: Okay, now this time you play yourself, and I'll be the boss again. Same situation.
CLIENT: Okay.
TRAINER: It's Friday afternoon again. I'm the boss and I approach you and say (*gruff voice*) "Hey, fellow, I need you to stay late."
CLIENT: (*low voice volume, eyes to the ground, slow speech*) I'm sorry, I can't stay tonight, but I can come in tomorrow. Will that be okay?
TRAINER: Look, fellow, I really need the help tonight, not tomorrow.
CLIENT: (*low voice volume, slow speech, eyes to the ground*) Well, I just can't help tonight, but I can come in tomorrow.
TRAINER: Okay, let's stop there.

After the client has rehearsed the new behavior, it is time to provide feedback. Had this practice or rehearsal been videotaped or audiotaped, the trainer could play the tape back and comment on the client's performance. If the performance is not taped, the therapist still makes similar comments, but does not have the benefit of the client's seeing himself objectively. As in other cases of feedback, it is important to keep feedback generally positive and specific, while still pointing out areas of needed improvement.

TRAINER: That was much better! You indicated that you couldn't help him tonight and still gave him an alternative. You weren't angry, and it made it much more difficult for the boss to get angry with you, and even when I persisted in giving you a hard time, you still didn't get aggressive.
CLIENT: Well, I can agree that it was better, but it still didn't feel comfortable.
TRAINER: That's to be expected at this stage. With more practice, it will become even more natural and comfortable. Now, let's role-play that situation again, but this time when you role-play it again use the same refusal and a suggestion for an alternative, as well as some indication that you understand the boss's situation. Be sure not to apologize for not being able to work. Its nothing that you have to feel sorry for. As long as you have made an attempt to understand his situation and be helpful, you have nothing to be sorry for.

At this point the sequence is again repeated. The feedback serves as additional instruction for what to do differently at the next role-playing. The trainer may have also modeled a somewhat different response for the client to give him even more options on the specific words to use. They would then rehearse the situation again, and more feedback would be provided. In this way, the skill is gradually built up over time. When the client has made good progress on this particular situation, they would then move on to another situation that presented more difficulty. For example, discussing a problem area with a co-worker. Another area for continued training is different behaviors. Besides working on the same kind of behavior in different situations, there are also other behaviors that need changing. In this instance, the client was still not using appropriate eye contact, voice intonation and volume, or hand gestures. All of these things would help him come across better. With repeated training sessions, the client develops the requisite skills to handle situations which were previously problematical.

Maintenance

The task of insuring that the client uses the new behaviors outside of treatment is always an important one. It takes on added significance when working with the aggressive individual since inappropriate aggression can have such devastating consequences. The general procedures used to enhance transfer of training to the natural environment are those identified in Chapter 6. Within the training situation every effort should be made to train effective behaviors, make the training as realistic as possible, train the client in the strategy of social skills as well as the specific behavior and, finally, insure that the client has adequate practice in the new behaviors. The reader will note that these strategies for enhancing transfer have already been included in the case example. The trainer went to some length to insure that the behaviors to be trained were effective ones. A thorough assessment was conducted to pinpoint the specific areas where the client needs to develop more effective skills. Another source of validation for the selection of effective behaviors has not been illustrated in the case example. The trainer could have drawn on other people from the client's same subculture to learn more about what behaviors work and what behaviors don't work in the client's particular setting. As we mentioned earlier, this strategy is especially effective when a group-training format is employed.

The trainer also attempted to make the training realistic. This was partly done through insuring that he had a good understanding of the individual's behavior in the critical situations.

TRAINER: You identified another problem area in negotiating conflicts with your wife.

CLIENT: That's right. We just can't seem to work out anything. We are fighting all the time.

TRAINER: Give me an example of this happening.

Here again the trainer is attempting to get a realistic assessment of another problem area. The trainer could go further in making training realistic by getting the client's wife in to role-play the situation, or, if that was not appropriate, to get a female role-playing partner. In other words, the training situation can be made more realistic by both insuring that the content or training material represents the actual situation and making sure that the context of training, that is, role-playing partner, setting, etc., is also realistic. Training in more effective interpersonal strategy is also a very critical element of the aggressive individual. As the case study illustrated, this particular client had a very limited range of alternatives. When faced with a conflict situation, he could either passively submit to the other person's demand, feeling resentment and anger, or attack the other person. Neither of these strategies is particularly effective in the long run. From the very beginning of training, care was taken to insure that the client realized that there were many possible ways of handling the situation. Enumerating these possibilities was an integral part of training.

TRAINER: In the situation you just described with your wife, you mentioned that you took all you could and then blew up at her. What other alternatives did you have?
CLIENT: I'm not sure. I guess just take some more.
TRAINER: What about using a similar strategy to the one we used with your boss. You acknowledged the needs that the boss had at the same time you disagreed with him.
CLIENT: I see what you are talking about. Sort of telling my wife that I know what she is talking about but I don't agree.
TRAINER: That's exactly right. Let's practice that situation.

Strategy training can also be used by varying the role-playing partner's response to the client. In one of the earlier role-playing situations, the trainer persisted with an unreasonable request even when the client's behavior was more appropriate. In subsequent practice sessions, the therapist could give in to the client's request, become angry with the client, make a counterrequest, etc. In this way, the client is taught to react to a number of possible situations. In other words, the client is taught to respond flexibly, based on the demands of the situation.

Finally, there is the notion of extending practice. With many individuals we are talking about a well-learned, engrained pattern of behavior that must be changed. It is not realistic for the trainer to expect to change a client's interpersonal style in a very brief time. The practice needs to be extended both by practicing the same situations repeatedly and by practicing a range of different situations until the client is comfortable with the new skills.

TRAINER: We've been practicing the situation where your boss approached you on a Friday night for quite a while, and you've become very good at handling it. What other kinds of situations cause similar problems?
CLIENT: Well, I'm not working, so there aren't any at work, but I'm still having problems at home.
TRAINER: Okay, let's pinpoint some of these situations.

Practice is extended until the client is comfortable in the full range of problematic situations. However, even when the client is comfortable role-playing the situations, he or she may not be fully utilizing the new skills outside the training situation.

   Four strategies that are centered outside training have been identified in Chapter 6: (1) use of graded homework assignments, (2) involving others in the treatment process, (3) development of self-management skills in the client, and (4) provision of follow-up or booster sessions. The use of graded homework assignments should be an integral part of training. It can begin at the same time as the skill development, and continue throughout training. Early assignments must be consistent with the client's level of progress. For example, at the beginning of training the assignment may involve a fairly easy-to-use skill in a nonproblematic situation.

TRAINER: Well, we had a good first session today. As I mentioned earlier, you will need to start practicing these skills outside training.
CLIENT: Well, I'm not sure I can do it as easily as I have done it here.
TRAINER: That's to be expected. For this week let's start out easy. We will take the skill we have been working on this week, and have you try it at least once before next session.
CLIENT: Okay.
TRAINER: This week I would like for you to identify at least one situation where somebody makes a request that you feel like refusing. Don't take the most difficult situation; take one that's fairly easy to refuse.
CLIENT: Okay.
TRAINER: Then when the person makes the request, I want you to refuse the request but tell the person making the request enough that he or she is sure you understand their situation, and also suggest an alternative. When you do this, I want you to jot down what the situation was, and how it went, so we can discuss it next time.
CLIENT: This sounds just like homework.
TRAINER: (laughing) It is.

As training progresses, the assignments become more difficult, reflecting the client's increasing level of skills. In this way the client is continually challenged to employ the skills, at the same time moving at a pace that allows ongoing success.

TRAINER: You've been doing real well on the negotiations with your wife. Let's tackle a more difficult homework assignment this week. This week I would like you to discuss the problem of money with your wife and try to negotiate a reasonable compromise.
CLIENT: That's going to be a tough one.
TRAINER: Yes, it is going to be more difficult, but if you use the principles we have been working on, I think you will make some progress. Remember that you don't need to reach a final solution, just work on it for this week.
CLIENT: Well, I think we can probably do that.

These graded homework assignments are then discussed at the sessions following their completion. On some occasions they will be successful, and on others, they won't. In instances where the success is less than hoped for, the homework can provide a good starting point for additional role-playing and working on those situations. In instances where the client is successful, it provides an excellent opportunity for praise and reinforcement for the progress that is being made.

In the example we have been presenting here, the trainer has not been very effective in involving others in training. As is quite often the case, this client has come in at a time when he is estranged from his family and isolated from many of his friends. This is often the case with very aggressive individuals. They do not seek treatment until the long-term consequences of their aggression have become quite severe. In the instances where the individual's family or friends are available, it is an excellent idea to involve them. This involvement can range from simply informing them of the progress all the way to having them an active part of the treatment. For this particular client, it would be useful to have his wife come in for training. However, the circumstances were such that, although she was available outside training, she was not willing to come in to the training sessions themselves. It is sometimes the case that, as the client begins to show improvement outside training, those in his or her environment become more willing to be active participants in the training process. This possibility should be considered and utilized whenever possible.

As we mentioned in Chapter 6, self-management skills offer an exciting but seldom-used technique for enhancing transfer of training. Covert modeling or rehearsal, prompting, self-monitoring, and self-reinforcement are all potential techniques that may be useful in a particular situation. In the case example described above, the trainer already begins to employ some self-management techniques. Specifically, he asked the client to monitor situations that presented problems. This technique could be still further refined to yield more detailed information.

TRAINER: Last time I had you jot down the situation that caused problems. Let's do the same thing next week, but this time let's get a little bit more information.
CLIENT: What kind of information?
TRAINER: Carry a little 3 × 5 notebook around with you, and each time you encounter one of the situations that makes you angry, record the day, the time, where you are, who you are with, and what the situation was. For example, the situation might be your friend John asking you to lend him your car for the weekend.
CLIENT: That would get me ticked off.
TRAINER: Then write a note about what you did, in other words, how you handled the situation, and the outcome of the situation, what happened afterward. Finally, I would like you to give yourself a rating of how angry you became with that situation. Let's use a 0 to 10 scale. Zero is not angry at all, and 10 would be extremely angry; as angry as you ever remember being.
CLIENT: That's a lot to record.
TRAINER: It is, but it will give us a lot more useful information on what kinds of situations present problems for you.

When the client returns the information, the trainer can then review it with him to establish patterns of difficult situations and make training more appropriate.

Finally, there is the issue of providing adequate follow-up and booster sessions. It is often convenient to develop a pattern of gradually lengthening time between training sessions. This makes the transition between regular training and follow-up a smooth one. For example, if weekly training sessions have been held, toward the end of training the trainer might start stretching the sessions out to one every other week, one every third week, and eventually one a month. In this way, the end of training is not abrupt, and the client does not feel that he or she is "pushed out" prematurely.

TRAINER: You've been doing very well both in here and outside training. How are you feeling about your progress?
CLIENT: Real good. I think I'm finally starting to get it.
TRAINER: Okay. Let's skip next week's session, and wait two weeks. This will give you a little bit more time to try some of the skills outside.
CLIENT: Okay. That sounds fine to me.
TRAINER: If you are successful with that, we can continue gradually to stretch out

the time between sessions, and start to deal with the difficult situations only as they come up.

Using this gradual *fading* procedure, the client has the opportunity to bring up problems and difficult situations without having the stigma of having failed and needing to return. The end of treatment is a gradual process. As the client starts to use the new skills in his or her natural environment, the need for additional training gradually disappears.

Summary

Inappropriate aggression is a problem of major importance to all of us. In attempting to understand the problem, one is faced with a number of difficulties. Among them is the fact that we use the term "aggression" to refer to behaviors that may be either positively or negatively valued by society. In addition, the same behavior may be viewed as aggressive in one context, but not aggressive in a different situation. A wide variety of theories have been used to explain the variety of behaviors labeled as aggression. Some of these have focused on innate instincts, or aggressive drives over which the individual has limited control.

One useful alternative is a social-learning approach to aggression. This approach recognizes that aggression is affected by the social context, the availability of skills to handle the situation, and the consequences that follow episodes of attack. One implication of this theory is that a useful approach to the problem of aggression is that of equipping the individual with more appropriate ways of handling interpersonal conflicts. The limited research that is available on the success of this approach indicates that it does seem to be useful in increasing effective social behavior and reducing inappropriate aggression.

Four phases of the treatment process were identified and illustrated with a case example. The first phase is *developing a working relationship* in which the approach to be taken is presented and discussed with the client in an effort to obtain the client's active support and agreement on a course of action. The second phase, *assessment*, involves a comprehensive evaluation of the client's interpersonal functioning with special emphasis on the skills used to handle conflict situations. *Skills training* is the third stage, involving the actual development of the client's new patterns of behavior. *Maintenance*, the final phase is concerned with insuring that the client actually uses these skills outside the training situation.

10

Training Social Skills at Work

Overview

- Effective interpersonal functioning is critical in the work setting.
- Traditional approaches to training have generally been oriented toward "fads" in the absence of empirical documentation of effectiveness.
- Social-skills training offers an effective alternative to producing changes in job-related behaviors. These changes are subject to documentation.
- Job-interview skills can be important in obtaining suitable employment. The available evidence indicates that they can be enhanced by using social-skills training procedures.
- Supervisory skills have traditionally been an important area of concentration. Social-skills training has been receiving increasing empirical support as an effective way to shape these behaviors.
- Effective communication skills (interviewing) is a third example of job-related social skills. A group-oriented workshop-training format is illustrated.

It is probably hard to overestimate the importance of the work place in our lives. For many of us it dominates our waking hours. It is not only the source of our livelihood, but also a source of joy and frustration. And many of those joys and frustrations, successes and failures, are intimately related to the nature of our interactions with others. The list of social skills that may be necessary in one's job is long and varied. Obtaining a job, presenting an idea to a superior, handling a complaint from a subordinate, attempting to secure one's rights, communicating with a client, or handling a complaint are just a few examples of the range of situations that require effective skills.

The need for effective social behavior on the job has not gone unnoticed. Millions of dollars are spent each year in attempts to train individuals to be more successful. Courses in sales training, effective communication, management and supervisory skills, and the like abound. Unfortunately, much of this attention is often directed toward the pursuit of the latest fad in the training literature. This infelicitous characteristic of the training literature is thus nicely summed up by John Campbell:

> By and large, the training and development literature is voluminous, non-empirical, non-theoretical, poorly written and dull. As noted elsewhere, it is faddish to an extreme. The fads center around the introduction of new techniques and follow a characteristic pattern. The technique appears on the horizon and develops a large stable of advocates who first describe its successful use in a number of situations. The second wave of advocates busy themselves trying out numerous modifications of the basic technique. A few empirical studies may be carried out to demonstrate that the method works. Then the inevitable backlash sets in and a few vocal opponents begin to criticize the usefulness of the techniques, most often in the absence of data. Such criticism typically has very little effect. What does have an effect is the appearance of another new technique and a repetition of the same cycle. (Campbell, 1971, pp. 565–566)

Against this rather discouraging background, the social-skills training approach has emerged as an important new perspective (cf. Kraut, 1976). There are probably several reasons for this emergence. First, social-skills training focuses primarily on observable behaviors and lends itself to quantification and verification. Put another way, the benefits of training can be more easily measured and documented with this approach (Goldstein & Sorcher, 1974; Kraut, 1976). Second, this approach takes into account what we know about principles of effective learning. Procedures such as providing a rationale and detailed instructions, modeling, practice, feedback, and principles to promote transfer of training are all based on knowledge of how people learn (Goldstein & Sorcher, 1974; Kraut, 1976). Finally, there is a growing body of empirical research to demonstrate that the techniques are in fact successful (e.g., Burnaska, 1976; Byham, Adams, & Kiggins, 1976; Moses & Ritchie, 1976). More than with most other approaches to training, here the practitioner can be guided by evidence rather than hunch, speculation, or opinion.

The range of situations to which skills-training may be applied is as diverse as are the interpersonal demands found in the world of work.

Relating to co-workers, clients, customers, superiors, and subordinates are all expected of us. Presenting one's ideas effectively, negotiating, securing one's interpersonal rights, making a sales presentation, handling a customer complaint, are just some of the examples of the range of skills that could be trained using this approach. We have selected three areas in which to illustrate job-related skills. These areas represent a cross section of the many possible applications. These skills are: (1) job seeking (employment interview), (2) supervisory situations, and (3) effective communication.

Job-Interview Skills

Regardless of its validity as a selection device, the job interview occupies a key role in the employee-selection process. Rightly or wrongly, the recruiter's impression of the job candidate can have a very pronounced impact on the decision to hire. The extent of this impact was partially documented in a survey of 195 corporate representatives of United States business firms conducted by Drake, Kaplan, and Stone (1972). They found that over three-quarters of the respondents indicated that the initial interviewer's impression was "very important" in making the decision to continue or terminate the employment process. In addition, nearly three-quarters of the respondents also felt that the interviewer's impression was more important than the candidate's resume. Further, 81% of the respondents rated the interviewer's opinion as more important than all the candidate's references. The importance of the interview, of course, varies with the type of job sought. For example, Norman (1976) found that behavior during the interview had a greater impact when the job being filled was that of a sales representative rather than an assembly-line worker. Nonetheless, behavior during the interview was still an important factor for technically oriented positions. In recognition of this need, a number of authors have suggested the systematic use of behaviorally based training procedures to develop the ability to make positive impressions during the interview (Forrest & Baumgarten, 1975; Hollandsworth, Dressel, & Stevens, 1977; Prazak, 1969).

The data that are currently available tend to support the notion that behaviorally based training procedures can aid effectively in developing job-interview skills (e.g., Barbee & Keil, 1973; Hollandsworth et al., 1977; Keil & Barbee, 1973; Kelly, Laughlin, Claiborne, & Patterson, 1979). Perhaps one of the best demonstrations of the impact that skills-training can have is a controlled single-case experiment reported by Hollandsworth and his associates (Hollandsworth, Glazeski, & Dressel, 1978). In this report, the authors describe their work with a 30-year-old male who had recently graduated from college with a degree in General Business. Although he had a three-year history of relevant work experience, over sixty job interieews conducted during a 5-month period following graduation resulted in not a single job offer.

During the initial assessment, the investigators conducted role-played job interviews to observe the client's performance. The results of these evaluations indicated that the subject's responses often were

> . . . rambling, disjointed, and difficult to follow. At times he lost his train of thought and lapsed into periods of silence accompanied by blank stares and an emotionless facial expression. The client reported extreme anxiety during these interviews. (p. 260)

Based on this analysis, the trainers came up with three target behaviors to be increased.

The first of these behaviors, *focused responses,* was defined as concise and unambiguous answers to the interviewer's questions. If the answer was rambling, disorganized, or otherwise difficult to understand, it was considered inappropriate. *Overt coping statements* were defined as any statement the client used in order to correct a verbal mistake or reestablish his composure. Examples might include statements such as "excuse me" or "let me start over." The importance of these statements were that they reflected a marked contrast to his previous pattern of total silence or continued speech dysfluency. The third target behavior was *subject-generated questions.* Any attempt to request additional information, feedback, or clarification of an interviewer's question was categorized as an instance of this target behavior.

To insure that the social-skills training had the desired impact, the investigators also conducted some additional assessments. At the beginning of training and again following its completion, the client was interviewed by an individual (previously unknown to the client) who had a good deal of experience in conducting employment interviews. This interview was entirely unstructured and represented a test of the client's skill. Investigators were also able to take recordings of the client's physiological reactions during this interview. The physiological recordings provided an index of the client's arousal or anxiety level during the interview. In addition, investigators also arranged to make unobtrusive observations of this client in his employment setting. This allowed them to determine whether his behavior changed in other work-related situations as well as in the role-playing and job-interview situations.

Training was sequentially introduced to each of the three target behaviors. On the *focused response* the client was first given a rationale for the importance of the focused response and then given instructions on the nature of focused responses. Next he viewed a videotape and live model demonstrating the use of the focused response to typical interview questions. The client was then given an opportunity to practice this new behavior as he and the trainer role-played an interview situation. Finally, a videotape of this role-playing was replayed, and the therapist provided feedback and encouragement on the positive aspects of his performance while pointing out ways in which his response might be further improved. This training sequence was continued until the client's ability to make focused responses reached nearly optimal levels. The training was then directed toward the use of *coping statements* at appropriate times. When coping statements had improved, the focus of training shifted to increasing *subject-generated questions*. In short, when the client mastered each interview skill, the training moved on to the next target behavior.

The results of this intervention were very encouraging. Over the course of training, the subject showed marked increases on each of the three target skills. These changes tended to occur only after training was introduced on each skill, indicating that improvement was the result of training and not simply of practice. In addition, the client also showed marked improvement in speech fluency. Prior to training, the client was showing a very high rate of speech disturbances, over 15 per minute. By the end of training, the rate of speech dysfluency was down to approximately one or two per minute. Importantly, the client also showed changes in his behavior during sessions in which he received no training. In addition, the physiological data from the pre- and posttraining interview indicated that this client was showing less anxiety during the interview situation. These data were in agreement with the client's self-report of feeling less anxious during the interview. Finally, the data from the unobtrusive observations in his work situation indicated that he was also showing better eye contact, more fluent speech, and was rated as improved in personal appearance, composure, and appropriateness of speech content. In short, this individual's behavior showed improvement, not only in the training situation, but also in a simulated employment interview, and in his work environment.

The bottom line on job-interview skills is of course whether the person gets an appropriate job. In this case, the results are impressive. At the end of training, the client had three additional job interviews. Each of these three interviews resulted in definite job offers, one of which the client accepted. Thus, he was successful in obtaining employment suited to his background and interests, at a salary that represented a 250% increase over his pretraining income. The authors also report follow-up at two-, four-, six-, and eight-month intervals. At each of these contacts, the client reported doing well.

Job-interview skills represents an important area of application for social-skills training techniques. The job interview is a critical link in the chain that leads to appropriate employment. Yet it can be a stumbling block to many individuals who are otherwise well qualified to meet the demands of a particular position. Further, it is usually a fairly well-circumscribed situation which lends itself nicely to role-playing, modeling, rehearsal, and feedback. Job-interview training also seems appropriate for a variety of different individuals. Kelly *et al.* (1979) successfully used social-skills training, conducted in a group format, with individuals showing marked deficits in social functioning. Each of the six clients were former psychiatric patients with severe emotional problems. On the other hand, Hollandsworth *et al.* (1977) reported success using a similar group-training procedure with college seniors showing normal social behavior. In short, it seems that the job-interview-skills training is effective with a wide variety of individuals, and can successfully be conducted in a group format. All these characteristics should add to the practical usefulness of this approach to preparing individuals for this very important social interaction.

Supervisory Skills

Effective supervsion of employees represents a key element in the success of any enterprise. As organizations are faced with demands for increased productivity, fair and equitable treatment of all employees, and the adaptation to ever changing environmental circumstances, the importance of effective supervision increases. However, the development of improved supervisory skills is not a simple matter. The supervisor is often faced with a bewildering array of problems and challenges. To many supervisors, their job seems to be an unending series of "putting out fires."

Social-skills training is being increasingly called on to meet the need for developing effective supervisory skills. Perhaps the seminal work in this area is a small volume by Goldstein and Sorcher (1974). In this volume, entitled *Changing Supervisor Behavior*, the authors outline their approach to the development of more effective supervisory skills. Their approach is labeled Applied Learning and involves training procedures very similar to those described in the first section of this volume. The social-skills training approach has been receiving increased attention under various labels, such as Behavior Modeling (Kraut, 1976), Interpersonal Skills Training (Burnaska, 1976), and Interaction Modeling (Byham *et al.*, 1976). The research on the effectiveness of social-skills training is encouraging. Goldstein and Sorcher (1974) report important increases in supervisor retention and overall worker productivity. Burnaska (1976) reports increases in supervisors' ability to handle specific difficult situations. Importantly, the supervisors showed greater skill in handling these situations four months after training compared with their performance immediately following its completion. Similar positive results were found in a study by Moses and Ritchie (1976). In this study, conducted at AT&T, matched supervisors were randomly assigned to either training or control conditions. When later tested in their ability to handle three difficult situations (absenteeism problem, discrimination problem, and theft problem), the trained supervisors were consistently rated as superior to their untrained counterparts.

An important question is the degree to which these new skills are actually used in the job situation. The study by Byham *et al.* (1976) looked at this question. Supervisors were trained in skills to handle common problems such as orienting a new employee, handling a complaint, etc. A randomly selected sample of subordinates working under both trained and untrained supervisors were then interviewed regarding how their supervisor handled the specific problem situations. These responses were then evaluated to determine whether the supervisors were using the skills that were previously taught. The results showed a consistent pattern of skill utilization by the supervisors. Finally, a study by Smith (1976) investigated the effects of social-skills training, given to managers, on their employees' morale and their customers' satisfaction. Managers were taught how to conduct effective meetings and how to communicate more effectively with customers. Results indicated that managers receiving training demonstrated superior social skills when later assessed. Importantly, these improved skills were associated with increased employee morale, improved sales, and greater customer satisfaction.

The above results must not be accepted uncritically. Each of the studies has methodological problems that limit the kinds of conclusions that can be drawn. Further, some of the changes reported are relatively weak. Thus, although they may be "statistically significant," their practical significance is open to question. Yet, the results are encouraging from two perspectives. First, the trainers are making an active attempt to evaluate the impact of the social-skills training. This stands in marked contrast to Campbell's description of the training literature in general (Campbell, 1971). If we are ever to break out of the cycle of one fad after another, this evaluation is an important first step. Second, the results tend to document the effectiveness of the social-skills training approach.

Although each individual study has its flaws, the aggregate results are clearly encouraging.

In training supervisory skills, it is important to remember that there is probably no single "supervisory skill." Rather, there are complex combinations of skills that are required for effective supervision. In one situation, the supervisor may need to ask the appropriate questions and be a good listener. In another situation, the supervisor may need to give clear, unambiguous instructions. In short, the required skills probably vary from situation to situation. The usual approach to handling this dilemma has involved specifying a series of situations that may be potentially problematic to the supervisor. The supervisor is then trained to handle those situations in which he or she shows skill deficits. Examples of some of these problem situations, taken from Goldstein and Sorcher (1974), are shown in Table IX.

It is important to remember that the demands that are placed upon the supervisor vary from one organization to the next. In some organizations, orienting new employees may be a critical part of the supervisor's job. For other supervisors, handling discrimination complaints may be critical. The point is that the areas assessed need to be relevant to the demands of the supervisor's job.

To illustrate this entire process, let us take the example of a supervisor having difficulty in delegating tasks and giving effective direction to subordinants. Barbara French is 31 years old. In her two years with the Universal Gear Corporation, she has consistently distinguished herself with the quality of her work, enthusiasm for her job, and overall productivity. Of particular note has been her ability to relate well to her co-workers and supervisors. Not surprisingly, she was spotted for her management potential and recently promoted to a supervisory position. However, shortly after her promotion, she began to run into difficulty. She was looking harried and overworked, and complained to her fellow supervisors that her subordinants appeared "lazy" and unwilling to "take the initiative."

Assessment of this situation first involved an analysis of what kinds of skills were required for effective functioning in her supervisory position. Did her job involve orienting new employees? Was she frequently faced with discrimination complaints? Was she required to conduct meetings or provide feedback to individual employees? This kind of specification allows the trainer to determine what kinds of skills are necessary. When the range of skills that are required has been specified, the trainer can then go about assessing those areas to determine where the supervisor may need to develop more effective skills. In some cases, the trainer may have a good idea of where to begin this assessment, based on the

Table IX. Examples of Situations Used in Supervisory Training[a]

- Orienting a new employee.
- Teaching the job.
- Motivating the poor performer.
- Correcting inadequate work quantity.
- Correcting inadequate work quality.
- Reducing absenteeism among disadvantaged workers.
- Reducing turnover among disadvantaged workers.
- Handling the racial-discrimination complaint.
- Handling the reverse-discrimination complaint.
- Reducing resentment of the female supervisor.
- Discussing personal work habits with an employee.
- Discussing formal corrective action with an employee.
- Giving recognition to the average employee.
- Overcoming resistance to change.
- Reducing evaluation resistance.
- Delegating responsibility.
- Conducting a performance review.

[a]After Goldstein and Sorcher (1974, p. 3).

history of a particular problem. In the example of Barbara French, the trainer might well suspect that delegating authority could be an important area to assess. However, the trainer should be cautious, lest he or she overlook important areas of functioning. As we have repeatedly stressed, we cannot assume that someone has adequate skills in an area simply because they report no difficulty. Many times the individual may be unaware or unwilling to admit that their behavior is less than effective. Assessment must replace assumption.

For the purpose of this example, we shall limit our discussion to situations requiring the delegation of responsibility. The starting place is obtaining a sample of the client's behavior in the relevant situation

TRAINER: The next area I'd like to take a look at is delegating authority. Can you think of a recent example in which you've tried to delegate some responsibility to a subordinate? In other words, a situation where you've needed to give one of the workers responsibility for completing a task.

CLIENT: Yes. There was a situation just the other day. The weekly quality-control reports were getting out of hand. I felt that completing these reports would be a job that one of the workers could handle.

TRAINER: Could you describe the situation in a little more detail, so we could role-play it?

CLIENT: Yes, I remember it well. I was going to give the job to Leo, but he reacted so negatively that I ended up doing it myself.

TRAINER: When did it happen?

CLIENT: Well, it was two weeks ago on Friday. I suppose it was about a quarter to five when I asked Leo to do the reports.
TRAINER: What was his response?
CLIENT: Well, he kind of hesitated and said that he'd rather not.
TRAINER: Then what happened?
CLIENT: Well, I got ticked off at him. He never seems to want to take responsibility.
TRAINER: O.K. Let's role-play that situation. I'll be Leo, and you approach me the way you did him.
CLIENT: Leo, I need to talk to you about something.
TRAINER: O.K., Ms. French.
CLIENT: (*eyes toward the floor, voice tone soft*) I really need these reports done sometime. (*pause*) They are the quality-control ones and they need to be done. Do you think you can do them?
TRAINER: Well, I'm not sure. I'd really prefer not to, if it's all the same with you.
CLIENT: (*cooly*) Don't bother.
TRAINER: Was that pretty close to the way it went?
CLIENT: Yes, it was. Do you see what I mean? That Leo is so lazy!

In this case, it is fairly obvious that the supervisor's way of delegating authority was ineffective. She made no attempt to explain the context of her request, or it's importance. Nor did she make the request in a definitive, assertive manner. Rather, the request was tentative and given at a time when most people are less than eager to take on a new project. When this tentative request was then denied, the client attributed the denial to a personality trait of the worker, rather than identifying her own behavior as a critical variable in Leo's willingness to take on the task. If this pattern of ineffective performance is found in other, similar situations, training is probably required.

Let us now move to the training phase. During assessment, we determined that there were probably a number of things that this supervisor could do to improve her performance. For example, she might make the request at a more appropriate time, explain the context of the request, state the request in more clear and unambiguous terms, and use better nonverbal skills, such as a firm, even voice tone and better eye contact, when making the request. Even if the request should be denied, she might inquire as to the reason, suggest alternatives, and so forth. In a situation like this, there is probably no single right way to do it. Rather, we are teaching this supervisor that she had more options on how to handle this situation. Presumably these options are ones that are likely to be more effective than previous patterns.

As we join the session our trainer is giving instructions on how to improve the process of delegation.

TRAINER: When you're trying to delegate responsibility for a job, it is a good idea to explain first the reason for that delegation. This helps put the request in its appropriate context and helps the employee see its importance. If you don't explain the context, you run the risk of the request's seeming as if it's coming "out of the blue."

CLIENT: Yes, that makes a lot of sense.

TRAINER: Let me give you an example. In the situation where you were attempting to get Leo to do the quality-control reports, you might have said something like "Leo, I have an important job I'd like you to take on. The quality-control reports need to be filed on a weekly basis. I think you can be very helpful in completing them."

CLIENT: That won't work with Leo. He's just too lazy.

TRAINER: It's possible that it might not work, but let's give it a try now and see how it works later.

CLIENT: O.K., fair enough.

After the trainer has covered the rationale, given instructions, and demonstrated the behavior, it is time to have the client actually practice it. This is usually done by role-playing the situation again.

TRAINER: O.K., let's practice the same situation again. This time, I want you to try and put your request in context. Ready?

CLIENT: O.K. Leo, I've got an important job for you. These quality-control reports are fairly routine, but they are important, and they do take some time. I'd like you to add these reports to your reponsibilities.

When the client has had an opportunity to practice the new responses, it is time to provide feedback. Feedback should highlight the positive aspects of the client's behavior, and make suggestions about how it might be improved further.

TRAINER: That was much better. You began to put your request in context. It was especially good the way you identified the request as an important one. Next time we practice it, you might also add another reason why it would be to the employee's benefit to take on the added responsibility. For example, you might point out that taking on added responsibility is viewed positively in the employee's evaluation.

CLIENT: It is! That would be a good thing to add.

TRAINER: Of course, it's important that you're honest with the employee. In the long run, conning the employee into accepting added responsibility on false pretenses will backfire.

CLIENT: I could also add that, by doing the quality-control reports, he could avoid some of the time on the clean-up crew.

TRAINER: That's another good point. I think you're getting the hang of it.

This feedback can then be followed by further practice and additional feedback, modeling, and instructions as required. The training cycle is continued until the skill is mastered.

Training effective supervisory skills represents an important and growing application of social-skills training. The current example focused on helping the supervisor develop a skill after the problem had already arisen. This need not be the case. Supervisory skills can be developed before a problem arises. Further, this example focused on individual training. It would seem quite feasible to conduct similar kinds of training in a group format. In fact, most of the research cited above has used a group training format. Such a format offers the opportunity for cost-effective skill development which may be an important consideration.

Effective Communication Skills

Communication is perhaps one of the most overworked terms in our language. At one level, virtually all human interaction can be analyzed as a form of communication. The examples of job-interview and supervisory skills can be conceptualized in these terms. However, as we use the term here, a much narrower focus is intended. Our focus is on the individual's skill in effectively gathering relevant information. Another way of labeling the same skill might be to call it "interviewing," or "gathering information."

Regardless of what we call it, this skill plays an important role in many work settings. Architects and engineers must understand the client's need before plans can be prepared. An attorney must be able to understand fully the client's situation in order to represent him or her most effectively. A consultant must understand the client's business problem before appropriate recommendations can be made. A salesman must understand a client's needs and desires if those needs are to be filled. In short, there is a wide range of occupational settings in which the ability effectively to obtain needed information is important.

Most attempts to train communication skills focus on the kinds of questions that are asked and how the interviewer responds to the answer (Frederiksen & Peterson, 1978). With respect to questions, a distinction is often made between *open-ended* and *closed-ended*. A *closed-ended* question is one that requires a concrete or specific answer. Examples of *closed-ended* questions are "How old are you?" "Do you want the package delivered on Thursday or Wednesday?" or "What is your total yearly income?" In each of these questions, the person is requested to give a specific, concrete answer. In most cases, there is little invitation to expand on the answer or explain. *Closed-ended* questions tend to limit the amount and kind of information given. *Open-ended* questions are those that require an explanation. The person must explain rather than simply give a limited bit of information. Examples of *open-ended* questions are "Why?" "Tell me about the situation that brought you here today?" or "Why is it important that you sell the property now?" *Open-ended* questions tend to increase the amount of talking required by the person being interviewed and to give broader sorts of information. If the interviewer is skilled in using both types of question, he or she can effectively direct the flow and quality of information.

The interviewer's behavior during the answer can also have an important impact on the flow of information. If the interviewer is attentive, does not interrupt, maintains appropriate eye contact, and encourages the person to continue talking, the flow of information is likely to be increased. These encouragements to talk often take the form of phrases such as "Go on," "Tell me more," and "Uh huh." By using attention and these verbal gestures selectively, the interviewer can direct the flow of information.

To illustrate this process, let us take the example of a training program designed to teach more effective communication skills to real-estate brokers (Frederiksen & Peterson, 1978). This example also illustrates how social-skills training can be conducted in a group-oriented workshop format.

The workshop begins with a dicussion of the general importance of the skills to be taught. The importance of thoroughly understanding the client's needs, resources, and desires is stressed. It is also pointed out that the satisfaction of those needs is the basis of all transactions. The lecture and discussion is supplemented by demonstrations of effective and ineffective communications skills, and a discussion of the impact they can have on communication, rapport, and trust. This general rationale sets the stage for instruction regarding a specific skill.

The workshop leader then presents the description of the first target behavior to be worked on, in this case, *open-ended questions*. This description restates the rationale for using *open-ended* questions, contrasts them with *closed-ended questions*, and concludes with several examples. Participants then generate examples which are evaluated by the group. Up to this point, the workshop participants have received the rationale for the use of the general skill as well as the specific target behavior, have had a chance to view modeling demonstrations, and have generated some examples of the target behavior.

Although the rationale, instructions, and modeling are important, they are not sufficient for skill development and maximum transfer of training. Thus, the next phase of the workshop involves actual practice and performance feedback. Participants are divided into small groups where they can practice using these skills in an interview situation. This is accomplished by having one of the members in the group conduct an interview while one or two of the other group members play the role of clients. To maximize transfer, the interview should be as realistic as possible. Consequently, participants playing the part of the customers are encouraged to model their behavior after actual customers with whom they have had experience. Participants then role-play the situation with the "interviewer" attempting to make maximum use of the target behavior, in this example, *closed-ended* questions.

INTERVIEWER: What can I help you with today?
CUSTOMER: I'm looking for some investment property.
INTERVIEWER: Oh?
CUSTOMER: I think I want to buy a duplex.
INTERVIEWER: Why is that?
CUSTOMER: Well, I've heard that they're good investments. Are they?
INTERVIEWER: Well, they can be. What location are you interested in?

These role-played interviews are videotaped to provide a basis for feedback. Although the trainer could observe the interviews and provide feedback based on that observation, the videotape adds clarity and impact to the feedback that may be missing from verbal feedback alone. Following a brief segment of role-playing (e.g., five minutes), the videotape is replayed to the small group. As it is replayed, the trainer can highlight and praise those aspects of the client's performance that were particularly strong. Opportune points for using the target behavior that were missed can also be identified and suggestions for more appropriate questions made. The videotape also allows for additional replaying of particularly important segments.

This group-training format can also take advantage of the other participant's feedback. For example, they might be queried regarding their reaction to a particular question or their assessment of how the interview "came across." Each trainee not only benefits from multiple sources of feedback (videotape, trainer, and other group members), but also has the opportunity to critique others and thereby learn to identify critical behaviors. Further, the group members may benefit from the modeling inherent in observing other people practice.

As we pick up the example, our participants have just completed role-playing an interview.

TRAINER: O.K. Let's stop there and take a look at it.

INTERVIEWER: Boy, I did a rotten job!

TRAINER: Not really. It actually looked pretty good. (*Directed to simulated customer*) How did it look to you?

CUSTOMER: I thought he came across very well.

TRAINER: Let's replay the tape and see how it looks. (*Trainer starts replay.*)

INTERVIEWER: Do I look like that?

TRAINER: It's sometimes a shock the first time you see yourself on T.V. Let's focus on these questions (*tape playing in the background. Interviewer on tape "What can I help you with today?"*)

TRAINER: That's a good question. A good way to start the interview.

CUSTOMER: I agree. (*Tape playing in background. Interviewer asks open-ended question "Why?"*)

TRAINER: That was another very good question. How did it come across?

CUSTOMER: It came across very well to me. I had to stop and think about why I was doing it. I think it was a very good question.

INTERVIEWER: I felt good about that question too.

TRAINER: Let's take another look at it. (*Trainer rewinds tape and replays the same question.*) Notice how the question not only gives you information but also forces the client to rethink his own needs. (*Tape playing in the background. Interviewer asks the question "What location are you interested in?" Trainer stops the tape.*) What about that question?

INTERVIEWER: That was a close-ended one. I guess I really got him off the track.

CUSTOMER: Yeah, I was surprised when you didn't follow up on your "why" question.

TRAINER: What else could you have done in that situation?

INTERVIEWER: I could have come back with another open-ended question.

CUSTOMER: He could have asked me more about my criteria for a good investment.

TRAINER: Can you give him an example of a question he could have used?

CUSTOMER: He could have asked "What's a good investment for you?"

INTERVIEWER: That's a good one.

TRAINER: All in all, that was a very good segment. You had at least three open-ended questions. Let's practice it again. Keep your open-ended questions and try to avoid cutting off the flow of communication by a change of subject or closed-ended questions.

The workshop participant who played the part of the interviewer now has another opportunity to practice the skill and receive additional feedback. When this cycle is completed several times, the small-group members change roles. The individual playing the part of the customer gets an opportunity to play the part of the interviewer and vice versa. This whole rotation sequence is continued until all participants have had an opportunity to practice the skill and receive feedback. The workshop then continues to the next skill to be taught. For example, listening skills (involving the appropriate uses of silence, encouragement to talk, and other nonverbal behaviors) may be taught next. Training continues in this general format until all behaviors have been demonstrated, and each participant has had an opportunity to practice and receive feedback on each behavior.

The group-training procedure illustrated by this example has some obvious advantages. It allows one to train a greater number of individuals and provides for input from multiple sources. It also seems that such a format is an effective way to teach communication skills. The report on which this example was based (Frederiksen & Peterson, 1978) found a 50% increase in the use of open-ended questions, and over a 100% increase in the use of encouragements to talk (a component of listening skills). In addition, this general training format is probably applicable to a wide variety of job-related skills.

Summary

The interpersonal demands of the work place are many and varied. The skill with which the individual handles these demands can have an important impact on productivity, satisfaction, and success. Although the traditional training literature has often followed one fad after another in the absence of sound empirical data, social-skills training offers a positive alternative.

The range of potential applications is illustrated by three examples: job interview skills, supervisory skills, and effective communication skills. The impression made during a job interview can have an important impact on the hiring decision. The use of social-skills training to aid in this area is illustrated by a controlled single-subject experiment reported by Hollandsworth *et al.* (1978). The training of effective supervisory skills has also been receiving increased attention. The process of assessing and training these skills is illustrated with the example of a newly promoted supervisor having difficulty in delegating responsibility. Finally, training in effective communication (interviewing) is illustrated by an example of a workshop conducted in a group format. Data from each of the above areas indicates that social-skills training can be a useful approach to changing job-related skills. However, caution must be exercised to avoid turning social-skills training into yet another "fad."

References

Alberti, R. E., & Emmons, M. L. *Your perfect right: A guide to assertive behavior.* San Luis Obispo, Calif.: Impact, 1974.

Argyle, M. *Social interaction.* Chicago: Aldine, 1969.

Argyle, M., Bryant, B., & Trower, P. Social skills training and psychotherapy: A comparative study. *Psychological Medicine,* 1974, *4,* 435–443.

Arkowitz, H., Lichtenstein, E., McGovern, K., & Hines, P. The behavioral assessment of social competence in males. *Behavior Therapy,* 1975, *6,* 3–13.

Azrin, N. H., & Holz, W. C. Punishment. In W. K. Honig (Ed.), *Operant behavior.* New York: Appleton-Century-Crofts, 1966.

Azrin, N. H., Naster, B. J., & Jones, R. Reciprocity counseling: A rapid learning-based procedure for marital counseling. *Behavior Research and Therapy,* 1973, *11,* 365–382.

Azrin, N. H., Flores T., & Kaplan, S. J. Job finding club: a group assisted program for obtaining employment. *Behaviour Research and Therapy,* 1975, *13,* 17–27.

Baer, D. M. Wolf, M. M., & Risley, T. R. Some current dimensions of applied behavior analysis. *Journal of Applied Behavior Analysis,* 1968, *1,* 91–97.

Bailey, K. G., & Sowder, W. T., Jr. Audiotape and videotape self-confrontation in psychotherapy. *Psychological Bulletin,* 1970, *74,* 127–137.

Bandura, A. *Principles of behavior modification.* New York: Holt, Rinehart & Winston, 1969.

Bandura, A. *Aggression: A social learning analysis.* Englewood Cliffs, N. J.: Prentice-Hall, 1973.

Bandura, A. Behavior theory and models of man. *American Psychologist,* 1974, *29,* 859–869.

Bandura, A., & Walters, R. H. *Social learning and personality development.* New York: Holt, Rinehart & Winston, 1963.

Barbee, J. R., & Keil, E. C. Experimental techniques of job interview training for the disadvantaged: Videotape feedback behavior modification and microcounseling. *Journal of Applied Psychology,* 1973, *58,* 209–213.

Birchler, G. R., Weiss, R. L., & Vincent, J. P. A multimethod analysis of social reinforcement exchange between maritally distressed and nondistressed stranger dyads. *Journal of Personality and Social Psychology,* 1975, *31,* 349–360.

Bellack, A. S., Hersen, M., & Lamparski, D. Role play tests for assessing social skills: Are they valid? Are they useful? *Journal of Consulting and Clinical Psychology,* 1979, *47,* 335–342.

Bornstein, M. R., Bellack, A. B., & Hersen, M. Social skills training for unassertive children: A multiple baseline analysis. *Journal of Applied Behavior Analysis,* 1977, *10,* 183–189.

Burnaska, R. F. The effects of behavior modeling training upon managers' behaviors and employee's perceptions. *Personnel Psychology,* 1976, *29,* 329–335.

Byham, W. C., Adams, D., & Kiggins, A. Transfer of modeling training to the job. *Personnel Psychology,* 1976, *29,* 345–349.

Campbell, J. P. Personnel training and development. In P. H. Mussen, and M. R. Rosenzweig (Eds.), *Annual Review of Psychology,* Palo Alto, Calif.: Annual Reviews, Inc., 1971.

Combs, M. L., & Slaby, D. A. Social skills training with children. In B. B. Lahey and A. E. Kazdin (Eds.), *Advances in clinical child psychology,* Vol. 1, New York: Plenum, 1977.

Cowen, E. L. Social and community interventions. *Annual Review of Psychology,* 1973, *24,* 423–472.

Curran, J. P. Social skills training and systematic desensitization in reducing dating anxiety. *Behaviour Research and Therapy,* 1975, *13,* 65–68.

Curran, J. P., & Gilbert, F. S. A test of the relative effectiveness of a systematic desensitization program and an interpersonal skills training program with date anxious subjects. *Behavior Therapy,* 1975, *6,* 510–521.

Disher, G. Discriminating violence emanating from over-controlled versus under-controlled aggressivity. *British Journal of Clinical and Social Psychology,* 1970, *9,* 54–59.

Dollard, J., Doob, L. W., Miller, N. E., Mowrer, O. H., & Sears, R. R. *Frustration and aggression.* New Haven: Yale University Press, 1939.

Drake, L. R., Kaplan, H. R., & Stone, R. A. How do employers value the interview? *Journal of College Placement,* 1972, *32,* 47–51.

D'Zurilla, T., & Goldfried, M. Problem solving and behavior modification. *Journal of Abnormal Psychology,* 1971, *32,* 47–51.

Edelstein, B. A., & Eisler, R. M. Effects of modeling and modeling with instructions and feedback on the behavioral components of social skills. *Behavior Therapy,* 1976, *7,* 382–389.

Edwards, N. B. Case conference: Assertive training in a case of homosexual pedophelia. *Journal of Behavior Therapy and Experimental Psychiatry,* 1972, *3,* 55–63.

Eisler, R. M., Hersen, M., & Agras, W. S. Effects of videotape and instructional feedback on nonverbal marital interaction: An analogue study. *Behavior Therapy,* 1973, *4,* 551–558.

Eisler, R. M., Hersen, M., & Miller, P. M. Effects of modeling on components of assertive behavior. *Journal of Behavior Therapy and Experimental Psychiatry,* 1973, *4,* 1–6.

Eisler, R. M., Hersen, M., & Miller, P. M. Shaping components of assertive behavior with instructions and feedback. *American Journal of Psychiatry,* 1974, *131,* 1344–1347.

Eisler, R. M., Miller, P. M., & Hersen, M. Components of assertive behavior. *Journal of Clinical Psychology,* 1973, *29,* 295–299.

Eisler, R. M., Hersen, M., Miller, P. M., & Blanchard, E. B. Situational determinants of assertive behavior. *Journal of Consulting and Clincial Psychology,* 1975, *43,* 330–340.

Eisler, R. M., Blanchard, E. B., Fitts, H.; & Williams, J. G. Social skill training with and without modeling for schizophrenic and nonpsychotic hospitalized psychiatric patients. *Behavior Modification,* 1978, *2,* 147–171.

Eisler, R. M., Frederiksen, L. W., & Peterson, G. L. The relationship of cognitive variables to the expression of assertiveness. *Behavior Therapy,* 1978, *9,* 419–427.

Elder, J. P., Edelstein, B. A., & Narick, M. M. Adolescent psychiatric patients: Modifying aggressive behavior with social skills training. *Behavior Modification,* 1979, *3,* 161–178.

Ellis, A. *Reason and emotion in psychotherapy.* New York: Lyle Stuart, 1962.

Fensterheim, H. Assertive methods and marital problems. In R. D. Rubin, H. Fensterheim, J. D. Henderson, & L. P. Ualman (Eds.), *Advances in behavior therapy.* New York: Academic, 1972.

Forrest, D. V., & Baumgarten, L. An hour for job interviewing skills. *Journal of College Placement*, 1975, *36*, 77–78.

Foy, D. W., Eisler, R. M., & Pinkston, S. Modeled assertion in a case of explosive rages. *Journal of Behavior Therapy and Experimental Psychiatry*, 1975, *6*, 135–137.

Foy, D. W., Miller, P. M., Eisler, R. M., & O'Toole, D. H. Social-skills training to teach alcoholics to refuse drinks effectively. *Journal of Studies on Alcohol*, 1976, *37*, 1340–1345.

Frederiksen, L. W., & Eisler, R. M. The control of explosive behavior: A skill-development approach. In D. Upper (Ed.), *Perspectives in behavior therapy*. Kalamazoo: Behaviordelia, 1977.

Frederiksen, L. W., & Peterson, G. L. *Training marital dyads in conflict negotiation skills*. Paper presented at the meeting of the Association for Advancement of Behavior Therapy, San Francisco, December 1975.

Frederiksen, L. W., & Peterson, G. L. *A behavioral approach to training communication skills in business and industry*. Technical report available from Behavioral Consultants, Ltd., 9024 Greenwood Ave. North, Seattle, Washington 98103, 1978.

Frederiksen, L. W., Jenkins, J. O., Foy, D. W., & Eisler, R. M. Social skills training in the modification of abusive verbal outbursts in adults. *Journal of Applied Behavior Analysis*, 1976, *9*, 119–125.

Friedrich, L. K., & Stein, A. H. Prosocial television and young children: The effects of verbal labeling and role playing on learning and behavior. *Child Development*, 1975, *46*, 27–38.

Gittlemen, M. Behavioral rehearsal as a technique in child treatment. *Journal of Child Psychology and Psychiatry*, 1965, *6*, 251–255.

Glass, C. R., Gottman, J. M., & Shmurak, S. H. Response-acquisition and cognitive self statement modification approaches to dating skills training. *Journal of Counseling Psychology*, 1976, *23*, 520–526.

Goldsmith, J. B., & McFall, R. M. Development and evaluation of an interpersonal skill-training program for psychiatric inpatients. *Journal of Abnormal Psychology*, 1975, *84*, 51–58.

Goldstein, A. P. *Structured learning therapy: Toward a psychotherapy for the poor*. New York: Academic, 1973.

Goldstein, A. P., & Sorcher, M. *Changing supervisor behavior*. New York: Pergamon, 1974.

Gottman, J., Gonso, J., & Rasmussen, B. Social interaction, social competence, and friendship in children. *Child Development*, 1975, *46*, 709–718.

Griffiths, R. D. P. Videotape feedback as a therapeutic technique: Retrospect and prospect. *Behaviour Research and Therapy*, 1974, *12*, 1–8.

Gronlund, N. E. *Sociometry in the classroom*. New York: Harper, 1959.

Gutride, M. E., Goldstein, A. P., & Hunter, G. F. The use of modeling and role playing to increase social interaction among asocial psychiatric patients. *Journal of Consulting and Clinical Psychology*, 1973, *40*, 408–415.

Hartup, W. W., Glazer, J. A., & Charlesworth, R. Peer reinforcement and sociometric status. *Child Development*, 1967, *38*, 1017–1024.

Hersen, M., & Bellack, A. S. A multiple-baseline analysis of social skills training in chronic schizophrenics. *Journal of Applied Behavior Analysis*, 1976, *9*, 239–245.

Hersen, M., & Eisler, R. M. Social skills training. In W. E. Craighead, A. E. Kazdin, & M. J. Mahoney (Eds.), *Behavior modification: Principles, issues, and applications*. Boston: Houghton Mifflin, 1976.

Hersen, M., Eisler, R. M., Miller, P. M., Johnson, M. B., & Pinkston, S. G. Effects of practice, instructions, and modeling on components of assertive behavior. *Behaviour Research and Therapy*, 1973, *11*, 443–451.

Hersen, M., Eisler, R. M., & Miller, P. M. An experimental analysis of generalization in assertive training. *Behaviour Research and Therapy*, 1974, *12*, 295–310.

Hollandsworth, J. G., Dressel, M. E., & Stevens, J. The use of behavioral versus traditional procedures for increasing job interview skills. *Journal of Counseling Psychology*, 1977, *24*, 503–510.

Hollandsworth, J. G., Glazeski, R. C., & Dressel, M. E. Use of social-skills training in the treatment of extreme anxiety and deficient verbal skills in the job-interview setting. *Journal of Applied Behavior Analysis*, 1978, *11*, 259–269.

Jacobson, N. S. Problem solving and contingency contracting in the treatment of marital discord. *Journal of Consulting and Clinical Psychology*, 1977, *45*, 92–100.

Kagan, S., & Moss, H. A. *Birth to maturity: A study in psychological development.* New York: Wiley, 1962.

Kanfer, F. H., & Phillips, J. S. *Learning foundations of behavior therapy.* New York: Wiley, 1970.

Kaufman, L. M., & Wagner, B. R. Barb: A systematic treatment technology for temper control disorders. *Behavior Therapy*, 1972, *3*, 84–90.

Kazdin, A. E. Covert modeling, imagery assessment, and assertive behavior. *Journal of Consulting and Clinical Psychology*, 1975, *43*, 716–724.

Kazdin, A. E. Effects of covert modeling and model reinforcement on assertive behavior. *Journal of Abnormal Psychology*, 1974, *83*, 240–252.

Kazdin, A. E. *The token economy: A review and evaluation.* New York: Plenum, 1977.(a)

Kazdin, A. E. Assessing the clinical or applied importance of behavior change through social validation. *Behavior Modification*, 1977, *1*, 427–452.(b)

Keil, E. C., & Barbee, J. R. Behavior modification and training the disadvantaged job interviewee. *Vocational Guidance Quarterly*, 1973, *22*, 50–56.

Kelly, J. A., Laughlin, C., Claiborne, M., & Patterson, J. A group procedure for teaching job interview skills to formerly hospitalized psychiatric patients. *Behavior Therapy*, 1979, *10*, 299–310.

Kornrich, M. *Underachievement.* Springfield, Ill.: Charles C Thomas, 1965.

Kraut, A. I. Developing managerial skills via modeling techniques: Some positive research findings. A symposium. *Personnel Psychology*, 1976, *29*, 325–328.

Lazarus, A. A. Behaviour rehearsal vs. non-directive therapy vs. advice in effecting behaviour change. *Behaviour Research & Therapy*, 1966, *4*, 209–212.

Lazarus, A. A. *Behavior therapy and beyond.* New York: McGraw-Hill, 1971.

Lazarus, A. A. On assertive behavior: A brief note. *Behavior Therapy*, 1973, *4*, 697–699.

Lewinsohn, P. M., & Shaffer, M. Use of home observations as an integral part of the treatment of depression. *Journal of Consulting and Clinical Psychology*, 1971, *37*, 87–94.

Lewinsohn, P. M., Weinstein, M. S., & Alper, T. A behavioral approach to the group treatment of depressed persons: A methodological contribution. *Journal of Clinical Psychology*, 1970, *26*, 525–532.

Libet, J., & Lewisohn, P. M. The concept of social skill with special references to the behavior of depressed persons. *Journal of Consulting and Clinical Psychology*, 1973, *40*, 304–312.

Linehan, M. M., Walker, R. O., Bronheim, S., Haynes, K. F., & Yevzeroff, H. Group versus individual assertion training. *Journal of Consulting and Clinical Psychology*, 1979, *47*, 1000–1002.

Locke, J. J. & Wallace, K. M. Short-term marital adjustment and prediction tests: Their reliability and validity. *Journal of Marriage and Family Living*, 1959, *21*, 251–255.

Lorenz, K. *On aggression.* New York: Harcourt Brace Jovanovich, 1966.

Mahoney, M. J. *Cognitive behavior modification.* Cambridge, Mass.: Ballinger, 1974.

Mahoney, M. J., & Thoresen, C. E. *Self-control: Power to the person.* Monterey, Calif.: Brooks/Cole, 1974.

Martinson, W. D., & Zerface, J. P. Comparison of individual counseling and a social program with nondaters. *Journal of Counseling Psychology*, 1970, *17*, 36–40.

Matson, J. L. & Stephans, R. M. Increasing appropriate behavior of explosive chronic psychiatric patients with a social skills training package. *Behavior Modification*, 1978, *2*, 61–76.

McFall, R. M., & Lillesand, D. B. Behavior rehearsal with modeling and coaching in assertion training. *Journal of Abnormal Psychology*, 1971, *77*, 313–323.

McFall, R. M., & Marston, A. R. An experimental investigation of behavior rehearsal in assertive training. *Journal of Abnormal Psychology*, 1970, *76*, 295–303.

McFall, R. M., & Twentyman, C. T. Four experiments on the relative contributions of rehearsal, modeling, and coaching to assertion training. *Journal of Abnormal Psychology*, 1973, *81*, 199–218.

McKinlay, T., Pachman, J., & Frederiksen, L. W. *Coaction: An innovative approach in the behavioral treatment of explosive behavior.* Paper presented at the meeting of the association for the Advancement of Behavior Therapy, Atlanta, December 1977.

Meichenbaum, D. *Cognitive behavior modification.* Morristown, N. J.: General Learning Press, 1974.

Meichenbaum, D. *Cognitive behavior modification: An integrative approach.* New York: Plenum, 1977.

Melnick, J. A comparison of replication techniques in the modification of minimal dating behavior. *Journal of Abnormal Psychology*, 1973, *81*, 51–59.

Michelson, L., & Wood, R. Behavioral assessment and training for children's social skills. In M. Hersen, R. M. Eisler, & P. M. Miller (Eds.), *Progress in behavior modification* (Vol. 9). New York: Academic, 1980.

Mischel, W. Toward a cognitive social learning reconceptualization of personality. *Psychological Review*, 1973, *80*, 252–283.

Moses, J. L., & Ritchie, R. J. Supervisory relationship training: A behavioral evaluation of a behavioral modeling program. *Personnel Psychology*, 1976, *29*, 337–343.

Nietzel, M. T., Martorano, R. D., & Melnick, J. The effects of covert modeling with and without reply training on the development and generalization of assertive responses. *Behavior Therapy*, 1977, *8*, 183–192.

Norman, K. L. Weight and value in an information integration model: Subjective rating of job applications. *Organizational Behavior and Human Performance*, 1976, *16*, 193–204.

O'Conner, R. D. Relative efficacy of modeling, shaping, and the combined procedures for modification of social withdrawal. *Journal of Abnormal Psychology*, 1972, *79*, 327–334.

Pachman, J., McKinlay, T., & Frederiksen, L. W. *Group versus individual social skills training.* Unpublished manuscript, University of Mississippi Medical Center, Jackson, 1977.

Peterson, G. L., Frederiksen, L. W., & Rosenbaum, M. S. Developing behavioral competencies in distressed marital couples. *American Journal of Family Therapy*, in press.

Phillips, L., & Zigler, E. Social competence: The action-thought parameter and vicariousness in normal and pathological behaviors. *Journal of Abnormal and Social Psychology*, 1961, *63*, 137–146.

Phillips, L., & Zigler, E. Role orientation, the action-thought dimension, and outcome in psychiatric disorder. *Journal of Abnormal and Social Psychology*, 1964, *68*, 381–389.

Prazak, J. A. Learning job-seeking interview skills. In J. D. Krumboltz & C. E. Thoresen (Eds.), *Behavioral counseling: Cases and techniques.* New York: Holt, Rinehart & Winston, 1969.

Rainwater, N., & Frederiksen, L. W. *Violent behavior: Assessment and treatment using multiple response systems.* Paper presented at the annual meeting of the Association for the Advancement of Behavior Therapy, Chicago, November 1978.

Redd, W. H., Porterfield, A. L., & Anderson, B. L. *Behavior modification: Behavioral approaches to human problems.* New York: Random House, 1979.

Rimm, D. C., Hill, G. A., Brown, N. M., & Stuart, J. E. Group-assertiveness training in treatment of expression of inappropriate anger. *Psychological Reports,* 1974, *34,* 791–798.

Rinn, R. C., & Markle, A. Modification of skills deficits in children. In A. S. Bellack & M. Hersen (Eds.), *Research and practice in social skills training.* New York: Plenum, 1979.

Robbins, L. N. *Deviant children grown up.* Baltimore: Williams & Wilkins, 1966.

Rose, S. D. In pursuit of social competence. *Social Work,* 1975, *20,* 33–39.

Schinke, S. P., & Rose, S. D. Interpersonal skill training in groups. *Journal of Counseling Psychology,* 1976, *23,* 442–448.

Simon, S. J., & Frederiksen, L. W. *Social skills training in the treatment of a physically abusive, "explosive personality."* Paper presented at the meeting of the Southeastern Psychological Association, Hollywood, Florida, May 1977.

Smith, P. E. Management modeling training to improve morale and customer satisfaction. *Personnel Psychology,* 1976, *29,* 351–359.

Spivack, G., & Shure, M. B. *Social adjustment of young children: A cognitive approach to solving real life problems.* San Francisco: Jossey-Bass, 1974.

Stahl, J. R., Thomson, L. E., Leitenberg, H., & Hasazi, J. E. Establishment of praise as a conditioned reinforcer in socially unresponsive psychiatric patients. *Journal of Abnormal Psychology,* 1974, *83,* 488–496.

Stuart, R. B. Operant-interpersonal treatment for marital discord. *Journal of Consulting and Clinical Psychology,* 1969, *33,* 675–682.

Stuart, R. B. (Ed.). *Behavioral self-management: Strategies, techniques and outcomes.* New York: Brunner/Mazel, 1977.

Stuart, R. B., & Stuart, F. Marital pre-counseling inventory. Champaign, Ill.: Research Press, 1972.

Stevenson, I., & Wolpe, J. Recovery from sexual deviations through overcoming non-sexual neurotic responses. *American Journal of Psychiatry,* 1960, *116,* 737–742.

Thibaut, J. W., & Kelly, H. H. *The social psychology of groups.* New York: Wiley, 1959.

Twentyman, G. T., & McFall, R. M. Behavioral training of social skills in shy males. *Journal of Consulting and Clinical Psychology,* 1975, *43,* 384–395.

Twentyman, G. T., & Zimmering, R. T. Behavioral training of social skills: A critical review. In M. Hersen, R. M. Eisler, & P. M. Miller (Eds.), *Progress in behavior modification.* New York: Academic, 1979.

Van Hasselt, V. B., Hersen, M., & Milliones, J. Social skill training for alcoholics and drug addicts: A review. *Addictive Behaviors,* 1978, *3,* 221–233.

Wahler, R. G. Some structural aspects of deviant child behavior. *Journal of Applied Behavior Analysis,* 1975, *8,* 27–42.

Wallace, C. J., Teigen, J. R., Liberman, R. P., & Baker, V. Destructive behavior treated by contingency contracts and assertive training: A case study. *Journal of Behavior Therapy and Experimental Psychiatry,* 1973, *4,* 273–274.

Watson, D., & Friend, R. Measurement of social-evaluative anxiety. *Journal of Consulting and Clinical Psychology.* 1969, *33,* 448–457.

Weinman, B., Gelbart, P., Wallace, M., & Post, M. Inducing assertive behavior in chronic schizophrenics: A comparison of socioenvironmental, desensitization, and relaxation therapies. *Journal of Consulting and Clinical Psychology,* 1972, *39,* 246–252.

Winder, C. L., & Rau, L. Parental attitudes associated with social deviance in preadolescent boys. *Journal of Abnormal and Social Psychology,* 1962, *64,* 418–424.

Wills, T. A., Weiss, R. L., & Patterson, G. R. A behavioral analysis of the determinants of marital satisfaction. *Journal of Consulting and Clinical Psychology,* 1974, *42,* 802–811.

Wolpe, J., & Lazarus, A. A. *Behavior therapy techniques: A guide to the treatment of neuroses.* New York: Pergamon, 1966.

Zigler, E., & Phillips, L. Social effectiveness and symptomatic behaviors. *Journal of Abnormal and Social Psychology,* 1960, *61,* 231–238.

Zigler, E., & Phillips, L. Social competence and the process-reactive distinction in psychotherapy. *Journal of Abnormal and Social Psychology,* 1962, *65,* 215–222.

Index